SECOND EDITION

Inclusion Strategies
for Secondary Classrooms

Keys for Struggling Learners

M.C. GORE

CORWIN
A SAGE Company

For information:

Corwin
A SAGE Company
2455 Teller Road
Thousand Oaks, California 91320
(800) 233–9936
Fax: (800) 417–2466
www.corwin.com

SAGE Ltd.
1 Oliver's Yard
55 City Road
London EC1Y 1SP
United Kingdom

SAGE India Pvt. Ltd.
B 1/I 1 Mohan Cooperative Industrial Area
Mathura Road, New Delhi 110 044
India

SAGE Asia-Pacific Pte. Ltd.
33 Pekin Street #02-01
Far East Square
Singapore 048763

Printed in the United States of America

Library of Congress Cataloging-in-Publication Data

Gore, M. C.
Inclusion strategies for secondary classrooms: keys for struggling learners/M.C. Gore.—2nd ed.
      p. cm.
Includes bibliographical references and index.
Rev. ed. of: Successful inclusion strategies for secondary and middle school teachers, c2004.
ISBN 978-1-4129-7544-5 (pbk.)
    1. Children with disabilities—Education (Secondary)—United States. 2. Inclusive education—United States. I. Gore, M. C., Successful inclusion strategies for secondary and middle school teachers. II. Title.

LC4031.G64 2010
371.9'045—dc22   2010001679

This book is printed on acid-free paper.

10   11   12   13   14   10 9 8 7 6 5 4 3 2 1

Acquisitions Editor:	Jessica Allan
Associate Editor:	Joanna Coelho
Editorial Assistant:	Allison Scott
Production Editor:	Amy Schroller
Copy Editor:	Jenifer Dill
Typesetter:	C&M Digitals (P) Ltd.
Proofreader:	Theresa Kay
Indexer:	Judy Hunt
Cover Designer:	Michael Dubowe

Contents

In memory of
Harold O. Gore, Esquire—father, gentle counselor, and friend—who spent
a lifetime working for the inclusion of people who are oppressed;
beloved aunt, Doris Gore Blair, rare and special soul;
and Little Man, my constant companion for 17 years, waiting
faithfully for me by Heaven's Gate.

Preface

During the fifteen years I spent teaching sixth-grade through twelfth-grade students who had learning problems, I learned many things, among them: middle and secondary school teachers love their disciplines. Their disciplines hold precious gems for them, rare and exquisite. They hunger to share the beauty with their students. When, in the vernacular, students "blow them off" with a sneer, their arms folded across their chests and eyes glazing over, content specialist teachers die a little inside.

I have listened to their laments in the teachers' lounge, not griping about students, but rather wondering how to reach the reluctant learner. In the thousands of hours I spent with my friend, Dr. Rosemary Grant of Monett, Missouri, the finest high school teacher I have ever known, I came to sense the fire she had in her breast to make every student love history and the humanities as she did. I came to feel her despair when a student seemed apathetic about the things to which she cleaved so dearly: democracy, freedom, rigorous intellectual inquiry, and intellectual integrity.

As a special education teacher, I desperately wanted to help. We knew how to work with students with special needs in the special education classroom in those years, but we did not know much about good inclusion strategies. We now have powerful research to guide us in including the learner with special needs in the general education classroom. But as Mastropieri and Scruggs (1994) wrote, "It is commonly agreed by educators that findings from experimental research are of little value unless it is shown how such findings can be adapted and implemented in actual classroom practice . . . ." How true. That is why I decided to write this book: to help practitioners access what the research tells us about teaching students with disabilities in middle school and secondary school classrooms.

Many inclusion books for elementary teachers are on the market, but those books do not satisfy the needs of middle and secondary school teachers. I wanted this overlooked population to have a quick resource for research-supported strategies, or for those showing great promise, that they could keep on their desk and reach for when needed. I wanted it to be a book of strategies that I or my students had field tested and found teacher-friendly. That was the sort of book I ached for when I was still working in public schools. The practitioners who reviewed the initial draft of this book for Corwin indicated that this, too, was the sort of book they wanted. I was greatly encouraged.

The first edition of this book met with success. Teachers across the world use it. Academic and public libraries throughout the United States, Canada, Europe, Africa, and Asia have it on their shelves. But a half-decade has passed since the first edition, so the time has come for a second—with information on Response to Intervention (RtI) and No Child Left Behind (NCLB), updated research, and new strategies.

From this point onward, I will write in the first person plural in order to represent, in addition to myself, the thoughts and feelings of the many special education teacher-researchers whose work led us to the findings I report, my students who have used and enjoyed these strategies in their fieldwork, and their teacher friends who have embraced the strategies as well.

May this book provide the keys that you need to help all of your students unlock the doors to learning so you can invite them in, introduce them to the jewels of your discipline, and help them develop the tools they need to turn rough gems into beautiful rings and tiaras.

Acknowledgments

Corwin gratefully acknowledges the contributions of the following individuals:

James Arnold, Alaska State Director of Special Education
Juneau, AK

Laura Cumbee, Special Education Math Teacher
Cartersville Middle School
Cartersville, GA

Wendy Dallman, Special Education Teacher
New London High School
New London, WI

Jackie Dorman, Special Education Teacher
Clay Middle School
Carmel, IN

Robert Krajewski, Professor of Educational Studies
University of Wisconsin—La Crosse
La Crosse, WI

Deborah D. Therriault, Special Education Teacher, POHI Classroom
Clarkston High School
Clarkston, MI

About the Author

M. C. (Millie) Gore, EdD, is Hardin Distinguished Professor in the Special Education Program of the Department of Counseling, Kinesiology, and Special Education at the Gordon T. and Ellen West College of Education at Midwestern State University in Wichita Falls, Texas. She is the author or coauthor of several books, including the Corwin title (with Dr. John F. Dowd) *Taming the Time Stealers: Tricks of the Trade From Organized Teachers.*

Dr. Gore received undergraduate and master's degrees from Eastern New Mexico University and a doctorate from the University of Arkansas. She and her husband, Don, spend their spare time with three adopted dogs: Sir, a Sheltie rescued from a puppy mill; Miss Winnie, an emotionally fragile Australian Shepherd cross; and Miss Ebbie Lou, three and a half pounds of fierce Chihuahua-Papillion independence.

The Letters Behind the Book

The young teacher education major furrowed his brow and frowned at me. "I'm going to be a high school history teacher, not a special ed. teacher. Why should I worry about inclusion strategies? After all, special education teachers are paid to work with kids who can't learn! Not me!" I smiled and thought to myself, *I've got a long way to go with this youngster!*

Every semester that I teach secondary and middle school teacher-education interns, I have to explain why a class on teaching students with exceptional learning needs in the general education classroom is required. I understand the question. The students who ask me were educated in school systems in which "those kids" went somewhere else for their academic core classes—no one knew exactly where they went for instruction or what they learned, but they didn't learn what everyone else learned, and teaching them was not the job of the history, science, English, or math teacher.

Thus, these aspiring teachers think that classes consist of the "brainy kids" and the "regular kids," none of whom need additional assistance or support from the general education teacher. The idea that every class has struggling learners—some of whom receive special education services, but most of whom do not—is new to these neophytes. Mine is the fun of introducing them to struggling learners and the strategies that can help them succeed in the general education classroom.

However, the neophytes demand more reasons for having to learn how to teach struggling learners, and that's the point at which No Child Left Behind (NCLB) and the Individuals with Disabilities Education Act (IDEA, officially IDEIA, the *Individuals with Disabilities Education Improvement Act*, but still known by the prior name) become involved; NCLB and IDEA are the first of the letters behind this book.

NO CHILD LEFT BEHIND

Every educator in America is familiar with NCLB. No Child Left Behind, commonly referred to as *nickelbee*, requires that every child be taught using teaching strategies that are scientifically based. *Scientifically based* means that educational researchers have investigated a teaching strategy using systematic, empirical methods that were based upon experiment or observation. The research methods and instruments must have been both scientifically valid and reliable. The researchers have then rigorously analyzed the data from the experiments or observations and have justified their conclusions. Their findings have been replicated and confirmed by other researchers and examined by peer experts who have concluded, "Yes, this teaching strategy has scientific evidence that it is effective."

I tell my teacher candidates, "If a teacher doesn't use strategies that are scientifically based, then he or she is using 'teacher folklore.' We're committing malpractice when we waste the time of struggling learners with teacher folklore. They are already struggling. We have a moral imperative to use best practice to help them learn. And *every single minute* counts."

In addition to requiring scientifically based teaching strategies, NCLB demands teacher accountability. Under NCLB, students are required to take high-stakes academic tests every year in third through eighth grade, and at least once during high school, to show that teachers are teaching and students are learning. The mandate is clear: Every teacher must teach every child. But what if a teacher doesn't use research-based teaching strategies? What if a teacher's students don't measure up on standardized tests?

Each state is required to report the test outcomes to parents and to the public according to disability status, socioeconomic class, level of English proficiency, and racial and ethnic group. This report is popularly called the "School Report Card."

This is in contrast to the previous requirement that only overall school performance be reported. It used to be possible for schools to receive high ratings yet have entire subgroups of students who scored consistently lower than their peers. Those days have passed. Teachers are now being held accountable for students with disabilities as well as those without, students who live in poverty as well as those who have socioeconomic advantages, and students of diverse racial and ethnic groups.

A school that is deemed "low performing" on standardized tests for two consecutive years will face consequences. Students in that school will be allowed to transfer to another school that is not low performing, and the school from which they transfer must pay transportation costs.

Schools that are deemed low performing for three years are required to pay for tutoring, afterschool programs, and summer school for students whose parents request such services. The parents are free to choose a tutor or afterschool program from a list of providers, and the school has to pay those providers.

Schools that receive low marks for four years may place heavy consequences on the teachers whose students score poorly on the standardized tests: They may fire those teachers. Firing teachers who have poorly performing students is considered part of restructuring a failing school. In addition to the termination of ineffective teachers, the school may hire outside consultants, implement new curricula that address shortcomings in the previous curricula, and train teachers in the new curricula. The schools may also overhaul their management structures.

If those changes are not effective after one year, schools that are low performing for five years may find their principal and staff replaced. Then the district may hire a private company to run the school and designate it as a charter school.

The few schools that are still low performing on standardized tests after the sixth year will find themselves in the position of being taken over by the state's department of education.

Principals are testy about having their schools listed in the media as being low performing. They are embarrassed personally and professionally. They intensely dislike losing students because that means losing funds, and they don't like having to reroute funds to pay for transportation to other schools. When they have to pay other organizations or individuals to provide afterschool tutoring or afterschool care, principals become irritable beyond belief. Few will hesitate to fire the teachers who are responsible for their school's poor performance if they hit the magic four-year low performing threshold. At that point, principals' faces flush crimson because they realize that without a dramatic turnaround the following year, they will be the ones on the chopping block.

RESPONSE TO INTERVENTION

The next set of letters in this book is *RtI*. If NCLB is the cake, RtI is the ice cream. RtI stands for *Response to Intervention,* and it is a requirement of the reauthorization of IDEA. RtI was developed as a general education initiative that could be implemented by general education teachers. RtI is an attempt to rectify a problem in the old system, in which we essentially had two educational systems: regular education for "regular" students and special education for students with disabilities. Special education is a service delivery system, not a physical location, but people thought of special education as a place—typically a portable building behind the school.

One of the problems with this system was that the children who were sent to the little building in the back progressed poorly: Special education teachers are experts in instructional strategies, not in curricula. History teachers are the experts in history curricula, science teachers are the experts in science curricula, English teachers in English. And as for math . . . let's not even go there. Students in special education suffered because their special education teachers were not experts in the variety of curricula for which middle school and high school teachers are responsible.

Another problem with that system was that many students who were struggling but not identified as eligible for special education were left in general education classes to fail without special support. Many of those students had learning disabilities but had not been diagnosed. Under the old system, we had to document that the student had a severe discrepancy between his or her IQ and classroom achievement before we could give the student help. This was called the *wait to fail* approach. We didn't intervene until the student was at least two years behind her or his peers. We needed to intervene sooner.

A third problem was that so many children of color and from various ethnic groups were being identified as eligible for special education. They were, and continue to be, proportionally overrepresented in special education. Those students who were inappropriately placed simply needed good, research-based teaching. RtI helps ensure that such students get the help they need in the general education classroom.

RtI means providing research-based instruction that accommodates the student's needs and then assessing the student to determine whether she or he has benefitted from the instruction (i.e., mastered the knowledge or skill). The assessment is ongoing, and the teacher scrutinizes the results. The process of assessment and close examination is called *progress monitoring*. Progress monitoring is conducted through curriculum-based measurement (CBM), which we shall address shortly.

Based upon the progress monitoring, the teacher determines whether the student doesn't know the material—has a *skill or knowledge deficit*—or knows the material and simply chooses not to apply it—has a *performance deficit*. If the student has a skill or knowledge deficit and is responding to instruction, then the teacher continues on with that type of instruction. If the student has a skill or knowledge deficit and is not responding to the teacher's instruction, the teacher tweaks that instruction until something works. If the student has a performance deficit, rather than a skill or knowledge deficit, the teacher seeks a way to motivate the student.

Curriculum Based Measurement

In Curriculum Based Measurement (CBM), the teacher provides a brief probe at least once each week. The probe, which takes from one to five minutes, is based upon the curriculum; the relationship between the curriculum and the assessment is transparent. Then the teacher graphs the student's performance. For example, one of the Montana competencies for high school seniors is to *give examples of scientific innovation challenging commonly held perceptions.* Clearly, this would be a one-sentence probe directing the student to provide such examples.

One of the New Jersey high school mathematics competencies is to *create and use representations to organize, record, and communicate mathematical ideas.* This could consist of a probe in which the student was expected to make a table or diagram that represented a problem provided by the teacher.

Arizona's eighth-grade content standards for reading include being able to *differentiate between primary and secondary source materials.* The teacher could provide a list of ten sources and then have the student circle the primary sources in a brief probe.

Whenever possible, the teacher graphs the student's performance. Clearly, this is difficult to do when assessing higher-order thinking; however, our struggling students are generally struggling with the most basic knowledge and skills in our disciplines. Because they have not mastered the basic building blocks of our disciplines, they cannot be expected to manipulate knowledge that they lack in order to analyze, synthesize, or evaluate. They are the students who are failing mathematical problem solving in eighth grade, in part because they simply have not mastered their multiplication facts. During the years that our college interns' field experience consisted of working with eighth and ninth graders who were in summer school for mathematics remediation, the interns were astonished and appalled to discover that the junior high students with whom they were working had not mastered the basic math facts. An intense 90 minutes a day for ten days inevitably resulted in the youngsters having mastered all of the facts that they did not know on the first day of summer school.

Likewise, the college interns discovered to their horror that the students who were in summer school for failing reading had not mastered the basic 220 Dolch sight word list: They could not read words such as *birthday, children,* and *please.* While this level of instruction is beyond what most middle school and secondary teachers are expected to provide, the example is instructive in assisting us to understand that students who are struggling often lack the most basic knowledge and skills that we assume they mastered years ago.

When we identify and assess the basic knowledge and skills that students lack, we can then graph their knowledge and skill acquisition using Microsoft Excel or some other spreadsheet program. We must be consistent in graphing only one type of content or skill on one graph: The number of math facts that a student has mastered each day or week goes on one chart; how long it takes the student to solve five problems using those facts goes on a separate chart. Similarly, the number of adjectives that a student correctly recognizes in one minute belongs on one chart, while the number of adjectives that the student uses appropriately on a five-minute writing probe belongs on a separate chart.

For more difficult performance-based assessments, carefully constructed rubrics can allow the teacher to assess a wide variety of performances. A plethora of rubrics are available free online from school districts, universities, textbook publishers, and other sources.

RtI Tier 1

RtI is a three-tiered approach that has been interpreted a number of ways depending on who is doing the interpreting. In general, in Tier 1 the teacher sets benchmarks (short-term instructional goals), provides research-based teaching to the entire class, and conducts progress monitoring (CBM) with the student who is struggling. Struggling students can be identified from daily performance, by examination of previous achievement scores or grades, or by screening assessments that all students take. At this point, the focus is on providing high-quality instruction for the entire class, although the teacher does provide appropriate accommodations for students who are struggling. The accommodations might include a partial-note lecture guide for students who cannot keep up with the teacher's presentation, a study guide for students who have difficulty identifying critical from salient information in a text, or written as well as oral instructions for an assignment. At this point, the teacher is closely monitoring the performance of the struggling students using CBM.

If the student is not making satisfactory progress in the whole-group, scientifically based instructional setting, then the teacher should meet with her or his campus's team (variously known as Campus Assistance Team, Teacher Assistance Team, Student Assistance Team, Instructional Support Team, Child Study Team, or some other similar term) that assists in generating instructional ideas and determining whether the student needs Tier 2 assistance. The students who are not making satisfactory progress after eight to ten weeks are known as *nonresponding* students because they have not responded to the scientifically based instruction.

RtI Tier 2

The campus team will use a problem-solving model to determine appropriate interventions and assessments to be provided to a small group of struggling students. This instruction will be more individualized (small homogeneous groups vs. whole group), more intense (of longer duration, greater frequency, more highly focused, and more closely monitored), and provided by personnel with more training in working with struggling learners than most general education teachers have. Tier 2 instruction is generally conducted for up to ten weeks.

Students who do not respond to Tier 2 instruction will move to Tier 3. Tier 3 instruction varies by state and even by district. Tier 3 may consist of 1:1 intensive instruction outside of special education. Tier 3 may mean that the campus team refers the student for a multidisciplinary evaluation for special education placement. In a few states, Tier 3 may mean that the student is immediately enrolled in special education without a multidisciplinary assessment. States that use this option do not label students as *learning disabled, behavior disordered,* and so on. They label the students as *eligible for special education.*

UNIVERSAL DESIGN FOR LEARNING

Universal Design is a term originally coined by architects to describe accommodations to facilities that could serve people who use wheelchairs: ramps, wide doorways, kitchen counters that could be raised and lowered. The idea was to build structures—rather than retrofit them—that would serve all people throughout their life span in order to address the requirements of civil rights legislation, such as Section 504 of the Rehabilitation Act and the Americans with Disabilities Act. Soon, engineers and product designers joined the movement, and they began designing disability-friendly products such as lever handles for doors, thick handles on cooking utensils, and cabinets with pullout shelves—all accommodations that enable people with physical limitations to live independently. The principles of Universal Design are that accommodations and products must

- Be equitable
- Be flexible
- Be simple and intuitive
- Have a wide tolerance for error
- Require low physical effort
- Provide adequate space and accommodate a variety of sizes
- Make information accessible to people who have sensory difficulties such as low vision or hearing

In 1984, several disability researchers came together to extend the concept of Universal Design to education. They established the nonprofit Center for Applied Special Technology (CAST) to investigate how technology could be exploited to improve education for all students: both those with and without disabilities. They named their approach Universal Design for Learning (UDL) and have won a plethora of awards for their contribution to education.

Like the Universal Design of architecture and engineering, UDL is based upon a set of guidelines:

- Provide multiple means of representation
- Provide for multiple means of student expression
- Provide for multiple means of student engagement

Multiple Means of Representation

Providing *Multiple Means of Representation* means presenting information to students in more than one way. Many of us know a Mr. Jones, whose entire teaching repertoire consists of standing in front of the class and lecturing while students are expected to take notes, sinking or swimming on their own when they need someone to point them to shore. Multiple means of representation means that Mr. Jones provides both auditory and visual input: He incorporates graphic organizers and other visual material into his lectures. He provides students with assistance in understanding concepts through providing graphic organizers and defining vocabulary. Finally, he provides students with assistance in comprehending material through highlighting critical elements and teaching them mnemonic strategies. These are simply a few examples of Multiple Means of Representation.

Multiple Means of Expression

We all know a Mrs. Barr, who only allows students to show what they know about history through writing the five-paragraph essay. Providing *Multiple Means of Expression* means that Mrs. Barr would provide options for physical action: She would allow students who could not write to record their answers in digital form, or she would allow students to create storyboards to demonstrate their knowledge. She would have them set learning goals and help them learn to progress toward their goals.

Multiple Means of Engagement

Finally, we all know a Mr. Adams, who expects his students to complete their biology homework simply because they should. Providing *Multiple Means of Engagement* means that he will find ways of showing his students how biology is socially relevant to them, allowing them to collaborate to exploit adolescents' natural urge to engage socially, and providing feedback that encourages persistence.

The CAST Web site, www.cast.org, explains the principles of UDL in great detail and even has a password-protected site where teachers can create and save their own UDL lesson plans.

THE PURPOSE OF THIS BOOK

The purpose of this book is to provide middle school and high school teachers with scientifically based UDL strategies for whole-class instruction that marry well with the types of teaching strategies that middle and high school teachers regularly employ. Many of the strategies in this book take little time or effort to incorporate into a good teacher's repertoire. Some take less than a minute of class time but yield significant results. Others are incorporated into lessons and provide a slightly different but important change in delivery; these strategies may take more time when they are initially developed, but will save time in subsequent lessons. They will result in improved learning for all students, not only those who are struggling. But they will make critical differences for our struggling learners.

To assist the reader, the book provides samples of reproducible graphic organizers and other forms in the Appendices.

A NOTE ABOUT PEOPLE FIRST LANGUAGE

Words are important. The words that we use to define people affect both the people we define and ourselves. Therefore, throughout this book, we will usually use the term *students with ELN*. ELN stands for *Exceptional Learning Needs*; ELN is the currently preferred term in a majority of the disability community when speaking of students with various disabilities who are grouped together, such as the students about whom this book is written: students with learning disabilities, mild intellectual disabilities (formerly known as *mental retardation*), and mild behavior disorders. We preface the letters ENL with the words *students who have*.

We derive our term from *People First Language*. People First Language puts the humanness before the disability and never uses a disability term as a substitute for a noun referring to a human. For example, we do not say *the learning disabled*; we say *a student who has a learning disability*. Calling people *the learning disabled* (or *the retarded*, or *the behavior disordered*, etc.) dehumanizes them and makes them seem monolithic.

I have a brain injury (and resulting neurological problems) from a brain tumor and the surgery to remove it. However, I am far more than simply *the brain injured* or *the neurologically impaired.* Having a brain injury is only one part of who I am. I am a teacher, a writer, a reader, a scholar, a Hardin Distinguished Professor, a staunch Episcopalian, a dog devotee, a classical music listener, a defender of the First Amendment, an advocate of people with autism and other developmental disabilities, a Tolkien lover, a Harry Potter fanatic, an amateur chef, a senior citizen, a loving wife, a good sister, a devoted cousin, and as Professor Dumbledore said of Cedric Diggory at his memorial service, a fierce friend.

I am not a monolith; I'm much more than simply *the brain injured* or *the neurologically impaired.* Do my brain injury and neurological impairments affect my life? You betcha; every day I gird my loins and do battle with them. But they are only *one* part of who I am. If, for some reason, you must to think of me in terms of my disability, then think of me as *a person with a brain injury,* or *a person with a neurological impairment.* Not *the brain injured* or *the neurologically impaired.*

Note that not everyone in the disability community prefers People First Language. The term is *not* preferred by people in the deaf and blind communities. The national organizations representing those individuals typically prefer to be called *blind people* or *deaf people.* In addition, many people with autism, primarily people with the Asperger's form of autism, prefer to be called *autistics.*

However, the majority of students for whom this book was written have learning disabilities, mild intellectual disabilities, or mild behavior disorders. They are the adolescents and young adults whom we have taught and loved for so many years. Therefore, we will generally use the term *students who have ELN.* Occasionally we will use the term *students with learning disabilities* when research has investigated exclusively students with that disability and we think that is the best term for clarification in this book. But we'd rather hit our thumb with a hammer than use the terms *the learning disabled, the retarded,* or *the behavior disordered.* After all, we don't want to be called the *brain injured* either.

2

The Locks on the Doors to Learning

We are high school and middle school teachers. We love our disciplines passionately. Unlike people in some other professions, we have not spent our lives chasing material wealth to adorn our bodies in gold and jewels. Instead, we have spent our lives pursuing ideas. The *big ideas* of our disciplines are our priceless jewels: diamonds, rubies, emeralds, and sapphires. Our jewels catch the light and fling it in a thousand directions. The tools that help us fashion the jewels are the fire over which we soften the gold that encases them, the jeweler's loupe, the gauges, and the cutting tools. Those are our scientific methods, our deconstructions, our primary documents, our peer-reviewed journals, and our stacks of reference books.

We want to share the wealth with young people, and we laugh out loud when students are wowed by the colors, and the shapes, and the way the light dances off the facets of our jewels. But some of our students—often those who have learning problems—appear apathetic about entering our stronghold and immersing themselves in the mounds of gems: They shrug their shoulders, roll their eyes, and yawn. They would much rather play videogames.

Sometimes our tempers flare at their cavalier dismissal. Sometimes we tell ourselves that they do not deserve our treasures, our priceless ideas for which the likes of Socrates, Galileo, Darwin, Alice Paul, Gandhi, Martin Luther King, and countless other great thinkers have suffered. Let those unappreciative, undeserving teenagers rot their minds with their vapid videogames.

What we teachers do not see are the invisible locks that bar those students from entering into our treasure rooms. Not one lock, but many, one after the other, bar their way. When they were younger, these students were as eager as their peers to get their hands on the jewels and to sort, cut, polish, and make jewelry of their own—but years of battling the locks reduced them to a fatalism that is apparent in their mantras of "Who cares?" or "Whatever."

We did not realize until relatively recently that they were bereft of the keys to the locks on the doors. Because the locks are invisible, we did not know they existed. Only in the last 30 years have we begun to know more about the keys that help students open the locks. The keys *do* work for our students with learning problems. They work, and they work well. All we have to do is learn which keys fit which locks and then use them to help all of our students access the treasure. This book is designed to help.

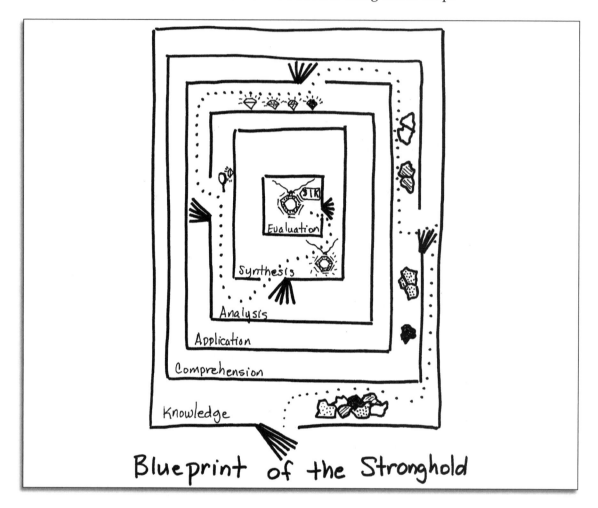

Blueprint of the Stronghold

The metaphor of the jewel and the stronghold works well for this purpose. The rooms are the levels of learning in Bloom's Taxonomy. The rooms are Knowledge, Comprehension, Application, Analysis, Synthesis, and Evaluation. In the first room, Knowledge, we collect the rough, uncut stones; in the second room, Comprehension, we study and sort the stones. The third room is Application, and here we cut and polish the gems. The first of the higher-order thinking skills rooms is Analysis, and in this room we study each stone to determine how best to use it. We decide whether the stone should be a solitaire in a ring or one of a dozen stones in a heart-shaped necklace. In the Synthesis room, we take the stone and create a lovely piece of jewelry. Finally, in the Evaluation room, we bring all of our knowledge together to appraise the exquisite adornment and establish its value.

The doors to each of those rooms are Acquisition, Proficiency and Fluency, Maintenance, Generalization, and Adaptation (Smith, 1981), and our students must go through all the doors to enter each room.

Theoretically, our students must *acquire*, become *proficient and fluent, maintain, generalize/ transfer,* and *adapt knowledge* before they are completely ready to move on to the next level of learning.

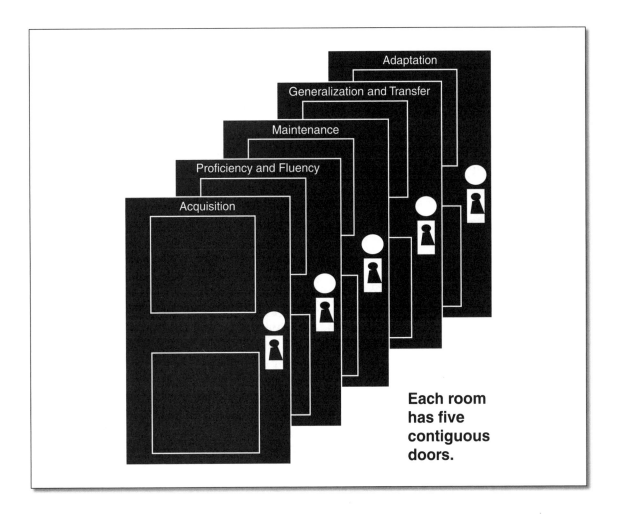

Currently, in pedagogical circles, discounting the importance of knowledge-level learning is de rigueur. We think that is unwise and that the phenomenon comes from a lack of deep understanding of Bloom and colleagues' (1956) Taxonomy of Cognitive Objectives. When we ask teacher friends exactly what the taxonomy means by *knowledge*, they are unable to tell us.

According to the taxonomy, knowledge consists of a discipline's

- Terminology
- Specifics
- Ways and means of dealing with the (1) conventions, (2) trends and sequences, (3) classifications and categories, (4) criteria, and (5) methodology of those specifics
- Universals and abstractions: (1) principles and generalizations and (2) theories and structures

Knowledge is significant, and it is a prerequisite to higher levels of thinking.

Bloom and his colleagues (1956) defined *comprehension* as *being able to translate the data, interpolate it, or extrapolate from a piece of information.* We cannot translate, interpolate, or extrapolate until we have the requisite knowledge, so our students must have full access to the first room before we can enter into the second room. If knowledge is, for example, mastery of the classification that 3, 7, and 9 are odd numbers, comprehension, then, would be interpolating 5 and extrapolating that 1, 11, and 223 are odd numbers.

Comprehension would also include telling someone else that an odd number is one indivisible by 2.

Like Knowledge, Comprehension has five doors. We must acquire comprehension, become proficient and fluent at comprehending, maintain our comprehension, generalize/ transfer, and adapt it. That is requisite to further manipulation of the data.

So it is with Application. We cannot authoritatively apply a concept or skill until we have mastery of its Knowledge and Comprehension. Without knowing that an odd number is indivisible by 2 and without being able to extrapolate that 23 is an odd number, we cannot apply the knowledge and decide whether we can have our students work in pairs when the class has 23 students enrolled.

When we reach the Higher-Order Thinking Skills of Analysis, Synthesis, and Evaluation, we find that each of them has five doors, too. We have to acquire the skills needed to analyze, become proficient and fluent with them, maintain the skill, generalize/transfer the skill when appropriate, and adapt it when necessary. The same sequence applies to Synthesis and Evaluation.

Although the doors are metaphorically and theoretically opened one at a time, in practice, students usually open multiple doors at once; for example, Knowledge and Comprehension often come hand in hand. Locating the rooms and their doors is the first step. Step 2 is understanding the locks, and we describe them next. In Chapter 3, we will discuss three master keys, and in subsequent chapters, we will describe specific keys for accessing specific rooms.

THE LOCKS ON THE DOORS

Rather than discussing each type of disability category separately, we will use noncategorical but useful terms, such as *students with exceptional learning needs (ELN), students with disabilities,* or *students with learning problems.* Unless we note otherwise, the information refers to this generic group.

For simplicity, we have organized the learning problems into categories drawn from the work of cognitive psychologists (Flavell, 1999) with the addition of an Affective category: Input Locks, Information Processing/Retention Locks, Affective Locks, and Output Locks. The Input Locks are Attention Problems, Perception Problems, Discrimination Problems, and Sequencing Problems. The Information Processing/Retention Locks are Confusion, Organization Problems, Reasoning Problems, Memory Problems, and Metacognition Problems. The Affective Locks are Frustration and Motivation Problems, and they are a direct result of the Input Locks and Information Processing/Retention Locks. The Output Lock is Persistence/Production; persistence/production problems are a result of the Affective Locks. We will discuss the Input Locks first because they contribute to the Information Processing/Retention Locks and the Affective Locks.

THE INPUT LOCKS

The Input Locks are problems with attention, perception, discrimination, and sequencing. They all involve difficulty in getting information from the outside world into the processing centers in the brain.

Attention Problems

Using neuropsychological evidence, Sturm and Zimmermann (cited in Schweitzer, Zimmermann, & Koch, 2000) developed a two-level taxonomy of attention. The upper level consists of two categories of attention: intensity and selectivity. Intensity has three subclassifications: alertness, sustained attention, and vigilance. Selectivity has three subclassifications: selective attention or focus, visual/spatial selective attention or change of visual focus, and divided attention.

The types of attention that are most important to the teaching and learning process are sustained attention and the selective attention that refers to focus. Klorman (1991) noted that selective attention refers to intentionally focusing on relevant information while ignoring

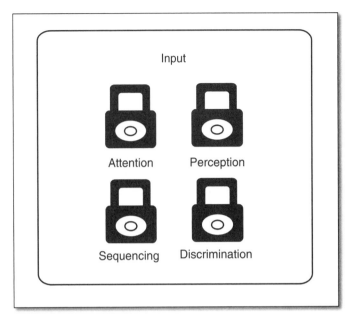

irrelevant information. She also noted that sustained attention refers to processes that are involved in maintaining attention over an extended period of time. If problems in sustained attention occur, they happen when an individual has been engaged in selective attention over a period of time. This is known to scientists and laypeople alike as *mindwandering.*

Unfortunately, many students with ELN exhibit both sustained attention and selective attention problems. For example, students with Attention Deficit Disorder have poorer comprehension on longer reading passages than on shorter reading passages. They also exhibit lower reading comprehension on longer passages than do their peers without attention problems. In addition, students with attention problems tend to be deficient in mathematics achievement, and their mathematics deficits appear to become more pronounced with age (Cherkes-Julkowski & Stolzenberg, 1991; Marshall & Hynd, 1997; Schweitzer et al., 2000).

Research on attention demonstrates that genes are in large part responsible for attention difficulties. At least part of the genetic influences involve multiple alleles on a gene that governs dopamine, dopamine receptors, and dopamine transporters (Bellgrove & Mattingley, 2008; Gizer et al., 2008).

However, regardless of the causes of attention difficulties, we have instructional keys that can help students unlock the locks caused by such problems. By using research-supported strategies, we can help them attend (selective attention) and remain (sustained attention) engaged.

Perception Problems

Visual and auditory perception deficits are hallmarks of learning disabilities (see Johnson & Myklebust, 1967), and their study has been voluminous. Our students with visual or auditory perception problems generally have good visual or auditory acuity; that is, they can see the letters on the eye chart or hear the tone on the audiometer. The problem is that the image or sound has a difficult time finding the right place in the brain so that the brain can make sense of it: The image or sound may travel down the wrong neural path and end up in some place in the brain that cannot make sense of it, or it might wander around before it finally finds the right place where the brain can make sense of it. Unfortunately, the perceptual training programs that characterized treatment of learning disabilities in the early days of the field do not help students' academic performance (Rosen, 1968).

Researchers continue to investigate visual and auditory perceptual problems. Boden and Brodeur (1999) found that adolescents who have reading disabilities are not only slower at processing visual information in the form of the written word but are also slower at processing all visual stimuli. For example, when such students see a dog walking down the street, it takes them longer to realize that what they have seen is a dog. While the difference may only be in milliseconds, the delay translates into significant difficulty in decoding text and other activities that require fluency. Other researchers have noted that students with severe reading disability can be identified by their deficiency in rapid naming ability when they are presented with items visually. Their eyes can see the object, but their brains cannot quickly make sense of what their eyes are seeing. As processing demands increase, the visual perceptual performance of students with ELN slows disproportionately, while the performance of nondisabled students remains strong.

But visual perceptual problems are not the only kind of perceptual problem that students with ELN may experience. Kruger, Kruger, Hugo, and Campbell (2001) found that the majority of the students with learning disabilities they examined had both visual and auditory perceptual disabilities. Not only did the students have difficulty processing visual input, they also had difficulty processing auditory input. Teachers, however, may be puzzled by the varying performance of students with sensory problems: New research with students with dyslexia revealed that while 30% of these students demonstrated visual and auditory processing problems, their performance on visual and auditory tasks was not stable across time (Wright & Conlon, 2009). When a student succeeds at a task one day and then does not perform well on a similar task the next day, we tend to think that the student is simply being lazy, rather than that he or she has a learning problem that waxes and wanes.

Perceptual problems create difficulties for our students outside as well as inside of the classroom. Most and Greenbank (2000) found that eighth graders with learning disabilities in visual and auditory perception were less able than their peers to discriminate the emotions of others, whether the stimulus was auditory, visual, or combined; this resulted in social difficulties. Itier and Batty (2009) noted that impaired visual processing of social partners' eyes and gaze may present a core deficiency in social relationship difficulties, and every secondary teacher recognizes the importance of social relationships in adolescence. Unfortunately, perceptual difficulties tend to remain stable throughout a person's life, so a teenager with perceptual problems that cause social difficulties will become an adult who has those same difficulties.

While we cannot fix their perceptual deficits, we can use teaching strategies that will help our students with ELN compensate for their difficulties. The strategies are easy to use, and research demonstrates that they are effective in helping students with ELN succeed.

Discrimination Problems

Discrimination, in this context, refers to the ability to differentiate between two or more entities. A high school student may have difficulty discriminating between communism and socialism, paramecium and bacterium, sine and cosine, or essential and nonessential information in writing a critical essay. Errors in discrimination often result in overgeneralization and undergeneralization; *overgeneralization* refers to incorrectly identifying an entity as a member of a class when it is not, and conversely, *undergeneralization* refers to failing to identify an entity as a member of a class when it does belong to a class.

In 1970, writing in the *Journal of Learning Disabilities,* Kidd noted that the discriminatory repertoire is the basis of all learning: Understanding an object or a concept consists of class inclusion and class differentiation. First, we must be able to determine to what class a thing belongs—such as a lemon belongs to the class of citrus fruit—and then we must be able to differentiate the thing from other members of that class—such as a lemon is yellow, sour, and more oblong, while a tangerine is orange, sweet, and more round. Such discrimination is difficult for students with ELN, and when the content is challenging, the student's difficulty is compounded.

In addition, Richards, Samuels, Ternure, and Ysseldyke (1990) discovered that students with learning disabilities are more likely to notice salient information than the critical information that teachers direct them to observe; they have difficulty discriminating between the critical data we want them to learn and the irrelevant. For example, they are far more likely to remember Franklin Delano Roosevelt's affair with Lucy Mercer than they are to remember his role in the New Deal. They focus on the wrong information, thereby studying for a test, failing the test, and then earnestly telling us, "I flunked because I studied the wrong stuff!"

Auditory discrimination problems affect many of our students. Watson (1991) examined the relationship of auditory discrimination to intelligence in college students. She found moderate correlations between auditory discrimination and intelligence scores. Subsequently, others have found that young readers who have dyslexia may not be able to maintain phonemic information in their short-term memories long enough to discriminate among sounds and that children with a learning impairment have poorer auditory discrimination on a two-tone discrimination task than do typical children.

Auditory discrimination difficulties also present difficulties for students with ELN; Newport and Howarth (2009) noted that an optimal auditory processing window for social interactions exists. Although the time differentials between normal and abnormal auditory discrimination may differ only by milliseconds, the slight delay may create subtle communication difficulties. Adolescents may be referring to such an auditory difficulty in a peer when they say, "I can't tell you what I don't like about him . . . . He's just weird. . . ."

Visual discrimination difficulties also affect many of our students. Students with learning disabilities are less able than typical peers at discriminating between orthographically legitimate and illegitimate pairs of letters, and some children with intellectual disabilities have difficulty with visual discrimination (Kavale, 1982).

Difficulty with discrimination extends to our students' problem-solving and reasoning ability. For example, McLeskey (1977) found that students with ELN have difficulty discriminating between when a response is and is not appropriate. Whereas McLeskey's nondisabled students tried a complex variety of responses in solving a novel problem, his students with disabilities could not discriminate between situations in which a problem-solving strategy was and was not appropriate. Other researchers have found that adolescents with learning disabilities performed worse on discriminant learning tasks that required them to code, recode, and recall information than did their nondisabled peers.

Discrimination problems extend outside the classrooms to our students' personal lives. Moffatt and others (1995) documented the difficulty persons with intellectual disabilities had in discriminating among emotions and expressing empathy—the greater the degree of intellectual disability, the greater the difficulty with discrimination. As noted earlier, eighth graders with learning disabilities were less able than their peers to discriminate between the emotions of others, such as telling fear from anger or anxiety from sadness.

The research consistently demonstrates that the discrimination tasks in which we engage so cavalierly every day are challenging to our students with learning problems. Fortunately, we can use good inclusion strategies to help them.

Sequencing Problems

The difficulty in sequencing that characterizes so many students with ELN has been documented since the early days of research on learning disabilities. Cohen, Spruill, and Herns (1982) found sequencing to be one of the six most problematic areas for students with auditory learning disabilities. (The others were attention, word retrieval, identification of antonyms, passive relationships, and memory.)

Even many gifted students who have learning disabilities experience difficulty with sequencing. Schiff, Kaufman, and Kaufman (1981) studied gifted children with learning disabilities. The children whom they studied had excellent verbal skills and many talents, but they were deficient in sequencing, as well as motor control and emotional development. The sequencing problems of students with learning disabilities do not retreat with high school graduation—they persist. For example, Blabock (1982) found that college students with auditory learning disabilities experienced persistent problems in sequencing. A number of strategies in this book are designed to help us help our students ensure that they can properly sequence ordered material in our disciplines. With our encouragement, they may be able to generalize/transfer the strategies to other classes and to their lives outside of school.

THE INFORMATION PROCESSING/RETENTION LOCKS

Once the information from the external environment enters the brain of a student with ELN, the student must then process and retain that information. Several locks bar the student from processing and remembering that information. Those locks include Confusion, Organization Problems, Reasoning Problems, Memory Problems, and Metacognition Problems.

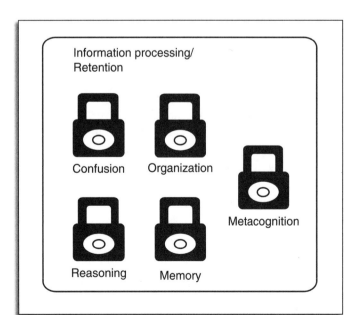

Confusion

Since the early days of learning-disability research, confusion has been documented as a learning problem that is characteristic of children with learning disabilities. Such findings continue to be confirmed and expanded across time. For example, Barkin, Gardner, Kass, and Polo (1981) documented left-right confusion; others have documented confusion in sequencing, sound-ground and figure-ground confusion, linguistic confusion, and cognitive confusion. In contrast to nondisabled peers, even after becoming acquainted with a task, students with learning disabilities continue to be confused about how to execute it.

In 1998, Scott and Nelson reported on the confusion in generalizing social responding experienced by students with learning disabilities, and others have identified their confusion about adult roles. Guyton (1968) even argued that students' confused emotions can compound their cognitive confusion.

A serious facet of confusion is that while nondisabled learners typically realize that they are confused, and can therefore ask for assistance from peers or teachers, students who have disabilities often fail to realize that they are confused. They are confused about their confusion. Because they think that they understand something when they are actually confused, they fail to ask for assistance or clarification. They are both astonished and deeply disappointed when they complete an assignment on which they thought they had performed well, only to find that they failed because they were confused about either the instructions or the content. When they fail an assignment, our students with ELN may document their failure when they tell us, "I was all mixed up about what we were supposed to do!"

The jury is in, and the verdict is not confusing: Our students with learning problems are confused much of the time. But we have the ability to help prevent much of their confusion if we use appropriate instructional strategies.

Organization Problems

Difficulty with organizational skills has long been documented in the literature on learning and emotional disability (Zera & Lucian, 2001). The National Dissemination Center for Children with Disabilities (NICHCY) explained that many students who are learning disabled have difficulty organizing bits of information to consolidate them into concepts, often learning multiple facts that they cannot draw upon to answer related questions. For example, the student may learn that the United States has a legislative branch that makes laws, an executive branch that enforces the laws, and a judicial branch that interprets the laws. However, he or she may not be able to organize this information to answer the question: "Explain the functions of the branches of the U.S. government." NICHCY noted that the entire context of their lives may reflect this disorganization.

Teachers, parents, and adolescent students with disabilities report that their poor organizational skills create problems with completing work, locating materials, and using time wisely. Adolescents with disabilities, and their parents and teachers, identify poor organizational skills as one of their three most problematic areas—the other two being communication and social skills. Such difficulty does not lessen with age; adults with learning disabilities report that poor organizational skills are an important impediment to their career and life success (Malcolm, Polatajko, & Simons, 1990).

Many of the strategies in this book are designed to help students organize information into meaningful wholes. Not only can we use the strategies to their advantage, but our nondisabled students will benefit as well.

Reasoning Problems

Many students with learning problems have trouble with reasoning skills. In fact, the problem is so pronounced that in 1993, Stanovich proposed a new category of learning disability: *dysrationalia.* Stanovich defined dysrationalia as *the inability to think rationally despite adequate intelligence.* Although leaders in the field promptly dismissed the concept with amusement (Sternberg, 1993, 1994), Stanovich's notion of irrationality as a separate learning disability points out the extent to which poor reasoning skills characterize the thinking of some of our students with ELN.

Students who have different subcategories of learning disabilities differ in their ability to reason. Schiff, Bauminger, and Toledo (2009) found that students with nonverbal learning disabilities demonstrate significantly more difficulty with analogical reasoning than do their peers without ELN or their peers with verbal learning disabilities. Students with learning disabilities demonstrate less coordinated thought structures than do their nondisabled peers; in addition, they are less likely to employ second-order logical structures than are their peers. They also display operational logic structures significantly less often than do their peers on mathematics tasks.

The problems persist. College students with dyscalculia differ significantly from their nondisabled peers in reasoning ability (McGlaughlin, Knoop, & Holliday, 2005). In addition, college students diagnosed as having learning disabilities demonstrate difficulty in learning to use logic and require explicit instruction in thinking skills—instruction that they may not receive in college (Utzinger, 1982).

Memory Problems

Mnemonic problems are generally present in students with learning disabilities (McNamara, 1999), and they continue to be investigated. In fact, Boudah and Weiss (2002), writing in the ERIC Digest *Learning Disabilities Overview: Update 2002*, called memory problems one of five common problems of students with learning disabilities. Likewise, writing in the ERIC Digest *Nonverbal Learning Disability: How to Recognize It and Minimize Its Effects*, Foss (2001) listed memory problems as one of the four difficulties she identified.

D'Amico and Passolunghi (2009) conducted a two-year longitudinal study investigating how well students with learning disabilities in mathematics could retrieve both mathematical and nonmathematical information from long-term memory. The students with ELN and their matched controls differed markedly in the speed with which they could retrieve information from memory. This finding applied to both the numerical and nonnumerical information, even though the students were disabled only in mathematics.

Swanson, Xinhua, and Jerman (2009) compared short-term memory and long-term memory among students with a broad range of ages, reading abilities, and IQ scores. They found significant differences in both types of memory between those students who had reading disabilities and those students who did not. The differences persisted across age groups and IQ scores.

Mnemonic problems affect students' performance across the curriculum, not only in reading and mathematics. Teachers in the social studies and sciences have noted the need for memory strategies for students with disabilities in those areas, too (Steele, 2007; Ward-Lonergan, Liles, & Anderson, 1998). Keyword mnemonic strategies have been found to significantly increase the social studies achievement of secondary students who were English Language Learners in an inclusive secondary classroom in a racially diverse, large, urban high school (Fontana, Scruggs, & Mastropieri, 2007). The course of study involved nationalism, imperialism, World Wars I and II, and the period between the wars; the vocabulary included words such as *ecumenism, protectorate,* and *reparations.* Scruggs and Mastropieri (2007) reviewed a variety of approaches to teaching science to students with ELN and stated that mnemonics instruction is an extremely effective and robust feature of good instruction for such students when teaching content knowledge. The studies that they reviewed involved the use of mnemonics instruction in paleontology, geology, chemistry, and biology.

Memory is important in every area of life, not only in academics. McNamara (1999) argued that memory problems contribute to the social relationship problems of students with learning difficulties. Being unable to remember social conventions, particularly when required to think on their feet, creates relationship difficulties for students with ELN. Forgetting appointments, dates, and promises all cause social difficulties—sometimes rupturing relationships.

Like the other characteristics of students with learning problems, mnemonic difficulties do not end with graduation. Adults with learning disabilities continue to experience problems with mnemonic functions (Jordan, 2000). Like the memory problems of our students, those of adults can be devastating, especially when they involve employers' demands, policies, or expectations.

Metacognition Problems

Metacognition, as discussed by A. L. Brown (1975, 1978, 1979) and J. H. Flavell (1971, 1979, 1999) in their extensive work on the subject, particularly in the area of reading comprehension, refers to thinking about thinking and controlling thinking; metamemory (thinking about and controlling remembering), meta-attention (thinking about and controlling attention), and metacomprehension (thinking about and controlling comprehension) are closely related to metacognition.

Students with ELN tend to be passive learners who are unaware of their own learning processes (Wang, 1987); they fail to monitor their own learning. For example, Garcia and Fidalgo (2008) examined the metacognition of middle school students with and without learning disabilities who were engaged in the writing process. The students who had learning disabilities were far more passive in the writing process, demonstrating far less self-monitoring of their writing than did peers and spending less time on pre-writing activities, revision, and the editing of their work.

Poor metacognition results in mnemonic difficulties, transfer and generalization problems, reading comprehension problems, and a host of other difficulties (Brown & Palincsar, 1982; Wong, 1985). We have all had students say, "But I read the chapter!" when they performed poorly on examinations. True, they pronounced the words on the pages, but they did not monitor whether they understood the meanings embedded in the words they pronounced. Typical learners would have realized that they did not understand what they were reading, and they would have employed strategies to improve their comprehension.

In *Research on Interventions for Adolescents With Learning Disabilities: A Meta-Analysis of Outcomes Related to Higher-Order Processing,* Swanson (2001) noted that metacognitive instruction produced large positive benefits for learners. This supports the large-scale study of learning strategies that students use in science, mathematics, and reading that Chiu, Chow, and Mcbride-Chang (2007) conducted. In their investigation of metacognitive and other strategies employed by 158,848 students in 34 countries, the researchers found that those students who used metacognitive strategies when they studied mathematics or science outscored peers who used other learning strategies.

Metacognition is critical for academic success across the curriculum. Wang, Haertel, and Walberg (1993/1994) used a knowledge base of 11,000 statistical findings to identify the magnitude of 28 categories of influences on student learning. Only classroom management was more influential on student learning than was the teaching of metacognitive strategies.

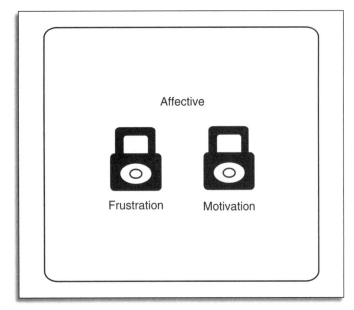

Metacognitive training extends beyond academics. For example, metacognitive training in social skills improves the social adjustment of incarcerated boys with learning problems and reduces the anger behavior and aggressive acts of elementary, middle school, and high school boys with anger management problems (Larson & Gerber, 1987; Smith, 1992).

In the context of our classrooms, we can use metacognitive strategies that will increase students' achievement in our discipline. That is good news. But the better news is that when we teach students to use metacognitive strategies, we may contribute to improving their lives both inside and outside of the classroom.

THE AFFECTIVE LOCKS

Frustration and Motivation Problems are the Affective Locks that bar our students' entry into the vault. Frustration and Motivation Problems are the direct result of Input and Information Processing/Retention Problems. Only by helping students unlock the previous locks can we help them unlock these barriers. But the phenomenon is cyclical in nature. Once we help them unlock these locks, our students will be better able to unlock the previous locks and, at the same time, the Persistence/Production Problems Lock.

Frustration

Writing in an ERIC Digest, Bergert (2000) noted that frustration is an early warning sign of learning disabilities; the frustration difficulties are evident in both academic and social arenas. As early as 1968, Beckman identified low frustration tolerance as a behavioral characteristic of children with learning disabilities. Toro, Weissberg, Guare, and Libenstein (1990) found that the poor social problem-solving skills of children with learning disabilities were complicated by their low frustration tolerance, and Murray and Whittenberger (1983) cautioned that frustration with learning problems contributed to the problems of many aggressive, severely behavior disordered children. In addition, Scime and Norvilitis (2006) found that students with Attention Deficit Hyperactivity Disorder not only became frustrated with difficult mathematics problems more easily than did their peers, but that they knew that they were more easily frustrated than nondisabled students were.

As early as 1978, Kronick noted that frustration characterizes the life experiences of adolescents with ELN both inside and outside of the classroom. But the problem of frustration does not end when high school does. Mays and Imel (1982), writing in an ERIC Fact Sheet, noted that low frustration tolerance is one of nine observable characteristics of adults with learning disabilities, and Lancaster, Mellard, and Hoffman (2001) reported that college students with learning disabilities reported frustration as one of their six major difficulties. (The other difficulties were concentration, distraction, test anxiety, remembering, and mathematics.) Even high ability students with learning disabilities who have earned college degrees have noted their frustration with certain academic areas.

Having learning problems frustrates our students who cope with them day in and day out, every day of their lives. Thank goodness we can help prevent much of their frustration when we use good inclusive practices.

Motivation Problems

The Input and Information Processing/ Retention locks prevent our students from being able to learn our disciplines, but they do teach them one thing: helplessness. In fact, the Motivation Problems Lock could easily be called the Learned Helplessness (Seligman, 1975) Lock because learned helplessness contributes to our students' low achievement motivation.

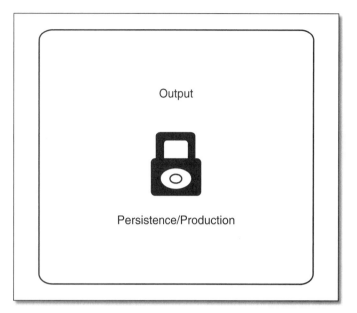

Low academic achievement motivation is a characteristic common to our students with ELN. In general, students with ELN tend to be extrinsically—rather than intrinsically— motivated to complete schoolwork, and of the various types of learning problems that students experience, our adolescents with learning disabilities demonstrate lower achievement motivation toward schoolwork than do their peers who have emotional disorders (Fulk, Brigham, & Lohman, 1998; Okolo & Bahr, 1995).

But some students with learning disabilities are highly academically motivated. Those students who are highly academically motivated are intrinsically, rather than extrinsically, motivated to excel in school (Dev, 1998). Also, many students who are not academically motivated are motivated in nonacademic areas. In areas in which they experience success, students with ELN are highly motivated (Adelman & Taylor, 1990). We have all known students who brag that they have worked for hours without food, rest, or sleep to master a complicated video game.

Learned helplessness appears to be at the root of low achievement motivation in students with disabilities (Valas, 2001). After repeated failures, students learn that they cannot succeed in school. This attribution becomes so deeply embedded that they may passively or actively refuse to try to achieve in schoolwork. A large-scale study in Sweden revealed that the more helpless a student feels, the more the student withdraws from engagement in school, the more depressive symptomatology the student exhibits, and the more the student engages in rule-breaking behavior (Määtt, Nurmi, & Stattin, 2007).

Once established, learned helplessness tends to persist, but fortunately, we can help combat learned helplessness by making assignments more approachable. Success breeds motivation.

THE OUTPUT LOCK

The Output Lock refers to Production Problems. However, we include the Persistence Lock with the Output Lock because combining them is intuitively appealing. Our students' problems with persistence are most observable when we have required them to produce some product.

Persistence/Production Problems

Persistence is a critical attribute for academic success. Somers, Owens, and Piliawsky (2008) investigated the predictors of academic success among 118 urban African American high school students. Personal persistence and educational intentions were the most powerful predictors of academic success of the multiple individual and social variables examined.

Our students with ELN often experience difficulty persisting in and completing classroom assignments and homework. Their teachers rate them as less persistent than nondisabled students and as deficient in quantity and quality of story production as compared to their nondisabled peers. In addition, while most students enjoy doing projects, students with ELN have difficulty completing them (Graves, Semmel, & Gerber, 1994; Salend & Gajria, 1995).

Adolescents and young adults with disabilities have difficulty completing their education; they comprise one of the three categories of students most likely to drop out of high school (the others being foreign-born students and those who were retained in one or more grades). Wave 2 of the National Longitudinal Transition Study published by the U.S. Department of Education in 2006 revealed that 28% of students with disabilities dropped out of high school; the group with the highest dropout rate was the students with emotional disabilities: 44% of the students in that group left school without graduating. College students with disabilities are less likely to have completed their degree in five years than are their peers without disabilities, and numerous studies have noted that adults and adolescents with mild intellectual disabilities have difficulty with work completion (Hurst & Smerdon, 2000a, 2000b; McMillen, Kaufman, & Klein, 1997).

From elementary school through adulthood, our students struggle with persisting in and completing what they need to do. While we cannot help in every arena, we can use supportive teaching strategies that will help students with ELN complete assignments in our classrooms.

THE SUM TOTAL OF THE LOCKS

Metaphorically, we do not think that multiple locks represent an additive relationship; we do not even think that the relationship is multiplicative. Instead, we think that the relationship of multiple locks on a student's learning is exponential. As with many other things, a synergy takes place among the locks, and the total damage that they do to our students is greater than the sum of their parts.

The news is serious: The learning problem locks make life and learning difficult for students with ELN. Reading about them could discourage us. But that is counterproductive. What we must do is learn how to use keys to help our students open the locks. Then we can invite them into the stronghold, and even into the vault, and offer them a handful of jewels.

3

Keys to the Effectiveness of the Inclusion Strategies

The locks on the doors to our students' learning can seem overwhelming to them and to us. The good news is that by using three master keys to effective instruction for students with disabilities, and the individual keys that are guided by those master keys, we can help our students unlock the doors to learning.

The three master keys to effective instruction for students with disabilities are (1) explicitness, (2) structure, and (3) repetition.

In "Instructing Adolescents With Learning Disabilities: A Component and Composite Analysis," published in *Learning Disabilities Research and Practice*, Swanson and Hoskyn (2001) noted the importance of explicitness in all phases of instruction for secondary students with learning problems. Their factor analysis of many studies showed that a factor called *organization/explicit* was the single most powerful factor of the strategies used in intervention programs for secondary learning disabled students; the explicit part of the factor referred to explicit modeling and explicit practice, with explicit practice being the single most important instructional component related to high effect sizes. The organization/explicit factor includes all three keys: *organization* refers to *structure*, and *explicitness* and *practice* are prima facie.

But the education community today is extremely concerned with higher-order thinking. So Swanson (2001) conducted a meta-analysis of 58 studies of the factors in interventions that led to higher-order processing, and his findings supported those of Swanson and Hoskyn (2001). He found that extended explicit practice and structure—in this case, the structure of advanced organizers—were the most critical factors in increasing the higher-order thinking skills of adolescents with learning disabilities.

In addition, in their mega-analysis of effective strategies for teaching students with learning problems, Kavale and Forness (1999) found Direct Instruction, a strategy that is a structured approach to explicit instruction that includes repetition through explicit practice with explicit feedback and review, to be one of the most effective strategies, having an effect size of 0.84; the only strategies more effective were mnemonic strategies (effect size [ES] 1.62), reading comprehension strategies (ES ranging from 1.13 to 0.98 depending on the particular strategy), and behavior modification (ES 0.93), all of which are structured approaches that include explicitness and repetition to a greater or lesser degree.

Swanson's (1999) study, presented at the National Summit on Research in Learning Disabilities, was an earlier analysis of the 58 studies he reviewed again in 2001; at that time, his analysis focused on instructional models instead of components of instruction within those models. This earlier analysis affirmed that Direct Instruction and strategy instruction were the two most effective strategies in teaching students with learning disabilities; both are structured approaches that include explicitness and repetition.

As compared to their nondisabled counterparts, students with mild disabilities tend to experience difficulty learning important information incidentally and inductively (Di Gennaro & Picciarelli, 1992; Hollingsworth & Woodward, 1993; Kavale & Forness, 1999; Mastropieri, Scruggs, & Butcher, 1997; Oetting & Rice, 1995; Rice & Buhr, 1992; Rice & Oetting, 1994), due to difficulty discriminating between the relevant and irrelevant dimensions of the task (Zeaman & House, 1961). Thus, they may incidentally learn irrelevant information (e.g., knowing the name of Harry Truman's dog, but not knowing who Harry Truman was).

Because discriminating between important and unimportant information tends to be difficult for them, students with learning problems benefit from direct instruction (Kavale & Forness, 1999) with its explicit focus on what is important. As part of that direct instruction, they need concrete hands-on experiences and multisensory, multirepresentational instruction (Clark & Paivio, 1991; Gellevij, Van Der Meij, De Jong, & Pieters, 2002; Moseley & Brenner, 1997).

In addition, because they tend to have difficulty encoding information into their memory systems and therefore lack basic skills and cognitions that must be in place before they can attempt higher-order thinking, students with learning problems require repetition in instruction, spaced practice, and frequent review. Each time a neural trace is activated, that arm of the neuron becomes stronger and easier to access the next time. An analogy for this is how we sometimes get into our cars to go to the store only to discover that we went the wrong way and headed for the office because that is where we usually go.

The brains of students with learning problems are not as efficient in making those neural traces stronger, so they need to activate the traces more frequently in order to strengthen the connections. Thus, repetition through multisensory, multirepresentational input, practice, and frequent review are necessary.

DUAL CODING THEORY AND TRI-CODING OF INFORMATION

Hebb's Law (Hebb, 1949) theorized that neurons that fire together simultaneously have a high likelihood to fire together again when stimulated. Siegel (1999), cited in Wolfe (2001, p. 76), paraphrased Hebb's Law: "Neurons that fire together, survive together, and wire together."

Wolfe (2001) explained that Information Processing Theory posits that memory starts with sensory input from the five senses. She cited Kotulak (1996), who wrote the following:

> The brain gobbles up its external environment in bites and chunks through its sensory system: vision, hearing, smell, touch, and taste. Then the digested world is reassembled in the form of trillions of connections between brain cells that are constantly growing or dying or becoming stronger or weaker, depending upon the richness of the banquet. (p. 4)

While the brain dumps 99% of its sensory input (Gazzaniga, 1998), the 1% that it stores in long-term memory is sensory data. Wolfe (2001) cited research that showed that the storage of that sensory data actually increases the size and weight of the brain due to larger number of synapses per neuron, large cortical neurons and synapses, and heavier branching of dendrites.

Although all sensory input is important, visual input is particularly powerful. Our eyes contain 70% of our sensory receptors, and we take in more sensory information visually than by any other means.

Paivio's (1990) Dual Coding Theory refers to teaching visually and auditorily at the same time and posits that the more neural paths that a memory involves, the more likely that memory is to be permanently recorded and to be successfully accessed at a later date. Simpson (1997) extended Dual Coding Theory to what he called Tri-Coding of Information by adding the kinesthetic pathway to the visual and auditory pathways.

Maria Montessori, a pioneer in the education of children living in poverty and children with disabilities, hailed the use of multiple sensory channel input as early as the middle of the nineteenth century. Grace Fernald, one of the twentieth-century pioneers of special education, developed a method she called VAKT, for visual, auditory, kinesthetic, and tactile teaching. Although more generally referred to as multisensory teaching than tri-coding of information, a number of researchers have produced research support for activities that employ tri-coding activities that employ visual, auditory, and kinesthetic channels. Sparks and Ganschow (1993) and other researchers have found positive effects when using multisensory teaching with at-risk high school foreign language learners, junior high special education social studies students, and mathematics students with learning problems. In addition, multiple studies have showed structured multisensory instruction to be effective in teaching reading to delinquents who have learning disabilities and college students who have learning disabilities.

Kubina and Cooper (2000) argued that the use of multiple learning channels within the same lesson adds variety to instruction and practice. They also added that varied instruction via multisensory teacher input and student output allows learners to experience different ways of learning; when teachers alternate the modalities that they instruct students to use as output, the novelty increases student motivation and attention to their task and, therefore, reduces students' failure.

Multicoding helps with attention problems by involving more than passive listening. Multicoding helps comprehension because the multiple representations increase the likelihood of the student connecting with the material in the way that he or she learns best. Multicoding also helps with retention by increasing the places in the brain where the information is stored.

Closely related to multisensory instruction is instruction that employs *multiple representations*. Multiple representations can be thought of as *multiple examples* or *multiple types of experiences of a concept*. The National Council of Teachers of Mathematics (see www.nctm.org) endorses the use of multiple representations in mathematics teaching. Herbel-Eisenmann (2002) found that multiple representations increased students' acquisition of mathematical vocabulary, and others have found that multiple representations increased junior high students' algebraic thinking significantly over students taught with traditional techniques. Using multiple representations in science, Wu, Krajcik, and Soloway (2001) found that students' understanding of chemical representation increased dramatically, and others have found positive effects in increasing high school students' conceptualization of the molecular structure.

When we use the master keys of explicitness, structure, and repetition and we employ those keys through multisensory and multirepresentational means, we will be able to help our students with ELN unlock the doors that block their way to the jewels in our stronghold. Those master keys provide the basis for the individual keys in this book.

Not only are the keys effective, but we teachers enjoy using them, and our students enjoy our lessons when we do.

4

Ensuring Students Understand Instructions

As teachers, we *try* to give clear directions. We *think* we give clear directions. For students without exceptional learning needs (ELN), our directions may *be* clear. But for students with ELN, our directions frequently are anything *but* clear.

The plethora of locks on students' learning are also locks on the ability to understand directions. They don't perceive the message we are sending; they don't discriminate between what they are supposed to do and what they are not supposed to do; they are confused; they have poor metacognition, so they think they understand our directions when they don't. From the get-go, they have problems with completing our assignments—in part because they don't get started on the right foot.

Instructions have received insufficient attention from researchers (Todd, Chiayasuk, & Tantisawetrat, 2008). This is surprising because giving instructions is a critical—albeit unglamorous—part of every teacher's daily life, and a teacher's skill at giving instructions impacts students' academic lives.

Studies on how to give instructions are far more common in law and medicine than in education; such studies constitute a robust, current, and ongoing field of inquiry in those fields—but not in ours. For example, multiple studies have examined how to improve juries' understanding of instructions given by judges. Many researchers in the medical field have investigated how to clarify instructions in a wide variety of contexts. For example, researchers have investigated how to improve (1) discharge instructions from hospitals, (2) prescription-use instructions, and (3) instructions on the proper use of medical devices, including home-pregnancy test kits and contraceptives.

From that body of knowledge in law and medicine, teachers can draw the following conclusions:

- Instructions should be explicit rather than implicit.
- Instructions should be worded clearly.
- Instructions should be worded simply.
- Subtle shifts in wording can produce significant differences.
- Instructors should have learners repeat back instructions to ensure understanding.

An education administrator who noted that he had observed over one thousand lessons being taught provided the following instructions on giving instructions:

- Make instructions concrete.
- List the materials needed.
- List the steps to be followed so students can mentally check them off; do not use paragraph form.
- Give multiple representations of directions: written and verbal, pictorial and diagrammatic, a demonstration of exemplary exemplars (examples of outstanding work).
- When multiple steps are involved, give instructions in "bite-sized chunks" (Dyrli, 1999), having students complete several steps before discussing the results and then presenting the next set of instructions (Dyrli, 1999).

The good news is that we can take quick, simple steps to increase our students' understanding of our directions. In this brief chapter, we will give instructions on improving instructions, thereby helping students get started correctly on their assignments:

↪ Key 1: Gain Students' Full Attention
↪ Key 2: Provide Written and Oral Instructions
↪ Key 3: Repeat Instructions
↪ Key 4: Chunk Instructions
↪ Key 5: Solicit Tell-Backs and Show-Mes

The poor metacognition of students with ELN is one of the hallmarks of cognitive disabilities, one of the locks on the doors to learning.

⚷➝ Key 1: Gain Students' Full Attention

Attention problems are one of the locks on the door of learning. When we are ready to have students start an assignment, we need to ensure that we scaffold them by helping them focus their attention on us while we give directions.

Tsal, Shalev, and Mevorach (2005) revisited the types of attention difficulties experienced by students with ADHD; they noted that few researchers have investigated the affects of ADHD and learning disabilities on various types of attention.

Executive attention refers to the ability to willfully inhibit attention from being drawn to irrelevant stimuli. The closely related *selective attention* refers to being able to focus attention on relevant stimuli while screening out the irrelevant. *Sustained attention* has traditionally been defined as *maintaining attention over a prolonged period of time in order to detect infrequent signals. Orienting attention* refers to the ability to direct attention to a specified location and reorienting to a new location.

The researchers had expected to find deficits in sustained attention, and while such deficits were present in most of the participants, what surprised them was that more than half of the participants had deficits in selective, executive, and orienting attention. Different participants demonstrated different profiles of attentional cluster problems.

Buchholz and Davies (2008) investigated the *Sluggish Attentional Shifting hypothesis,* the hypothesis that people with dyslexia have difficulty with orientation of attention (i.e., a deficit in the ability to move their attention from one stimulus to another). Their participants were Australian adults who had dyslexia. The researchers found that the participants did have sluggish attentional shift and that the difficulties shifting attention were strongest when they were directed to attend to a stimulus at the periphery of their vision.

The strategy that we have used at all levels, including the graduate level, is to use the following two-cue system consistently. We teach students from the first day that the signal for getting quiet and attending is raising our hand at the front of the room. The first student who notices us with our hand raised immediately stops talking and raises his or her hand. Other students quickly notice, stop talking, and raise their hands. In only seconds, the class is quiet, and most of the students are looking at us.

We engage in whatever talk we need, be it lecture or housekeeping duties. Then, when we get ready to give instructions, we use the instruction cue. We point to our eyes, and then our ears, and finally the middle of our chest while saying the chant, "Eyes and ears on me." We say the mand three times to ensure that everyone has processed it. Only when we have everyone's eyes do we give the instructions. This two-part strategy ensures that students with difficulty shifting attention are engaged and ready to receive instructions.

Using attentional cues to prepare students for receiving instructions is a good strategy for students with ELN because

- ♪ Attention is ensured
- ♪ Confusion is eliminated when we have students' attention

⚷ Key 2: Provide Written and Oral Instructions

What teachers call *giving directions,* researchers call *procedural discourse.* Procedural discourse has attracted less attention from researchers than coordinate forms of discourse, such as *narrative, expository, argumentative,* and *descriptive* (Wikberg, 1992). Were researchers to ask practicing teachers what we would have them research, we'd give them some discourse, imploring, "Procedural discourse! Help us learn to give directions better!" Indeed, as Catrambone (1988) wrote, "Poor instructions are ubiquitous" (p. 40).

Processing difficulties are a hallmark of cognitive disabilities. Some students have better auditory perception, and others have better visual perception. Students with poor auditory perception need written directions to supplement oral directions. Students with poor visual perception need oral directions to supplement written directions. Providing both serves the needs of all students and is effective, efficient, and absolutely economical—three criteria for determining the feasibility of an instructional strategy.

When instructions are written on a handout or in the exercises in a textbook, the teacher simply needs to read them aloud to the class. When the teacher is providing oral directions for an activity, she or he needs to write them on the board, an overhead, or a PowerPoint slide before she gives them orally.

Perhaps delivering comprehensible instructions is never more important than when a judge delivers instructions to a jury. In a study published in *Forensic Reports,* an actor portraying a judge delivered instructions to 52 undergraduate students on video. The instructions regarded a complex set of intervening causations of the type that a judge would deliver to a jury. The experiment examined two treatments: (1) revising and simplifying the instructions or (2) receiving a written copy of the instructions as well as the oral instructions. Both treatments—revised/simplified and oral paired with written—produced improvement in the students' understanding of the original directions. The researchers concluded that juries are smart; judges simply give directions poorly (Prager, Deckelbaum, & Cutler, 1989).

Hursh, Schumaker, Fawcett, and Sherman (2000) compared two types of instructional delivery. They gave instructions to 12 undergraduates in a psychology class on behavior modification. Half of the students received written instructions to follow as they carried out a behavior modification process. The other half of the students received oral direct instructions. Written instructions produced increases in the student performance on 58% of the possible applications; oral direct instructions produced increases on 87% of the possible applications. However, on a delayed assessment, the improvement in applications was maintained by only 50% of the instances in the oral direct instruction condition as compared to 75% of the students in the written instructions condition. This suggests that the oral directions had an initial advantage, whereas the written directions had an advantage over time. The researchers did not compare the combined strategies to either strategy alone.

Providing oral and written instructions helps students with ELN succeed because

- ♪ Perception improves with multicoding of information
- ♪ Confusion is eliminated when perception is supported
- ♪ Sequencing is facilitated when students both hear and see instructions
- ♪ Frustration is reduced when students understand what they are supposed to do

🔑 Key 3: Repeat Instructions

What teachers call *repetition*, cognitive scientists call *repetition priming*. A robust body of research demonstrates that priming increases the brain's ability to attend to and learn new material while reducing the cognitive load. Gagnepain and colleagues (2008) measured the effect of repetition priming using an fMRI. They found that repetition sharpens the brain's ability to recognize a word in subsequent presentations. They noted that their research is the first to demonstrate long-term spoken-word memory traces within the auditory cortex.

Brunye, Taylor, and Rapp (2008) examined repetition by giving Tufts University undergraduate students instructions on how to assemble toys in either a repetitious or nonrepetitious format. They found that repetitious instructions provided benefits as compared to nonrepetitious instructions, crediting the natural function of inherent redundancy.

Pugh and colleagues (2008) used neuroimaging from an fMRI to study the effects of repetition on reaction time and accuracy of word identification for adolescents with dyslexia and adolescents without dyslexia. Repetition produced a facilitative effect on both reaction time and accuracy for both sets of participants. The researchers call the increase in activation under such conditions *latent functionality* and note that repetition is one of the factors that will increase activation in the brains of people with dyslexia.

Worsdell and colleagues (2005) investigated the use of repetition in improving the reading of adults with developmental disabilities. When the participants incorrectly read a word, they were asked to repeat the correct word either once or multiple times. All the participants learned more sight words with the multiple-response procedure than with the single-response procedure.

Some teachers argue that once should be enough when giving directions. Unfortunately, for students with ELN, once isn't enough. Some teachers take the position, "Students must learn to listen. I give directions once. If I repeat directions, I'm not teaching them responsibility." These teachers might as well say of their students who use glasses, "Students must learn to see. I write instructions on the board. If I let them use glasses, I'm not teaching them responsibility." The logic is absurd. Students with ELN have a biological neurologic basis for their disabilities. Denying them simple accommodations that would assist them is illogical. Refusing to repeat instructions is not even a civil way for one human to treat another—it's downright rude.

We repeat directions at least once, and sometimes twice, for a total of three exposures. This primes and gives our students' brains the opportunity to decode a piece of the message at a time. With luck, they may have been able to decode the entire message by the end of the third presentation.

Repeating directions is an effective key for increasing students' ability to carry out assignments correctly because

- 🎵 Sequencing is facilitated when students have more than one opportunity to listen to steps of an assignment
- 🎵 Confusion is eliminated when students are repeatedly exposed to directions
- 🎵 Memory is enhanced by multiple exposures
- 🎵 Frustration is reduced when confusion is eliminated

☐⊸ Key 4: Chunk Instructions

Chunking, a strategy specifically recommended as a Universal Design for Learning (UDL) strategy by the Center for Applied Special Technology (CAST), was initially studied in chess. Chunking means *to combine small, meaningful units of information.* DeGroot (1965) and other researchers found that experts and novices differed in their ability to reconstruct the placement of pieces on a chess board after a brief exposure. The experts, who chunked the pieces into meaningful groups, could replace most of the chess pieces perfectly, whereas the novices could remember where to place few of the pieces. The difference in performance of this task was not due to a difference in memory of the two groups; when the chess pieces were placed randomly during the exposure, the experts could not reproduce the board any better than the novices could—the random placement of the chess pieces did not produce units that were meaningful to the experts. Such findings were replicated with expert and novices in reconstructing circuit board diagrams and computer programming (Cocking & Mestre, 1989).

The benefit of chunking is derived from the learner's reduced memory load when compared to a condition in which she or he doesn't chunk (Mislevy, Yamamoto, & Anacker, 1991). Instead of remembering one long string of information, the learner needs only to remember several short strings.

In an early study, Rosner (1971) examined the effects of various types of instruction on free recall, organization, and subjective groupings. Participants received either (1) standard instructions, (2) pictorial instructions accompanied by overt rehearsal, or (3) chunked instructions in which the students were given several instructions, allowed to complete the corresponding part of the task, and then provided with another chunk of instructions. Chunking instructions facilitated fifth-graders' performance in all dependent measures. Chunking produced a slight improvement for ninth graders.

Lancioni, O'Reily, and Oliva (2001) investigated the impact of chunking instruction on people with intellectual and visual disabilities. Three adults were taught tasks using a self-operated verbal instruction system. Under the training condition, verbal instructions were presented one task-step at a time; after the participants completed that step, another step was provided. After the complete task was learned, the device presented instructions in clusters of two. The participants demonstrated and maintained correct task performance exceeding 90% as long as the chunked instructions were maintained; however, performance deteriorated when the instructions were no longer provided.

British researchers Duggan and Payne (2001) investigated the effects of chunking instructions in a drama class. In two experiments, the researchers found that chunked instructions of three or four steps in a read-act cycle improved subsequent performance of the procedure over standard conditions.

Chunking makes instructions easier to remember by reducing the memory load. Chunking of instructions is a successful inclusion strategy because

- Confusion is eliminated when students are not overwhelmed with input
- Memory is enhanced when smaller numbers of items must be remembered
- Frustration is decreased when students know exactly what to do

⚷ Key 5: Solicit Tell-Backs and Show-Mes

In a landmark study, Keenan, Betjemann, Wadsworth, DeFries, and Olson (2006) investigated the genetic contribution to listening comprehension. They examined 382 participants: 70 pairs of identical twins, 61 same-sex pairs of fraternal twins, and 60 opposite-sex pairs of fraternal twins. Of the participants, 133 had a school history of reading difficulty. The participants were assessed as to word-reading difficulty and listening comprehension. The results showed that the fraternal twins differed from the identical twins in highly statistically significant ways; unlike the fraternal twins, if one identical twin had poor listening comprehension, the other twin was highly likely to also have poor listening comprehension. The results clearly demonstrated that word-reading and listening comprehension are both genetically determined.

Banai, Nicol, Zecker, and Kraus (2005) investigated the speed of brainstem response in (1) students who had learning disabilities without listening comprehension difficulties, (2) students who had learning disabilities with listening comprehension difficulties, and (3) normal controls. The students with learning disabilities who had listening comprehension problems demonstrated abnormal brainstem timing. The researchers concluded that abnormal brainstem timing in people with learning disabilities is related to reduced cortical sensitivity to sound and may be a reliable biological marker of students in this group.

Students with ELN often have difficulty with verbal comprehension for what are clearly biological reasons. Add to that their notoriously poor metacognition and we have a recipe for disaster when we give directions: They don't understand, and they don't know that they don't understand! We give instructions. They think they understand what they are supposed to do. We say, "Do you understand what you are supposed to do?" and they reply in the affirmative. Then, they proceed to do the wrong thing.

Brown, Dunne, and Cooper (1996) investigated a method by which to overcome the difficulties that students with ELN have with listening comprehension. The participants were ten junior high students with developmental disabilities. The participants were subjected to three conditions: different listening, repeated listening, and repeated listening with immediate retells. The results demonstrated that repeated listening to information with immediate retells produced improvement in delayed retells for nine of the ten students.

This research supports what we call *Tell-Backs* and *Show-Mes*. We never ask, "Do you understand what you are supposed to do?" We always repeat the directions three times while we have students look directly at us. After we complete the instructions, we then ask several students, including at least one with ELN, "Tell me what you are supposed to do," or "Show me what you are supposed to do." We then allow the class to start on the assignment. We quickly walk the room and stop at the desks of our students with ELN, quietly saying again, "Tell me (or show me) what you are supposed to do." This strategy accommodates for the genetic influences on poor listening comprehension. Blaming the victim is counterproductive. What we need to do is stop asking, "Do you understand?" and start using Tell-Backs and Show-Mes.

Tell-Backs and Show-Mes are good inclusion strategies because

- ♪ Confusion is eliminated when students know exactly what to do
- ♪ Memory is enhanced when students repeat back or demonstrate instructions
- ♪ Metacognition is increased when students know that they know what to do
- ♪ Frustration is eliminated when confusion is eliminated

5

Teaching the Concepts and Vocabulary of Our Disciplines

This is the longest chapter of the book because mastery of the vocabulary concepts of a discipline provides the basic building blocks for comprehension and all higher-order thinking skills in that discipline. Teaching the vocabulary concepts is the most elemental activity in teaching a discipline. Most of us who became teachers learned our discipline's vocabulary inductively: We discerned the meanings of our discipline's tongue through context clues. As highly able learners, we have trouble understanding why everyone doesn't pick up our vernacular as a matter of course.

Our students with exceptional learning needs (ELN), however, don't learn that way; so, in order to ensure that they master the vocabulary that is essential to our field of study, we must explicitly teach it. In this chapter, we will discuss several ways to add multisensory dimensions and structure to teaching new vocabulary by using simple keys to unlock the doors barred by problems of confusion, discrimination, memory, attention, and motivation.

Words are concepts. Concepts are categories. McCoy and Ketterlin-Geller (2004), who developed a concept-based model of instruction, characterized concepts as "a broad class of objects or events bearing a unique label and spanning multiple instances and examples" (p. 89). Those classes have critical attributes that thoroughly describe the concept and differentiate the concept from similar concepts.

For example, in our subterranean office, a six-foot tall, three-legged object topped with an enormous frosted-glass bowl casts a soft, yellow light on the ceiling. In the same office, a one-foot tall object with a pull-chain and a green glass top throws a bright light onto the desk. A third object, about two feet tall, consists of three Grecian maids standing back-to-back, and above their heads sits a petal-shaped, translucent silk object through which light is diffused throughout the room. A fourth object is a fierce-looking brass raven from whose mouth hangs an amber globe. This amber globe glows gently in its dark corner and serves no useful purpose except for making us smile. Each of these objects has a cord that is inserted into an electric socket in the wall. We group those rather disparate objects together based upon their function and create the concept *electric lamp.*

In order to identify the critical attributes of the concept *electric lamp*, we must venture further, to wit: Inside the four electric lamps are diverse objects that, grouped together, we call *incandescent lightbulbs.* One is a clear glass tube shaped rather like a sausage, one is a pear-shaped white-frosted globe, another is a yellow pear-shaped globe guaranteed not to attract bugs. The one in the amber globe that hangs from the raven's mouth is a clear, flame-shaped, two-inch-long furrowed bauble. These objects differ greatly, yet we group them together as a concept based upon what they have in common: They produce light from a thin filament that heats up when an electric current passes through it. And of course, *filament* and *electric current* are also concepts.

Having identified the concepts of lightbulbs and electric current, we can then identify the critical attributes of *electric lamp*: (1) It is an artificial source of illumination, (2) it employs a lightbulb, and (3) it is powered by electric current.

Those groups of objects, or concepts, are the building blocks from which we create generalizations, principles, and natural laws. A *generalization* is *a statement about the relationships between two or more concepts.* For example, as we have noted, lamp is one concept and lightbulb is another concept. We can then make the generalization that *lamps require lightbulbs in order to produce light.* Based upon our own preferences, we might also make the generalization that *people tend to find certain types of lightbulbs more aesthetically pleasing in certain types of lamps.*

Principles can be thought of as generalizations that are true in most cases, and principles tend to be the domain of the liberal and fine arts, such as the economic principle *wants exceed resources necessary to obtain them,* or in the lamp and lightbulb case, our second generalization: *People tend to find certain types of lightbulbs more aesthetically pleasing in certain types of lamps.*

Natural laws are generally the domain of the natural sciences, and they can be thought of as principles that are true in every case, such as the natural law of gravity: *Objects with mass attract each other.* In this case, *objects, mass,* and *attraction* are the concepts. In the case of our little analogy, *lamps require lightbulbs in order to produce light* is the natural law.

Unless we begin at the beginning—with vocabulary—we have no concepts with which to begin the process of developing higher-order thinking through the manipulation of generalizations, principles, and natural laws.

Greenwood (2002) wrote that knowing the vocabulary, the words of a discipline, is the key to reading comprehension in that discipline. Hennings (2000) wrote that vocabulary is a key factor not only in reading but also in listening comprehension—especially in secondary and postsecondary education. She warned that students who have limited vocabularies in our disciplines have problems understanding what they read in their textbooks and what they hear in our classes because words are building blocks, and students with limited word knowledge have "too few building blocks' with which to construct meanings" (p. 269). We encounter the same problem when we pick up an advanced-level text in an area completely outside of our own realm of study, such as engineering or nutrition. We lack the building blocks, the concepts, with which to construct meaning.

Graves and Penn (1986) identified three levels at which a word is known: *unknown, acquainted,* and *established.* Greenwood (2002) described a word at the acquainted level as one in which the user has heard and recognizes the word, but is "fuzzy" about its meaning

(p. 269). He stated that our goal as content area teachers is to help students move words from the acquainted level to the established level (and, of course, from unknown to established), at which they become automatic.

In a free monograph, *What Content-Area Teachers Should Know About Adolescent Literacy*, The National Institute for Literacy (2007) identified one typology of vocabulary: *oral, aural,* and *print* vocabulary. *Oral vocabulary* refers to the words in a person's lexicon: those words that a person actually speaks. *Aural vocabulary* refers to the words that a person understands in the speech of other people; these words may or may not be in one's oral vocabulary. *Print vocabulary* refers to the words that a person understands in text and uses in writing.

The National Institute for Literacy (2007) also noted that another typology of vocabulary categorizes words as (1) high-frequency, everyday words; (2) nonspecialized academic words that are common across subject matter areas; and (3) specialized content-area words. Examples of the nonspecialized academic words include *investigate, solution,* and *alternative.* While we each have the responsibility for teaching our discipline-specific vocabulary, we share the responsibility for teaching the nonspecialized academic words.

The task of understanding a word exists, in part, in determining (1) to what class of concepts that word belongs and (2) how the word is differentiated from other words in that class. Let's go back to our lamp and lightbulb example. Our four lamps differ enormously from each other. A time-traveler from the distant past would be hard-put to understand why we classified them together when they look so different from each other, yet we do classify them together because we recognize their common function. The superordinate concept is *electric lamp.* The concepts that are subordinate to lamp, and coordinate to each other, are the *types of lamps,* the typology by which we differentiate them. In this case, we can discriminate between the floor lamp, the banker's-task lamp, the ambient lamp, and the rather useless (but enormously endearing) decorative lamp.

McCoy and Ketterlin-Geller (2004) warn that only high-achieving students ever fully understand the concepts and principles presented in textbooks. Either the teacher or the students must assume the responsibility for developing the understanding required. Few students are going to assume such responsibility, and students with ELN, by definition, lack such skills. The responsibility for explicating the concepts and their relationships then logically and ethically falls to the teacher.

Having determined that we, as ethical teachers, should teach vocabulary to our students with ELN, how should we go about it?

In the *Handbook of Reading Research* (Vol. 2) about teaching general education students, Beck and McKeown (1991) wrote

> The following four statements about the effects of vocabulary instruction on word learning can be made with a high level of confidence: First, all instructional methods produce better word learning than no instruction. Second, no one method has been shown to be consistently superior. Third, there is advantage from methods that use a variety of techniques. Fourth, there is advantage from repeated exposures to the words to be learned. The simple version of these findings is that people tend to learn what they are taught, and more attention to what is being taught is useful. (p. 805)

The National Institute for Literacy (2007) concurs that no one method of vocabulary instruction is better than all others, that multiple instructional practices are more effective than the use of any one instructional practice, and that multiple exposures to new words are critical. The institute also warns that although traditional dictionary assignments may be part of vocabulary instruction, they should be used only in conjunction with other pedagogical practices and only *after* the student has had multiple encounters with the word.

We argue that students with ELN are not well-served by traditional dictionary assignments. Research supports our claim. Bos, Anders, Filip, and Jaffe (1989) examined the effectiveness of having students with ELN use a dictionary to look up vocabulary words. Their participants in the study were middle-class high school students with ELN who were in social studies or English classes. One group of participants looked up new vocabulary words in the dictionary and then wrote both definitions of the words and sentences that used them in the traditional dictionary-vocabulary type of assignment that teachers have been using since the days of one-room schoolhouses. The second group received explicit, direct teaching of the definition by use of Semantic Feature Analysis (SFA; see Key 2). The words included general academic words, such as *anonymous,* and discipline specific terms such as *search and seizure.* Students in the SFA group outperformed the students in the dictionary group on both the initial test and the six-month follow-up (i.e., the results were highly statistically significant).

In "Guidelines for Evaluating Vocabulary Instruction," published in the *Journal of Reading,* Carr and Wixson (1986) identified four guidelines for evaluating vocabulary instruction:

- Instruction should help students relate new vocabulary to their background knowledge.
- Instruction should help students develop elaborated word knowledge.
- Instruction should provide for active student involvement in learning new vocabulary.
- Instruction should develop students' strategies for acquiring new vocabulary independently.

The strategies in this chapter meet Carr and Wixson's (1986) guidelines and use the keys to teaching students with ELN.

When we want to focus the attention of students with ELN on the vocabulary we want them to learn, we need to use explicit instruction, and multisensory methods help us increase explicitness because they help students see, hear, feel, and move to experience a word. Multiple representations provide the many different types of exposures to a word that students with ELN require.

A wide variety of strategies allows us to provide multisensory instruction and increase cognitive structure for students in our classes who have special needs. These 14 multisensory strategies are keys that will help us unlock many of the doors that have barred our students with special needs from accessing our disciplines:

    ⌐ Key 6: Taxonomic Tree
    ⌐ Key 7: Semantic Feature Analysis Matrix
    ⌐ Key 8: Compare and Contrast Vocabulary Matrix
    ⌐ Key 9: Typology
    ⌐ Key 10: Word Analysis Diagram
    ⌐ Key 11: Semantic Map
    ⌐ Key 12: Quick Sketching a Definition

↪ Key 13: Total Physical Response and Vocabulary Drama
↪ Key 14: Keyword Mnemonic Strategy
↪ Key 15: Teach Greek and Latin Morphemes
↪ Key 16: Vocabulary Word Wall
↪ Key 17: Learning Games
↪ Key 18: Peer Tutoring
↪ Key 19: Vocabulary Word Card Ring

Keys 6 through 11 are types of graphic organizers (GOs). GOs are one class of teaching devices. Horton, Lovitt, and Slocum (1988) explained that teaching devices help teachers to increase the explicitness of their instruction, to elaborate on critical content, and to increase students' active learning. Fisher, Schumaker, and Deshler (1995) explained that teachers use teaching devices to increase student understanding and application, memory storage, and subsequent retrieval. Egan (1999) found that GOs have been reported to be effective teaching devices at all levels of learning and that their use in education is widespread.

Fisher, Schumaker, and Deshler (1995) reviewed the literature for validated inclusive practices. They found that GOs were one of the only two teaching devices that met their criteria to be declared validated practices that "benefit most, if not all, students in a class, that allow the integrity of the curriculum to be maintained, and that are practical in terms of time and implementation" (p. 1). GOs provide visual input and a visual structure that helps students organize, comprehend, analyze, and retain information.

Kim, Vaughn, Wanzek, and Wei (2004) conducted a synthesis of the research on the effects of GOs on the reading comprehension of students with ELN. Across the board, they found impressive results from the GO strategies employed with secondary and upper elementary students.

Boyle and Yeager (1997) explained that GOs are learning frameworks. They stated that in the same way that a house needs a framework, learning needs a framework. Here, learning frameworks are called *cognitive frameworks.*

> Cognitive frameworks support student learning by presenting component information in an organized manner and by linking related information together. More specifically, during academic activities cognitive frameworks aid students by highlighting the important points, visually displaying the relationships between ideas, and serving as guides for studying after the lesson. (p. 27)

Horton, Lovitt, and Bergerud (1990) agreed that GOs work by helping students consolidate what they may perceive as a set of unrelated facts rather than an interrelated set of facts and concepts. They develop relational knowledge that is necessary in order to conduct deep processing of new concepts, serve as a vehicle for higher-order thinking, and assist in retrieval of information. They help students see information as an integrated whole.

GOs can be categorized as *expert-made, student-made,* or *co-constructed.* The category of GO that seems most effective in terms of student understanding and retention appears to be co-constructed. Expert maps are best when first introducing mapping to students; a benefit of expert maps is that teacher time is saved and students receive a preview of the material. Chang, Sung, and Chen (2002) explained that a drawback to the continued use of expert maps is the passive nature of student learning—no autonomous learning takes place. Students do not actively engage with the text, so they miss the crucial benefits of multicoding through the kinesthetic experience of drawing the map.

The two main problems with student-generated maps are time constraint and cognitive overload. Having students construct their own GOs is time consuming, and time is always a concern for teachers. The more important problem, however, is cognitive overload; even college students find generating their own maps to be difficult.

One solution is for the teacher and students to co-construct the organizer: The teacher works on the chalkboard or overhead projector while the students work at their seats. As the teacher and students engage in discourse, the teacher scaffolds the students' thinking so that they discover how to best construct the device.

The other solution is map correction. In this strategy, the teacher provides the map with approximately 40% of the information incorrect. The students must then correct the map. This approach provides the best of both the expert-made and student-generated organizers; students have the expert map as a framework, but they must then think critically about the map (Chang, Sung, & Chen, 2002).

Horton, Lovitt, and Bergerund (1990) found support for GOs when they compared the use of teacher-directed GOs to self-study with 180 seventh- and tenth-grade students. Of those students, eight had ELN. When the students with ELN used self-study on a reading passage (i.e., read the material and took notes) for 45 minutes, they scored 19% on a test. When they completed a teacher-prepared blank GO while reading material of similar difficulty for 45 minutes, they scored 71%. The nondisabled students also improved from 56% with self-study to 89% with the GO.

With GOs, students become active instead of passive learners and benefit from the kinesthetic involvement as well as the auditory and visual involvement. This is supported by Horton, Lovitt, and Bergerund's (1990) second experiment. Whereas in the first experiment (see preceding paragraph) the teacher directed the GO construction, in the second experiment, the students directed their own construction of a GO and that was compared with a self-study condition. In the student-constructed GO condition, the mean score of the students with ELN was 71% on a quiz; their mean score on the self-study condition quiz was 19%. Likewise, the students who did not have learning problems benefited from constructing their own GOs; they averaged 89% on the self-directed GO condition quiz and 56% on the self-study condition quiz.

Moore and Readence (1984) found that GOs are especially effective in teaching technical vocabulary. Because the technical vocabulary of mathematics is the most difficult vocabulary for students to understand, GOs are especially important keys to learning in mathematics.

Because GOs are grounded in schema theory (Dye, 2002), they help students connect new vocabulary to their existing concept networks. In learning a new word, students start with what they know. They then engage in two processes: (1) determining class inclusion and (2) determining class differentiation of the concept. In other words, students must first determine to what class of concepts the new word belongs and then determine how the word differs from other members of that class. GOs help students connect the new information to what they already know and then make the inclusion-differentiation determinations in learning the new vocabulary.

A Taxonomic Tree is one visual tool we use to teach vocabulary through showing the concept class in which the term is included and the classes from which it is differentiated. Other tools include Semantic Feature Analysis Matrix, Compare and Contrast Matrix, Typology, Word Analysis Diagram, Semantic Web, and Word Walls.

🔑 Key 6: Taxonomic Tree

Egan (1999) noted that GOs are used to structure information, and the Taxonomic Tree structures information so that a concept is clearly situated in context for learners. In a Taxonomic Tree, the row above a new word represents the class to which the word belongs—the *superordinate concept.* The words on the same row as the new word represent the classes from which the word is differentiated—the *coordinate concepts.* The words directly beneath the new word are the subclasses of that word—the *subordinate concepts.* Taxonomic Trees have sometimes been called *Expository Graphic Organizers* or *brace maps.*

Taxonomy is the science of classification. Written taxonomies can be traced to ancient Greece and the philosopher Theophrastus, a disciple of Aristotle. Theophrastus was classifying plants into taxonomies as early as 300 BCE. However, it was Carolus Linnaeus who essentially invented modern taxonomy, listing over 12,000 species of plants and animals. Although the scientific use of taxonomies originated in the natural sciences, every discipline employs taxonomies of concepts. The Taxonomic Tree as a graphic organizer takes thought that is ambiguous and amorphous to the student with ELN and makes the organization of that thought visible and clear (Tarquin & Walker, 1997). We find that we understand our own disciplines much more clearly when we construct Taxonomic Trees because making thought visible helps teachers as well as students.

Vinther (2004) compared having students draw their own Taxonomic Trees to having them use a computer program that assisted them in creating the trees. The experiment was in the context of teaching the syntax (grammar) of English and an additional European language to advanced university students in southern Denmark. She found that while the students in the computer-aided group were more highly motivated, both the hand-generated method and the computer-aided method were successful in assisting students in learning syntax.

The Taxonomic Tree (see adjacent example) helps students open the Acquisition and Fluency and Proficiency doors that block access to Knowledge and Comprehension because

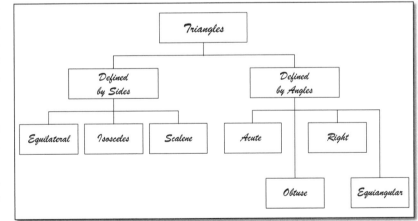

- 🔑 Auditory perception is enhanced by the visual and kinesthetic dimensions
- 🔑 Discrimination is sharpened because the coordinate concepts are clearly delineated
- 🔑 Memory is enhanced because of the depth of processing
- 🔑 Organization is provided because of the strategy's inherent organization
- 🔑 Attention is assured because the student is actively involved
- 🔑 Frustration is decreased because the concept is presented in a highly explicit manner

⚷ Key 7: Semantic Feature Analysis Matrix

The Semantic Feature Analysis (SFA) Matrix is a tool that is used to teach class discrimination: How are these members of a class different from each other? The SFA helps students understand the fine shades of meaning between and among similar words (Pittelman, Heimlich, Berglund, & French, 1991). The SFA was designed to be used in the following way: (1) The teacher writes a list of words on the board that are in a common category. (2) The teacher asks the students to list characteristics of one of the words and writes these characteristics across the top of the board to make a matrix. The students then complete the matrix with pluses or minuses; if the characteristic is not completely present or absent, the students use a rating scale of 1 to 10. (3) After the students have finished, the class discusses the matrix and adds more items.

Brunn (2002) said that GOs further students' understanding of difficult concepts, and understanding the fine distinctions that differentiate a concept from a similar concept is a difficult task for novices in a subject. The SFA Matrix is designed to help students open the door that makes discrimination difficult, highlighting those fine distinctions between such coordinate concepts. We are all familiar with apples; in almost every first-grade class in America, apples are used in an autumn thematic unit that covers an entire month. In addition, most of us have eaten thousands of apples over the years; but if called on to explain the difference between a Fuji apple and a Braeburn apple, most of us would be hard-pressed to do so. With an SFA Matrix, we could learn those distinctions.

Anders, Bos, and Filip (1984) investigated the effects of SFA among 62 high school students with ELN. Half of the participants looked up words in a dictionary. The other half of the participants participated in an SFA activity. The SFA group scored significantly higher than the dictionary group on both vocabulary and conceptual items.

Toms-Bronowski (1982) compared SFA with semantic mapping and a traditional contextual approach for vocabulary acquisition. Her participants were 36 fourth-, fifth-, and sixth-grade classes. The students were taught 15 target words a week, one week under each condition. The students were tested on the 15 words that they studied each week; a week after the instruction was completed, the students were tested on all 45 words. Both mapping and SFA were significantly more effective than the traditional contextual approach, but SFA produced better results on more target words than did the mapping strategy.

The intellectual work involved in using the SFA Matrix is challenging, but having that kind of mastery over concepts is empowering. This is a key to accessing the door to increasing student motivation. High school students with disabilities sometimes tell us that they actually help their friends without disabilities study if they have a class in which their teacher does not use these tools. The SFA Matrix is effective because

- ♪ Perception is enhanced by using all three sensory dimensions
- ♪ Discrimination is acute because the very fine differences between coordinate concepts are clearly explicated
- ♪ Memory is enhanced because of the depth of processing
- ♪ Organization is provided because of the strategy's matrix organization
- ♪ Attention is enhanced because the student is actively involved
- ♪ Frustration is decreased because the subtle shades of meaning between and among the concepts are highlighted

Here is an example we used in an English class to clarify clauses.

Semantic Feature Analysis for Clauses/Phrases

	Expresses a complete thought	Can stand alone as a sentence	Contains a predicate and its subject
Independent clause	+	+	+
Dependent clause	−	−	+
Phrase	−	−	−

⚷→ Key 8: Compare and Contrast Vocabulary Matrix

The Compare and Contrast Vocabulary Matrix is an offshoot of the SFA Matrix. Langan-Fox, Waycott, and Albert (2000) heralded the fact that GOs can help students grasp concepts much more quickly than most other methods of instruction, and the Compare and Contrast (C&C) Vocabulary Matrix is a tool that maximizes the speed of understanding. The C&C, while not allowing for the razor-edge distinctions afforded by the SFA Matrix, provides sufficient understanding for all but the most critical shades of meaning in coordinate concepts, and for most of the concepts we teach, the C&C works well.

In the C&C, instead of placing the critical attributes at the top of the matrix's columns, the students write more general attribute categories. They then write each concept's characteristics in the squares of the matrix. In general, students tend to prefer using the C&C Vocabulary Matrix instead of the SFA Matrix strategy because it does not demand such rigorous thinking. We use C&C Vocabulary Matrices far more frequently than we use the SFA Matrices. Occasionally, we start with the C&C, and if students have difficulty distinguishing the fine differences between coordinate concepts, we add an SFA Matrix to clarify.

Alvermann (1981) explored whether tenth-grade social studies students increased their understanding of key vocabulary terms encountered in an expository passage with and without a C&C matrix. She found that both the poor and the strong readers benefited from the C&C organizer; the organizer was a key to increasing comprehension and helped students acquire and organize the new knowledge in their schema.

In their meta-analysis on improving comprehension of expository text, Gajria, Jitendra, Sood, and Sacks (2007) found graphic organizers to be a valuable tool for assisting students with ELN. They found that content enhancements such as graphic organizers were effective for students in high school and middle school. The effects of treatments were strong whether the students received less than four hours, between four and eight hours, or more than eight hours of intervention.

The C&C Vocabulary Matrix works because

- Auditory perception is ensured by using all three senses
- Discrimination is enhanced because differences in the confusing coordinate concepts are delineated
- Memory is strengthened because of the depth of processing
- Organization is enhanced because of the strategy's inherent organization
- Attention is focused because the student is actively involved
- Frustration is decreased because the similarities and differences between the coordinate concepts are made explicit

When students with disabilities use this key, their problems in discriminating among concepts are mediated, and their confusion is prevented. For example, in the earth science example that follows, the matrix we created helped students understand the critical vocabulary terms that are related to tectonic plate boundaries: *convergent*, *divergent*, and *transform*.

Tectonic Plate Movement

	Type of Movement	Lithospheric Consequence	Resulting Geographic Features
Divergent	Plates spread apart	Lithosphere produced	Seafloor spreading; fractures; rifts
Convergent	Plates collide	Lithosphere consumed	Lithosphere subducted into mantle; oceanic, continental; deep ocean trench . . .
Transform	Plates slide past each other	Nothing produced or consumed	Transform faults; usually in oceanic floor

⌗ Key 9: Typology

Typology is a system by which concepts can be classified into a particular type. The word *typology* comes from Greek and can be translated as *study of types*. We consider taxonomies and typologies to be different tools with different advantages, disadvantages, and uses. Taxonomies give us the big picture: an overview of a concept's class membership, the members of its class that differ from it, and its subclasses. However, the information about any particular concept in taxonomy is shallow. Taxonomies provide no more than information about the relationship between a concept, its superordinate concept, coordinate concepts, and subordinate concepts.

In contrast, we use the word *typology* to designate a graphic organizer that shows us how a concept differs from three coordinate concepts along two dimensions. In a typology, a one-by-two or two-by-two matrix is used in which dimensions are listed along the side and the top of the matrix. Within the intersection of each dimension falls the name of each concept being taught.

Using a taxonomy matrix to give the big picture that situates the words we are targeting and following that with a typology to clearly differentiate among those words in relation to each other is a powerful strategy.

We have found that, in general, the distinctions between words taught in a typology are more easily remembered than those taught in other ways. This is a good key for opening the door that causes discrimination problems. With only two critical attributes on which to focus and only two to four terms to consider, the student's cognitive energy that is invested in the multicoding of seeing the words in relationship to each other while listening to an explanation of the terms, followed by constructing a matrix in his or her own notebook, results in an impressive degree of comprehension, retention, and retrieval. Comprehension is increased because the trouble with discriminating among critical attributes is mediated and confusion about which term to use when is reduced.

We have found that memory retrieval is especially high when students with disabilities are explicitly taught to draw the typology whenever they need to access the information from their memory banks. Students without disabilities may do this automatically, but those who have learning problems may need the explicit instruction. With this key, motivation is increased because feelings of competence are generated, success is ensured, and the expectation of future success is created.

The Typology is an effective key because

- ⌗ Perception is enhanced by using all three senses
- ⌗ Discrimination is ensured because only four concepts are presented, only two dimensions are addressed, and the differences among them clearly explained
- ⌗ Memory is enhanced because only two dimensions and four concepts are addressed and thoroughly processed
- ⌗ Organization is enhanced because of the strategy's inherent binary organization
- ⌗ Attention is ensured because the student is actively involved
- ⌗ Frustration is decreased because two dimensions that differentiate among only four coordinate concepts are made explicit

Here is an example used with secondary students in a science class to show the dimensions that characterize the concept *air mass*.

Typology of Air Masses

Air mass originates . . .	In high latitudes	In low latitudes
Over land	*Continental Polar*	*Continental Tropical*
Over water	*Maritime Polar*	*Maritime Tropical*

⊶ Key 10: Word Analysis Diagram

The Word Analysis Diagram examines one word in great detail. This strategy is an extension of the Frayer Model of Concept Attainment (Frayer, Frederick, & Klausmeier, 1969). In that model, essential and nonessential attributes, examples and nonexamples, and superordinate, subordinate, and coordinate concepts are listed.

In an important study, Peters (1974) compared the Frayer model to a textbook method of teaching social studies vocabulary concepts to 360 ninth-grade students. He found that both the good and poor readers in the Frayer group significantly increased their achievement and that the Frayer group outperformed the textbook method group.

Monroe and Pendergrass (1997) compared the Frayer model to the definition-only model in teaching mathematics vocabulary. The definition-only model involved having students write the definition of the new word after an oral review of the word. The Frayer group outperformed the control group after two weeks of instruction, which led Monroe and Pendergrass to declare that the model is an effective model for teaching mathematics vocabulary.

Curtis (2008) compared the Frayer model and semantic mapping (two socially mediated strategies of vocabulary development) to contextual and morphemic analysis. Her participants were fifth-grade students in 14 classrooms. Although all students made gains, only the students in the Frayer model-semantic mapping group sustained gains on a follow-up assessment.

In the Word Analysis Diagram, we modify the Frayer method in two ways. First, we use Graves's (1985) modification that adds a definition of the word, and second, we include its origin, root word and affixes, and synonyms and antonyms. We also place the entire structure in a graphic form.

Including the word origin is more important than many teachers realize. Hennings (2000) noted that a critical problem in reading and listening comprehension is students' lack of understanding of the history of the English language and the origins of words. Simply knowing that many of our scientific words come from Greek and that *ology* means *the study of* is useful and empowering. After having taught a student with an IQ below 70 that *geo* means *Earth* and *graph* means *write* or *draw,* we were pleased weeks later to hear her pass this information on to a nondisabled student in a meaningful context. Her peer was impressed, and her self-concept as a competent member of a learning community was boosted.

The Word Analysis Diagram is best reserved for use on crucial concepts that require extended discussion and deep processing. The strategy is effective because

- ♪ Perception is ensured by using all three senses
- ♪ Discrimination is strengthened because differences in the confusing coordinate concepts are delineated
- ♪ Memory is enhanced because of the depth of processing
- ♪ Attention is enhanced because the student is actively involved

A good use of the diagram in social studies can be found in introducing each of the five big ideas in geography: location, place, relationships within places, movement, and regions. The figure that follows represents how we used a Word Analysis Diagram to introduce the concept *place.* When we finished, the students with disabilities (and without) had a solid understanding of place.

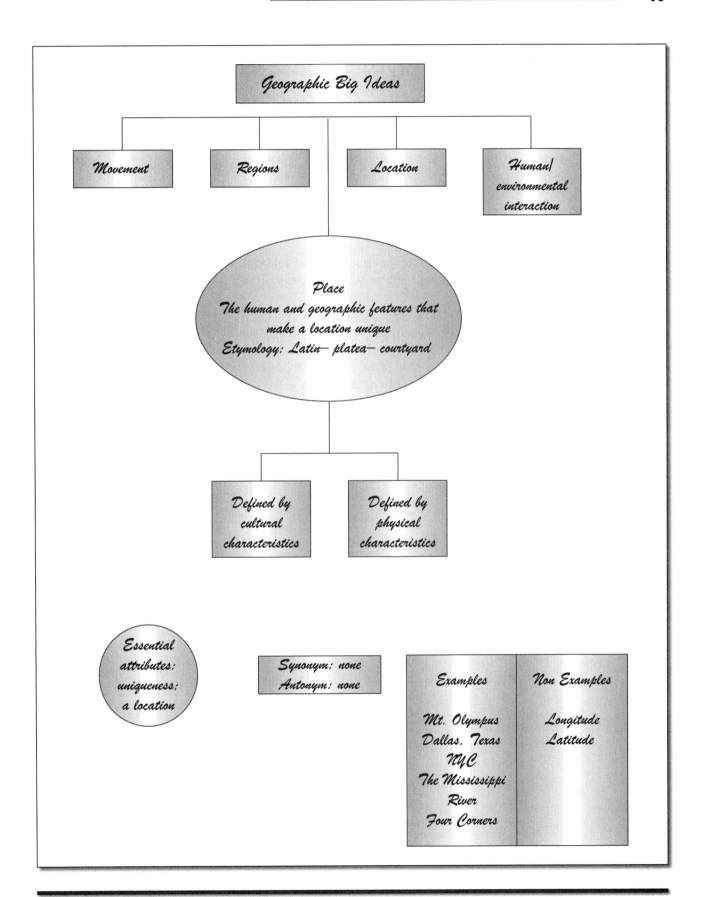

☞ Key 11: Semantic Map

The National Institute for Literacy (2007) recommends that middle school and secondary school teachers use Semantic Maps in the content areas. A *Semantic Map* (Harste, 1980), which is sometimes called a *Semantic Web* (Freedman & Reynolds, 1980), a *Word Web* (Kerber, 1980), or a *Concept Map* (Rowell, 1975), is a complex representation of the multiple facets of a word.

The semantic map can include word origins; definitions; superordinate, coordinate, and subordinate concepts; attributes; examples; causes; effects; emotions evoked by the term; and so forth. A word related in any way to the core concept is fair game in a semantic map.

Carr and Wixson (1986) noted that we must relate new vocabulary to students' background knowledge and that semantic mapping is an effective tool for stimulating that schemata.

Polloway, Patton, and Serna (2001) explained that a Semantic Map is created when the teacher writes a stimulus word on the board and has students brainstorm to generate words that are related to the stimulus word. Then, with the teacher's help, the students group related words and draw connecting lines to show the relationships between them and the stimulus word. Semantic mapping is also useful after the new learning takes place to demonstrate how the new learning fits into the old learning.

Darch and Eaves (1986) explained that Semantic Mapping involves the "use of lines, arrows, and spatial arrangements to describe text content, structure, and key conceptual relationships" (p. 310). They recommended using keywords and, when possible, pairing those keywords with simple drawings; they warned against the use of complete sentences and too much detail.

Guastello (2000) investigated the effects of concept mapping on the science concept comprehension of inner-city seventh graders who were low achieving. With 64 students in both the experimental and control group, Guastello taught a unit on the circulatory system that lasted for eight days. The groups were introduced to the unit and then read and discussed the chapter together in class. At the end of the unit, the group that was taught each day with the concept mapping increased its performance by six standard deviations over the control group.

A Semantic Map is an effective key to unlocking Acquisition and Fluency and Proficiency to word or concept Knowledge and Comprehension because

- ♪ Perception is assured by the use of all three senses
- ♪ Memory is enhanced because of the depth of processing
- ♪ Attention is focused because the student is actively involved
- ♪ Motivation is enhanced because the students have serious fun with the activity

The following shows how a biology teacher used a Semantic Map to demonstrate the relationship of flowers to plants.

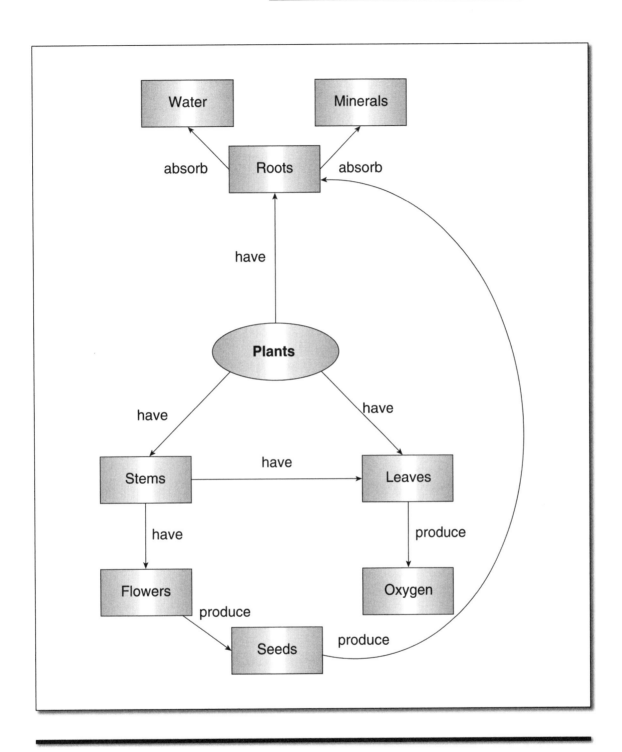

⚷ Key 12: Quick Sketching a Definition

In Quick Sketching a Definition, students take a new word and sketch a picture that represents the word to them. They then can share their sketches and rationales with a small group of other students. By drawing and explaining their drawings to each other, the students are using their kinesthetic sense. By seeing their sketches and the sketches of other students, students are using their vision. By hearing the other students' explanations, students are using their auditory sense. By experiencing their own and each other's drawings, the word also becomes multirepresentational and is thus stored in multiple places in the students' brains—resulting in a greater likelihood that the word will be remembered and retrieved when needed.

The multiple representations also increase students' comprehension by extending their conceptualization of the word. A student may construct a drawing, thinking that he or she understands the word, but after seeing the drawings of other group members, the student may discover that he or she had misunderstood the concept. One student with disabilities discovered by this method that *unanimous consent* did not mean that *no one knew who was consenting.* She had confused *anonymous* with *unanimous*. The misunderstanding would have gone uncorrected if we had not used the Quick Sketching strategy.

The National Council of Teachers of Mathematics endorses the use of multiple representations. Multiple representations increase junior high students' algebraic thinking significantly over the thinking of students taught with traditional techniques. Using multiple representations in science has resulted in positive effects in increasing high school students' conceptualization of the molecular structure of water, and students' understandings of chemical representation also increased dramatically (Kendall & Stacey, 2000; Wu, Krajcik, & Soloway, 2001).

Bull and Wittrock (1973) compared a sketching technique for enhancing understanding and memory of vocabulary words to rote memorization. The retention of the words by the sketching group was much higher than the retention of the control group. One of the recommendations from the Teachers' Curriculum Institute's (1999) *History Alive* curriculum is to stop periodically during lectures to have students sketch a scene to assist them in remembering the concept discussed. Wolfe (2001) recounted the experience of a freshman English teacher who had her students choose partners and create two-minute or three-minute presentations on vocabulary words to teach the rest of the class. Many of the students used sketches to represent their words; the students were delighted with their experiences. Swiderek (1996) recommended having middle school students draw representations of words that they frequently misuse.

Quick Sketching a Definition is effective in ensuring Acquisition and Proficiency and Fluency in Knowledge and Comprehension because

- ♪ Perception is ensured by using all three senses
- ♪ Memory is assured because of the depth of processing
- ♪ Attention is enhanced because the student is actively involved
- ♪ Motivation is enhanced because the class is often filled with laughter

The example that follows is from a science class we were teaching on the definition of *entropy*.

⚷ Key 13: Total Physical Response and Vocabulary Drama

In addition to the kinesthetic act of creating the graphic organizers and quick sketching definitions, we use Total Physical Response (TPR). TPR adds a dynamic kinesthetic dimension to our vocabulary instruction, and our junior high and high school students have fun doing it after they get over their initial hesitance. Our college students also enjoy TPR and demonstrate no initial resistance to the activity!

TPR was first described by Asher in 1969 in the *Journal of Special Education* as a tool for teaching children with disabilities. Then, in 1981, Asher published a book on the method as a strategy for teaching foreign language. We first learned about TPR from a high school Spanish teacher, Joe Lesue, whose students all talked about how much they learned from him. Lots of noise, laughing, and the sound of desks being moved about in Joe's class led us to ask what good things were happening in his room. He invited us to come watch him teach with TPR. First, he provided the students with a new word in Spanish, and then he demonstrated a motor movement that symbolized the word. Next, the students all stood up and performed the movement. For example, he used the Spanish word for *airplane*, and the students all flew around the room like airplanes, a key to great motivation and memory retention.

Research supports the effectiveness of the strategy. Wolfe and Jones (1982) taught one group of high school foreign language students using TPR for 20 minutes per day and taught the control group using a traditional method. The TPR group not only scored substantially higher on their unit test, but like Joe Lesue's students, they also expressed more enjoyment in the unit as compared to their control counterparts.

We tested the strategy in two graduate educational research classes. Using a traditional method, we taught ten unknown Scottish words in ten minutes. Next, we taught ten unknown Scottish words using TPR for ten minutes. Two hours later, the students remembered more of the words taught under the TPR condition than the words taught under the traditional condition.

In 1980, Blaine Ray, a foreign language teacher in Bakersfield, California, developed Total Physical Response by Storytelling (TPRS). Whereas TPRI is taught mainly through commands, TPRS includes asking the students personalized questions employing the target words and creating fanciful stories from the answers. Kariuki and Bush (2008) compared the use of TPRS to the traditional method of foreign language teaching. Their participants were 30 randomly selected high school students who were then randomly assigned to the experimental or control group. The experimental group outscored the traditional group by 20 points on a 100-point test.

Closely related to TPR is what we call *Vocabulary Drama*, which employs the use of brief skits. Writing in *English Journal*, Hardwick-Ivey (2008) described her use of vocabulary skits in the secondary English classroom. Hardwick-Ivey often used teams to spark competition.

Jacobson, Lapp, and Flood (2007) recommend skits or pantomimes as one of seven activities to teach vocabulary to adolescent and adult English language learners. The skits or pantomimes are the sixth step in their process. They assign students to work in pairs to prepare a skit or pantomime (or pictorial representation) of a pair of confusing words—homonyms, homophones, or homographs. The pair of students then presents the creation to the class. The class tries to decide which word was presented. The word meanings and pronunciations are then reviewed.

TPR is a key to unlocking Acquisition and Proficiency and Fluency in Knowledge and Comprehension because

- ♪ Perception is assured by incorporating all three senses
- ♪ Memory is assured because of the depth of processing
- ♪ Attention is focused because the student is actively involved
- ♪ Motivation is assured because the activity is such fun

In chemistry, our students were confused about the meaning of single and double replacement reactions. We had Maria, a female student, and Aaron and Jared, two male students, come to the front of the room. We told the class that Jared and Maria went on a date; they then moved together and held hands. Next we said, "But along came Aaron. Maria took one look at Aaron and said 'good-bye' to Jared and left him for Aaron!" Maria dropped Jared's hand and moved over to stand by Aaron, taking his hand. After seeing the demonstration, our students acted out the reaction in groups. They never forgot the meaning of *single replacement reaction*.

Then, to teach double replacement reaction, we used two females and two males to demonstrate and explained that on a double date that the students decided to switch partners. The two couples acted it out, and the students never missed the definition of either *single* or *double replacement reactions* again.

Double Replacement Reaction

⚷→ Key 14: Keyword Mnemonic Strategy

Mnemonic strategies are memory strategies. When Forness, Kavale, Blum, and Lloyd (1997) conducted their mega-analysis of meta-analyses of what works in special education, mnemonic strategies were in first place. The effect size of mnemonic strategies was far ahead of the strategy in second place. Mnemonic strategies are the single most effective way to raise the achievement level of our students with ELN.

Wolegmuth, Cobb, and Alwell (2008) conducted an extensive review of research on mnemonic strategies employed with secondary students with ELN. Compared to such strategies as Direct Instruction and free study, students in mnemonic conditions had better immediate and delayed recall in English, mathematics, social studies, and science than did their peers in the control conditions.

A number of mnemonic strategies are successful, but for vocabulary learning, we have chosen to focus on the Keyword Mnemonic Strategy. The Keyword Mnemonic Strategy was developed by Atkinson (1975) and was simplified by Levin (1988) as recording, relating, and retrieving. In recording, the student changes the word to a well-known, similar-sounding word. This word is the keyword. Then, the student practices saying the target word and the keyword together. Next, in the relating stage, the student visualizes and draws a picture that symbolizes the keyword. Finally, in the retrieving stage, the student hears the target word, thinks of the keyword, and visualizes the picture and retrieves the meaning of the target word. Visualization and drawing employ the Universal Design for Learning (UDL) guideline of adding nonlinguistic methods of instruction to linguistic methods.

Brahler and Walker (2008) taught medical terminology to students in Anatomy and Physiology classes. The classes were divided into three groups: The first group was a control, in which the terms were taught by rote memorization; the second group was taught by keyword mnemonics; the third group combined the keyword method and rote memorization. The students who studied the keywords alone outperformed both the rote memorization group and the group that combined the keyword method with rote memorization (i.e., the results were highly statistically significant). The explanation for the findings was that the time spent with rote memorization in the combined group decreased the time spent in the keyword condition.

Terrill, Scruggs, and Mastropeiri (2004) investigated the usefulness of a pictorial mnemonic keyword approach on the vocabulary of high school students with ELN. Eight tenth-grade students with ELN participated. The students were all members of a self-contained special education class. The students received either keyword instruction or direct instruction on ten vocabulary words on alternating weeks. Instruction included words such as *diffident* and *turbulent*. On the posttest for the 30 words taught under each condition, the students defined 92% of the words correctly under the mnemonic condition and defined 49% of the words correctly in the control condition.

Mastropieri, Scruggs, and Mushinski (1990) investigated the use of keyword mnemonics with 23 adolescents with learning disabilities. The students were assigned either to the keyword condition or to a rehearsal condition. The students were taught eight difficult concrete vocabulary words, such as *chiton,* and eight difficult abstract vocabulary words, such as *vituperation.* When the students were tested on both production recall and on comprehension, the keyword students significantly outperformed the rehearsal condition students; on the production test, the keyword students remembered about five abstract and six concrete words as compared to one abstract and two concrete words remembered by the rehearsal group. On the comprehension test, the keyword group scored correctly on about seven concrete and six abstract concepts as compared to scores of four concrete and four abstract concepts by the rehearsal group.

Mastropieri and Scruggs (1991) described their investigations of the effect of the keyword strategy on the memory for and comprehension of abstract words taught to junior high school students who had ELN. Using keyword strategy, they taught incredibly difficult words, such as *catafalque* and *saprophytic*, to one group of students; the second group used a rehearsal-based strategy. The comprehension task required the participants to identify the word in a new context. The keyword group not only outperformed the rehearsal group for memory, but they also demonstrated superior comprehension. The researchers concluded that if they found success even with these difficult words, then they could teach anything to anyone using this method.

In our classes, we use index cards for the Keyword Mnemonic strategy, following the Levin (1988) strategy. The student writes the target word on the front of the card. On the back of the card, the student writes the keyword and draws the picture. The student self-quizzes by looking at the word on the front of the card and then checking the back to self-check.

Students with mild disabilities have serious difficulties with memory. The Keyword Mnemonic Strategy is successful in increasing students' Acquisition, Proficiency and Fluency, and Maintenance of Knowledge and Comprehension because

- Memory is ensured because of the depth of multisensory processing
- Attention is captured because the student is actively involved
- Motivation is enhanced because the strategy is serious fun

Here is an example that a student used to learn the word *calumny*.

⚷ Key 15: Teach Greek and Latin Morphemes

Secondary students suffer when they are not explicitly taught academic vocabulary (Flynt & Brozo, 2008). Cunningham and Moore (1993) found that when students were asked reading comprehension questions employing academic vocabulary, their ability to answer the questions decreased. They may have understood the reading passage about which they were queried, but their vocabulary deficiencies prevented them from understanding the questions. Borzo and Simpson (2007) defined academic vocabulary as "word knowledge that makes it possible for students to engage with, produce, and talk about texts that are valued in school" (as quoted in Flynt & Borzo, 2008, p. 500).

A critical key to teaching academic language is explicitly teaching Greek and Latin (G-L) roots, combining forms, and affixes. Corson (1983) referred to G-L facility as a "lexical bar" that is easily jumped by students from homes in which G-L words are frequently used, but that is formidable for students without such a home language. Of no surprise to secondary teachers is the fact that few struggling students grow up in families in which G-L words are used (Hennings, 2000).

Holmes and Keffer (2001) employed a computerized program to teach G-L root words to 115 college-bound high school students whose mean age was 15.6. Over a six-week period, the students used the program for an average of 7.9 hours to learn 90 Latin roots and 11 Greek roots; these roots resulted in approximately 800 English derivatives. After completing the program, the students in the experimental group outperformed the students in the control group by 40 points on the SAT.

Roberts (2009) taught high school freshmen orthographic conventions and morphological features in the form of G-L roots, suffixes, and prefixes over the course of a semester. The students were from eight freshman-English classes at a full-inclusion high school. The classes were randomly assigned to either the experimental condition or to a control condition in which they were provided class time for independent reading that equaled the amount of time that the experimental group participated in the word study. At the end of the semester, the experimental group significantly outperformed the control group on reading comprehension.

In our summer dyslexia clinic taught by undergraduate students who are Special Education majors, children from third through sixth grade are taught G-L roots and combining forms through Keyword Mnemonics and Direct Instruction methods. As the instructor circulates the room, she hears children respond to cues from tutors to chant, "Tele, distance. Visi, to see. Television, to see at a distance," and "Auto, self. Mobile, to move. Automobile, self-moving." That elementary children with dyslexia can master dozens of such G-L morphemes in only 15 hours of instruction ensures that middle school and secondary students with ELN can easily master such word elements.

In our clinic, interns employ the UDL principle of multiple representations to teach the children. Strategies they use include Keyword Mnemonics (Key 14), direct instruction, Word Card Rings (Key 16) that they review daily, and Word Walls (Key 17) to teach students Greek and Latin morphemes.

Multirepresentational teaching of Greek and Latin morphemes is successful in increasing the vocabulary of students with ELN in Acquisition and Proficiency and Fluency of Knowledge and Comprehension because

♪ Perception is increased by using multiple representations
♪ Discrimination is acute because differences in subtle word meanings are highlighted and explained
♪ Memory is enhanced because of the depth of processing
♪ Attention is ensured because the student is actively involved

In addition, the strategy is a key to Application and Generalization/Transfer of the word comprehension because

♪ Discrimination is enhanced, allowing the student to understand in which contexts to use the G-L root and affix
♪ Motivation is ensured because mastery of G-L root and affix is powerful and immediately useful in many contexts outside the content area class

Below are examples of G-L morphemes that the interns teach many third- through sixth-grade children using multiple representations.

Greek and Latin Morphemes

Anthrop	L	Man	Anthropology–study of man
Aud	L	Hear	Auditorium–place to listen
Bibl	G	Book	Bibliography–books written (from)
Circ	L	Round	Circulatory–going around
Derm	G	Skin	Dermatology–study of skin
Eth	G	Nation	Ethnicity–nationality
Geo	G	Earth	Geology–study of earth

⚡ Key 16: Vocabulary Word Wall

Interactive Word Walls are ubiquitous in elementary classrooms, occasionally seen in middle schools, and seldom used in secondary settings. Interactive Word Walls can be an important part of the vocabulary development of secondary students. We use them in our university classes for juniors and seniors to great effect.

Writing in the *Journal of Adolescent & Adult Literacy*, Harmon, Wood, Hedrick, Vintinner, and Willeford (2009) argued that secondary and middle school students deserve print-rich classrooms. The researchers noted that they observed Word Walls in secondary English classes where teachers displayed difficult spelling words, in social studies classrooms where teachers classified critical historical terms, and in mathematics classes where teachers displayed mathematical symbols.

In order to investigate how Interactive Word Walls could be best used with middle school students, the researchers conducted a six-week experiment. Their participants were 44 seventh graders, of whom 30% were Hispanic, 63% were Caucasian non-Hispanic, and 7% were biracial and Asian. The students were enrolled in two heterogeneous reading classes taught by the same teacher. Half of the students were in the experimental group and half were in the control group. The experimental students self-selected words for vocabulary study and participated in evidence-based instructional activities that involved Interactive Word Walls. The control students worked with activities from a commercial vocabulary workbook. In a delayed test two weeks after the last lesson, the researchers found that the Interactive Word Wall students demonstrated a "sustained higher level of understanding of the word meanings and were able to successfully apply them to meaningful prompts" (Harmon, Wood, Hedrick, Vintinner, & Willeford, 2009, p. 406).

The researchers then wanted to compare two word walls: one with only words, and one with colorful pictures and symbols that the students had created. When the researchers asked the students which word wall was more helpful, the students selected the one with the pictures that they had drawn and colored. When the researchers asked what was most helpful about the word wall, the students responded that the pictures provided cues as to the meanings of the words and even gave contexts for word use. For example, the word *tantalizing* was illustrated by a drawing of a chocolate candy drop; a student discussed how candy can be tantalizing. The students also explained that the word wall was especially useful in helping them select words when completing writing assignments and in reviewing for tests.

Hennings (2000) used two specific types of word walls in her college English classes: Linguistic Link Lists and Verb Towers. Linguistic Link Lists are Greek and Latin roots and affixes. The roots are written in red uppercase letters, and the affixes are written in black lowercase letters. Verb Towers show prefixes modifying a common verb. For example, Henning shows the *cede* tower. *Cede* means *to go* or *yield*. In front of a tower in which *cede* is written ten times are ten prefixes and their definitions, such as *pre* (for *precede*) and *inter* (for *intercede).* She urges middle school and secondary teachers to employ such devices.

Researchers who investigate Word Walls are quick to offer this caveat: Word Walls must be *interactive* tools in order to be effective. A teacher who simply lists words on the wall and leaves it at that will find little effect on student learning. In our college classes, we start each session with a quick review of our pedagogy words by asking students to do something with five or six of the words on our Interactive Word Walls. One day we might have the students write a paragraph about child development using any five words that they select. Another day we might have students share with their partners an example of a specific word on the wall that they have observed in a classroom: For example, one word on the wall is *routinization*. Students will tell their peers how they have observed routinization in their field experiences. Another day we might have students quiz their partners on the words that we added during the previous class. The key is to require students to interact with the words on the wall.

Interactive Word Walls helps students with Acquisition and Proficiency and Fluency and Maintenance of word Knowledge and Comprehension because

- Memory is enhanced because of repetition and judicious review
- Memory is enhanced because of the depth of processing
- Attention is ensured because the student is actively involved

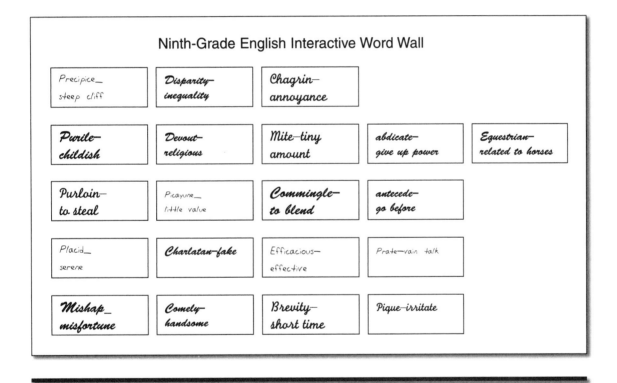

Ninth-Grade English Interactive Word Wall

Precipice— steep cliff	Disparity— inequality	Chagrin— annoyance		
Puerile— childish	Devout— religious	Mite—tiny amount	abdicate— give up power	Equestrian— related to horses
Purloin— to steal	Picayune— little value	Commingle— to blend	antecede— go before	
Placid— serene	Charlatan—fake	Efficacious— effective	Prate—vain talk	
Mishap— misfortune	Comely— handsome	Brevity— short time	Pique—irritate	

⚸ Key 17: Learning Games

We refer to *learning games* as *Serious Fun* because we stress to our education majors that they must provide a laser focus on the selected learning objectives. Learning games, whether in traditional format or electronic format, should provide high amounts of Opportunities to Respond (OtR) coupled with fun. Lacking either, a game is not Serious Fun.

For 15 years, our special education majors have conducted clinics every summer with students who have ELN. Some years, we worked with eighth and ninth graders who had failed the previous year; other years, we worked with elementary and middle school students. Some years we targeted mathematics, and other years reading. Each year, we employed multisensory direct instruction with multiple representations, formative assessment, and instructional games.

The games we used were traditional board-type games; in some cases, tutors hand-created boards on half-sheets of poster board. Other tutors created their games on computers and then printed them on photocopy paper. In other cases, tutors used commercial games (purchased at garage sales or scavenged from family) and created new rules for them. The rules usually involved answering a question on an index card that the student was studying; if the student answered correctly, she or he rolled a die and moved that many steps forward. If the answer was incorrect, the student did not roll the die. Other tutors used a *Jeopardy* format. In 15 hours of instruction over 10 days, our results were consistently astonishing.

Scottish researchers Gray, Topping, and Carcary (1998), at the University of Dundee, examined the effectiveness of board games in teaching the Highway Code (drivers' education) to secondary students. Students either studied the book individually or as part of a group, or they played a game individually or as part of a group. The game condition, regardless of whether a student played individually or as part of a group, was far more effective than the book study condition.

Whereas we use board games, many researchers are now investigating the effects of computer games on achievement. For example, Chuang and Chen (2009) compared Computer Aided Instruction (CAI) to a computer-based video game in teaching facts to Taiwanese students. The game format increased students' knowledge of the facts at a statistically significant level as compared to CAI without the game format.

Ke (2008) found that computer games that were cooperative in nature, as opposed to competitive and individualistic, significantly enhanced students' attitudes toward learning mathematics.

Learning Games are great inclusion strategies because

- ♪ Attention is acute because students are having fun
- ♪ Memory is enhanced because of the repetition of the words
- ♪ Motivation is increased because the students are having fun
- ♪ Persistence is increased because of the enjoyable nature of the activity

⊶ Key 18: Peer Tutoring

The excellent strategy called Classwide Peer Tutoring (CWPT) was developed at the University of Kansas's Juniper Gardens Children's Project by R. C. Greenwood, J. Delaquadri, and others. More information for CWPT can be found on the KU Juniper Gardens Web site: www.jgcp.ku.edu. However, here we suggest a simplified form that we refer to as *peer tutoring* or *peer-delivered tutoring*.

Peer tutoring studies have shown varied results depending upon the amount of explicitness and structure involved. When teachers simply tell students to work together on an assignment, achievement may not increase. However, when teachers have students use structured routines with explicit scripts, such as those employed in CWPT, achievement is accelerated.

We use the term *peer tutoring* for reciprocal tutoring of students with similar achievement. We use the term *peer-delivered tutoring* for when the tutoring is not reciprocal, but the tutee earns points for the class. Peer-delivered tutoring can be either *heterogeneous tutoring*, in which the tutee is taught by a tutor in the same class with a higher level of skill, or *cross-age tutoring*, in which a tutee in one grade is taught by a student in a higher grade.

In peer tutoring, the teacher pairs students; one acts as tutor and the other as tutee for five minutes. The students then exchange roles. The tutor uses an explicit script created by the teacher. The tutor shows the tutee the front of a vocabulary card. The tutee gives the definition. If the tutee is correct, the tutor says, "Correct. Two points," and marks two points on a point sheet. If the tutee is incorrect, the tutor says, "Incorrect." The tutor then shows the tutee the definition, and the tutee says the definition three times and writes the definition three times. The tutor then shows the tutee the front of the card again, the tutee gives the definition, and the tutor says, "Correct. One point." The process is repeated for the entire five minutes. At the end of the two five-minute sessions, the students give the point sheet to the teacher. The teacher adds all the class's points together. When the class achieves a predetermined number of points, the class receives a reward. The teacher may wish to set the number of points so that the class has an opportunity to earn a reward once a week or every two weeks if all students work diligently.

Kamps, Greenwood, and others (2008) conducted a three-year study of CWPT with 975 middle school students in 52 classrooms. The CWPT resulted in strong academic improvement, although the results varied with classrooms and content.

Hannah (2009) employed peer-delivered tutoring with African American high school students in mathematics classes. Hannah paired 46 tutees in algebra and geometry with tutors in Advanced Placement calculus. An additional 46 algebra and geometry students served as a control group. The tutoring sessions occurred in an afterschool tutoring program. After six weeks, the tutees' course grades were compared to the previous grading term's course grades. The difference in scores was statistically significant.

Stenhoff and Lignugaris (2007) conducted a review of research on peer tutoring in high school classrooms. They found peer tutoring to be an effective strategy. They also found that explicitly training students in the tutoring strategy before the actual tutoring begins is critical; turning students loose without explicit training and practice may render chaos. They also found that teachers should monitor the tutoring pairs.

Peer tutoring is an effective inclusion strategy because

- Attention is engaged when students work together
- Memory is enhanced from repetition and explicit feedback
- Motivation is increased because of the social drive of adolescents
- Persistence is increased because of adolescents' social drive

🔑 Key 19: Vocabulary Word Card Ring

The American Council on the Teaching of Foreign Languages' 2008 Teacher of the Year, Janet Glass, employs the use of index cards to teach beginning vocabulary to students studying Spanish. When our students with special needs confront an important new vocabulary word in a content area, they create a word card from an index card and add it to their Vocabulary Word Card Ring (VWR). Using index cards to learn vocabulary words and concepts is recommended by a number of researchers for use across a number of disciplines and created in a variety of ways (Barbetta, Heron, & Heward, 1993; Carr & Wixson, 1986; Dreyer, 1974; Ellis, 1992; Foil & Alber, 2002; Greenwood, 2002; Kagan, 1992; Mosher, 1999; Walker, 1989).

We use the strategy by having students write the word on the front of the card and then write the definition and a Keyword Mnemonic on the back. Though no individual's name emerges from the literature, special education teachers have used such cards and provided their students with metal binder rings for many years. We have then had students punch a hole in the upper left-hand corner of each card, place all the cards on the ring, and carry them around in a pocket or purse for review during odd moments. When a card is well-mastered, we remove it from the ring and file it.

After we have taught the strategy in special education pedagogy classes, we have even had our college juniors and seniors tell us that this simple strategy has revolutionized their study skills. We commonly see our students flipping through their cards while sitting in hallways waiting for classes to start or sitting in the student union in a group studying together. The strategy is not flashy or fun, but it is a good key to memory retention and retrieval because spaced practice and judicious review are major keys to accessing learning for all students—but especially for special needs students. (See *Vocabulary Acquisition: Curricular and Instructional Implications for Diverse Learners* [Technical Report No. 14] from the National Center to Improve the Tools of Educators and the National Council of Teachers of Mathematics Standards for more information.)

The Vocabulary Word Card Ring is a reliable tool to increase information retrieval. *Information retrieval* refers to *testing*. Our students use their word cards to conduct daily self-testing. Karpicke and Roediger (2007) investigated the effects of repeated testing on memory. The researchers provided college students with 40 Swahili-English word pairs. Once a

Tessellation

student correctly identified a word pair, the word was assigned to one of four conditions: (1) the word pair was again studied and tested on subsequent days, (2) the word pair was dropped from further study but tested on subsequent days, (3) the word pair was dropped from further testing but was studied on subsequent days, or (4) the word pair were neither studied nor tested. A week after the final session, participants were tested on the words. In the two conditions in which students were continuously tested, they correctly recalled 80% of the words whether or not they studied. In the two conditions in which students were not continuously tested, they remembered only 36% and 33% of the word pairs whether or not they studied. The researchers called Information Retrieval, which we call *repeated testing*, the key to long-term memory.

The Vocabulary Word Card Ring serves as a device that assists our students in the frequent self-testing that assists them in remembering new vocabulary words.

The VWR helps students become fluent and proficient in knowledge and comprehension because

- 🎵 Memory is enhanced because of repetition and judicious review
- 🎵 Motivation is enhanced because students often pull out the handy ring cards and use them with friends when studying for quizzes or exams

6

Teaching Devices
for Increasing
Student Learning
From Lectures

In this chapter, we will add to our key ring new keys that will help make us more powerful teachers. With only small adaptations to the ways we typically teach, we can teach all of our students—not simply the average and bright ones. When all of our students are educated citizens, we all win.

The different strategies in this chapter serve a variety of needs. Many lessons we teach can be enhanced by using several of the strategies in one lesson, thereby allowing us to accommodate more needs. When students find that we are meeting their needs, they become more highly motivated to learn. The success cycle escalates, and everybody wins.

We wish that teachers never felt like they had to lecture, but it is a fact that many teachers rely heavily on lecturing (Brophy, 1988; Good & Brophy, 1984). In fact, Hawkins and Brady (1994) asserted that despite the fact that many instructional options are available to us, lecturing is the most frequently used instructional technique in secondary schools. Thirty years ago, 70% of class time was spent in lectures, and although we have made progress, Putnam, Deshler, and Schumaker (1993) found that we still lecture half the time in junior high and high schools. They interviewed 120 teachers in three states and found that the teachers spent half their time lecturing, with tenth-grade teachers lecturing slightly more frequently than seventh-grade teachers. Of course, one goal of secondary teachers is to prepare students for success in college, and 80% of college class time is spent listening to lectures.

Brown and Manogue (2001) provide the following caveat regarding lectures:

(Lectures) can be boring and, worse, useless. If they are merely recitations of standard texts then they are not fulfilling adequately their functions of developing understanding and motivating students to learn. If the lecture is used only to provide detailed coverage of facts and findings then the students would gain more from reading a good textbook. If lectures are the only method of teaching used then the students are not being well prepared for their future roles. (p. 231)

Brown and Manogue (2001) explained that every teacher who lectures has at least one style, and better teachers who lecture employ a variety of styles depending on the context. Styles are "habitual sets of responses to situations perceived as similar" (p. 232). At the ends of the lecture continuum are the *reading aloud* style and the *associating aloud* style. The read-alouders read their prepared lectures verbatim. The associate-alouders say whatever pops into their heads regardless of relevance to the topic at hand. The median style is the *think-aloud* style. Think-alouders share their thinking about a topic, engaging in Vygotskian cognitive modeling so that their cognitive apprentices can learn how an expert thinks about a subject.

Brown and Bakhtar (1987) identified five styles of lecturing. The types they identified are as follows:

- *Oral Presenters* strictly talk, using no visual supports.
- *Visual Information Givers* are confident providers of visual information, using the board or overhead (and ostensibly in the twenty-first century, video monitors) to provide diagrams, and they give students time to transfer the diagrams to their notes.
- *Exemplary Performers* are confident, well structured, and capable. They employ a menu of oral and visual strategies. They carefully decide on the objectives of each lecture and share those objectives with students. They use aids to cue important points. They often use questions to structure their lectures.
- *Eclectic Lecturers* use a variety of strategies, including humor. They use multiple sources for their lectures, but find selecting and structuring their materials difficult. They lack confidence and tend to be disorganized; they often digress from their notes.
- *Amorphous Talkers* are overconfident, poorly prepared, and vague. They don't think about their objectives until they stand up before the class.

Researchers (Bligh, 2000; Brown & Bakhtar, 1987) identified five methods of structuring lectures.

- The *Classical lecture* is the easiest. The lecture is divided into broad categories that are subdivided into more specific categories. This is not only the simplest method, but it easily becomes the most boring.
- The *Problem-Centered lecture* can pique students' interests. This lecture starts with a problem to which potential solutions are suggested.
- The *Sequential lecture* can easily lose students' interest because they get lost. This lecture starts with a problem and is followed by a sequential chain of logic that leads to a conclusion.
- The *Comparative lecture*'s main problem is that the lecturer assumes that the students know more about the topics to be compared than they actually know. This lecture compares two or more concepts, methods, and so on. The comparative lecture is best accomplished through the use of graphic organizers.
- The *Thesis lecture* can be hard to follow, but when well presented, it interests students. The thesis lecture begins with an assertion that is then supported or refuted through argument.

When Brown and Bakhtar (1987) asked students what they disliked about lectures, they found that students did not dislike lectures—they disliked poor-quality lectures. Specifically, the students disliked teachers who (1) were inaudible, (2) talked too quickly, (3) tried to cram in too much information, (4) were incoherent, or (5) used visual aids poorly.

Brown and Bakhtar (1987) noted that lecturing was useful and economical, and Hawkins and Brady (1994) concurred that lecturing is a cost-effective method of instruction; however, they cautioned that many students who have exceptional learning needs (ELN) do not learn well from traditional lectures. Students with ELN need accommodations.

When Suritsky (1992) asked college students who had a learning disability what their instructors could do to help them learn better from lectures, they identified five strategies: (1) giving the students lecture handouts or outlines, (2) slowing down the rate of delivery, (3) explicitly identifying the most important lecture points, (4) using overhead transparencies regularly, and (5) making the tests reflect the lecture content.

The keys presented here will help unlock the doors to Acquisition and Knowledge.

- ↪ Key 20: Simply Slow Down
- ↪ Key 21: Pause Procedure
- ↪ Key 22: Solicit Students' Examples
- ↪ Key 23: Cue Critical Points
- ↪ Key 24: Explicitly Teach the Big Ideas
- ↪ Key 25: Provide an Advance Organizer
- ↪ Key 26: Provide a Plethora of Examples
- ↪ Key 27: Provide Nonexamples
- ↪ Key 28: Teach CSA/CRA
- ↪ Key 29: Role Play Difficult Content

⚷ Key 20: Simply Slow Down

Hughes and Suritsky (1993) asked college students with learning disabilities what they most needed lecturers to do in order to help them learn more effectively. The students' biggest complaint was that their instructors lectured too quickly.

A lecture is fast if the rate of speed is 120 or more words per minute. Students who have ELN cannot make sense of what the instructor is saying or write quickly enough to process what is being said and keep up with notes.

A morpheme is a unit of meaning. For example, *president* is one morpheme in English, but *presidents* is two morphemes because the letter *s* in this case carries the meaning of *more than one*. Nine morphemes per statement is the maximum that people can understand without loss of meaning. Some listeners can only process five morphemes per statement, yet Moran (1980) found that teachers average ten morphemes per statement. If the average listener has difficulty understanding the teacher, the task must be nearly insurmountable for students with disabilities.

The task of understanding a lecture becomes more complex if the listener and the lecturer do not share a native accent (i.e., if both speaker and listener are English speakers, but they come from different parts of the country). Adank, Evans, Stuart-Smith, and Scott (2009) conducted experiments to determine the effect of disparate accents on a listener's understanding. They found that under adverse listening conditions, the difference in accents employed by the speaker and the listener reduced the listener's speed of processing. As might be expected, when the speaker had a nonnative accent, the processing load was even greater for the listener—so our rate of speed is critical when we are teaching students who are English language learners.

High information density means that a lecture contains many ideas, also called *information units* (Hughes & Suritsky, 1993). Structural complexity and information density can lead to cognitive overload when the required cognitive resources exceed the student's available cognitive resources (Fox, Park, & Lang, 2007). Potts (1993) recommended that information density be kept low, with no more than 50% of the material in a lecture being new to the students.

Gordon, Daneman, and Schneider (2009) found that when adults listened to 10- to 15-minute lectures at the rate of normally encountered fast speech (240 words per

minute), they had more trouble remembering details and integrating the information into their schema than when the information was delivered at a slower pace. When background noise was present, the difficulty was aggravated.

When our Special Education majors and master's students teach in our dyslexia clinic, we have them videotape themselves. We then have them calculate both the speed and the information density of their speech and adjust accordingly. We heartily recommend this technique. Most newer laptop computers have webcams that can be used to allow teachers to record themselves and assess their rate of speech and information density.

Teachers can increase their students' understanding by simply slowing down.

Simply Slowing Down is an effective inclusion strategy that helps students acquire knowledge and comprehension because

- ♪ Frustration is decreased when students can keep up with their notes
- ♪ Motivation is enhanced when students see that they are keeping up with their notes
- ♪ Perception is increased when students have time to process auditory information

⊶ Key 21: Pause Procedure

If a lecture is both fast and dense, students with ELN are overwhelmed. In addition to slowing down the rate of presentation, we can use the Pause Procedure (Rowe, 1976, 1980, 1983) to let students retrieve information they missed due to attention problems and also to increase their attention. This is an important strategy for our students with attention deficit disorders. Tileston (2000) reported that in middle school and high school, students stop listening or attending after 15 to 20 minutes of lecture.

During the Pause Procedure, students catch up on their notes and ask their group members or neighbors to clarify statements about which they are unclear. Kiewra (1985) reviewed the literature on the Pause Procedure and recommended what he called *segmenting lectures*; this refers to lecturing for six or seven minutes and then pausing three or four minutes while the students take notes and consult with each other.

Dyson (2008) incorporated three 1-minute pauses into his lectures—20 minutes, 30 minutes, and 40 minutes into the lectures. At each pause, the students were told to write one thing that they had learned. The students were also asked to record their level of attention every five minutes. The intervention significantly increased student engagement. In contrast, when the students were given the 1-minute pauses but told either to write down a question they would like answered, or to simply take a 1-minute break, their engagement was not increased.

Ruhl (1996) also found differences in the usefulness of activities employed during the Pause Procedure. In a college context, 27 students who had ELN attended a class in which the professor used the Pause Procedure. One condition instructed the students to use the pause for reflection and note taking. The second condition instructed the students to use the pause to discuss the lecture with their peers. The discussion condition resulted in more ideas recorded in the students' notes than did the reflection and note taking condition.

Davis (1995) also found that the type of activity an instructor required during the Pause Procedure affected student achievement. Davis's participants listened to a 21-minute videotaped lecture in which they were given three 4-minute pauses. In one condition, the students were told to write a summary of the lecture since the last pause. In the second condition, students were told that they might review their notes if they wished. In the

third condition, the control, the lecture did not have pauses. While all three groups scored comparably on the test immediately following the lecture, the summary group significantly outperformed the other two groups on a delayed posttest.

Ruhl and Suritsky (1995) investigated the effects of three 2-minute pauses at logical stopping points in a videotaped lecture. The 33 college students who participated in the study had learning disabilities. The Pause Procedure increased the students' immediate recall of the lecture content. In addition, the Pause Procedure increased the completeness of the students' notes.

The Pause Procedure is an effective inclusion strategy because

- ♪ Frustration is decreased when students can keep up with their notes
- ♪ Motivation is increased when students can see that they are keeping up with the other students and the teacher
- ♪ Perception is increased when students can check with each other to complete their notes and correct as necessary during pauses

🔑 Key 22: Solicit Students' Examples

Researchers have extolled the use of everyday examples in such fields as psychology (Baldwin & Baldwin, 1999), chemistry (Jones & Miller, 2001), physics (Prigo, 2007), and mathematics (Suh, 2007). Students' lives are a rich source of everyday examples that can be more meaningful to students than the examples found in their textbooks.

Gersten, Baker, and Marks (1998) recommended soliciting concrete examples of new concepts from the lives of English language learners with learning problems. Their recommendation was based on a review of the literature and on professional focus groups of practicing teachers.

Concrete examples from students' lives activate prior learning. When a teacher solicits students' experiences of a concept they are learning, the teacher is tying the new learning into the students' existing schema, a principle of teaching and learning that dates back to Piaget's notion of accommodation and assimilation.

When we were teaching our students the concept of *cycles of change* in science, we asked them to relate examples of cycles of change in their own lives. With nudging from us, one student identified such cycles as the school year starting, Thanksgiving holiday, Christmas holiday, spring break, and the end of school. Another student identified wearing hot-, warm-, cool-, and cold-weather clothes. Another identified being born, growing up, growing old, and dying. The cycles they identified from their own experience created a neural network for cycles of change, and they could connect the new information we gave them to the network they had created. We turned this information into graphic information on a table and further strengthened the connection.

When we were teaching about migration and asked volunteers to share their reasons for moving from one place to another, we were surprised by the candor with which they talked about how their lives demonstrated the usual causes of migration: economic problems and human rights problems. The students volunteered such economic problems as a parent being laid off and no longer being able to afford the upscale apartment, or the birth of a new baby that put a financial strain on the family, or the unexpected cancer of a sibling that caused a mother to quit working to stay with the child. The human rights violations were reflected by problems with neighbors, unreasonable landlords, or abuse by housemates. We never had a student miss a test question on the causes of migration, and we were consistently impressed with their essay responses on the topic.

Solicit Students' Examples

When we taught about propaganda techniques in a language arts class, we asked the students to give us examples of the various types of propaganda they had encountered. All of our students, especially those with special needs, understood the concept much more clearly when we contextualized it in this way than when it was contextualized in other ways.

Soliciting Students' Examples is a powerful inclusion strategy because

- 🎵 Motivation is stronger when students see how a concept applies to themselves
- 🎵 Attention is secured when motivation is stronger
- 🎵 Confusion is avoided when students have a concrete example in their schema to which to attach the new learning
- 🎵 Memory is activated when students process deeply to find their own examples and when they develop multiple representations from hearing other students' examples

☛ Key 23: Cue Critical Points

Because we know that students who have ELN have difficulty discriminating between critical and nonessential information, we need to make the main points explicit by cueing them. We do this by explicitly teaching our students with disabilities a set of cues and teaching them to make notes of that cued information (Titsworth, 2001).

Titsworth and Kiewra (2004) compared the performance of students when listening to lectures that were or were not cued as to important points. When teachers provided spoken cues, the students increased their number of noted main ideas by 39% and the number of important details by 35%. The cueing raised students' test scores from 15% to 45% as compared to noncueing during lectures.

Cueing is even more important when learners are not native English speakers. Jung (2003) compared the academic performance of 80 Korean students who were English language learners and who did and did not receive cues when listening to a lecture. Compared to the noncued group, the cued group accurately remembered significantly more information from the lecture. Pollio (1990) noted that teachers must explicitly teach their cues to students who are not native English speakers because the cues that are typical in their cultures may be different from the cues that are typical in American classrooms.

Nevid and Mahon (2009) employed mini-quizzes at the beginning of lectures to signal key concepts. Students learned significantly more lecture material with the pre-lecture quizzes than without them. The researchers explained that the quiz served to signal the key concepts of the lecture.

We must explicitly teach our cueing system to our students because students are often unaware of an instructor's cues. Researchers have found that written cues are more effective than verbal cues, so we should be certain to cue by writing essential information on the board or the overhead (Fahmy & Bilton, 1990a, 1990b; Scerbo, Warm, & Dember, 1992).

We develop and explicitly teach a cueing system at the beginning of the school year. For example, some cues we use and teach include the following:

- ♪ Writing the essential points on the board in bullet style.
- ♪ Stating, "This is a critical detail. Be sure to write this in your notes," and then writing it on the board or overhead.
- ♪ Stating, "You will see this on a test. Count on it," and then writing it on the board or overhead.

Many researchers recommend the use of repetition as cueing (Belfiore, Skinner, & Ferkis, 1995; Cahnmann, 2000; Powell & Thomson, 1996) in widely diverse arenas. We frequently repeat an important point three times, sometimes speaking in a stage whisper as though we were sharing a secret.

In addition to repetition, we use choral responding. Researchers have recommended choral responding for mastery and for checking for understanding with all students, but they have strongly recommended the strategy with special needs students in both academic and vocational classes (Heward, Gardner, & Barbetta, 1996; Kagan, 1992). We have used it extensively with high school students and found it to be not only effective but also fun for the students.

We explicitly teach cue words such as *first, next,* and *finally; alternatively, in contrast,* and *on the other hand;* and *if, therefore,* and *because.* Not only should we verbally teach our students the code words we select, but making a chart and posting it in our room is imperative. Not only will it help our students in the early stages of learning the new words because we can point to a word as we say it in our lecture, but it will remind us of the agreed-upon words when we forget for a moment as we are lecturing.

Cuing critical points and explicitly teaching lecture cues is an effective strategy because

- ♪ Motivation is increased when students see that they are able to write down what the teacher thinks is important
- ♪ Discrimination between critical information and less important information is ensured when the teacher explicitly cues the critical information
- ♪ Frustration is decreased when students are certain that they recorded the critical information
- ♪ Attention is activated when the student sees or hears the cue

My Lecture Cues	_Cue Words_
I am cueing you if I . . .	First, second, third
Say it three times	Then, after, finally
Hold up one finger	Alternatively
Write it on the board	In contrast
Ask for a "drum roll"	On the other hand
Say to write it down	Therefore
Have you echo me	Because

⊶ Key 24: Explicitly Teach the Big Ideas

A number of researchers have argued that explicitly teaching the *big ideas* of a discipline is crucial for students with disabilities (Carnine, 1994; Coyne, Kame'enui, & Simmons, 2001; Grossen, 2002; Grossen et al., 2002; Kame'enui & Carnine, 1998; National Center to Improve the Tools of Educators [NCITE], 1998). Grossen and her colleagues (2002), writing for the U.S. Office of Special Education Programs, wrote that Big Ideas is one of the six principles of accommodation for students who have ELN:

> Big ideas, concepts and principles that facilitate the most efficient and broad acquisition of knowledge across a range of examples are presented. Big ideas make it possible for students to learn the most and learn it as efficiently as possible, because "small" ideas can often be best understood in relationship to larger, "umbrella concepts." (p. 71)

Olson (2008) argued that one of the central problems in science teaching is that students are missing core concepts in favor of learning isolated facts. She gives the example of students learning that butterflies have larva, pupa, and so on but failing to internalize the big idea: *life cycles.* She argues that science teachers must focus on the Big Ideas rather than topics.

Writing in the *Kappa Delta Pi Record,* Conderman and Bresnahan (2008) argued that instead of trying to teach middle school students every idea in a textbook, teachers should ask themselves, "What are the one or two main ideas or core concepts from this lesson that all students should learn? In other words, what big ideas should all students learn today?" (p. 176).

Every subject has its Big Ideas that are identified by the learned societies of that discipline. During the first week of school, we explicitly explain to the students that every discipline has its Big Ideas around which the study of that discipline revolves. Then, we explicitly teach the big ideas of our discipline. Each day, when we are ready to begin our lesson, we explicitly identify the big idea(s) that we will be addressing that day.

The American Association for the Advancement of Science does not use the words *Big Ideas* in *Science for All Americans,* from its Project 2061, but rather uses the term *Common Themes.* Those themes are generally called Big Ideas by practitioners.

While average students and those who are intellectually gifted may be able to infer the big ideas of a discipline inductively, few students with ELN will be able to make that cognitive leap. They need explicit, didactic instruction on the Big Ideas and frequent reminders. A permanent poster on the bulletin board to which the teacher refers each day will not only provide needed instruction to the student with ELN but will also remind the teacher to keep focused on "keeping the main thing the main thing."

Teaching the Big Ideas is good for all learners, but especially for students with special needs because

- ♪ Motivation is ensured when we continuously return to a small number of known ideas
- ♪ Attention is captured when the new information is tied to something we know well

♪ Discrimination is enhanced when we make the most important ideas explicit

♪ Memory is strengthened when we have fewer, but more important, things to remember and when well-known schemata are elaborated

Big Ideas in Geography

1. *Location*
2. *Place*
3. *Movement*
4. *Regions*
5. *Human/environmental interactions*

⊶ Key 25: Provide an Advance Organizer

Ausubel (1968) developed the advance organizer. Ausubel stated that what the student already knows is the greatest predictor of how much the student will learn from a lesson. He said that in contrast to an overview, which simply states key ideas, an advance organizer is a bridge between what the student already knows and what he or she is going to learn. However, the teachers we know use the term *advance organizer* for almost any activity that engages students before a lesson and helps them prepare to learn the new material, and the majority of the research on advance organizers uses the term in the same way.

Advance organizers can consist of a list of important points that will be covered, a short discussion, a list of questions, a graphic organizer, or any other tool that will prepare the student for the lesson.

Stacey (2001) examined the use of advance organizers with secondary students who have ELN. The students attended a resource room for a geography class. The students were provided an advance organizer, guided notes, and a 10-minute review after the lecture. The intervention was compared to one in which the students were provided guided notes and the review but no advance organizer. The advance organizer improved students' quiz scores on the material covered.

Willerman and MacHarg (1991) taught a control group of 40 eighth-grade science students a unit on elements and compounds. Then, the researchers taught an experimental group the same lesson but employed a concept map as an advance organizer. The advance organizer group outperformed the control group.

Lenz and Alley (1983) investigated the use of advance organizers with secondary students who had learning disabilities and were trained to attend to their teachers' use of the advance organizers; their knowledge of information in a lecture was compared to that of a control group whose teachers did not use the organizer. First, the students in the organizer group demonstrated their increased awareness of their teachers' use of the organizers. Then, the students in the advance organizer group significantly outperformed their control group peers. The students in the advance organizer group remembered more important information from the lecture than did their peers, whereas the students in the control group remembered more unimportant information than did their peers in the experimental group.

However, Lenz, Alley, and Schumaker (1987) provided a caveat on the use of advance organizers with students with ELN. When they compared the performance of students who have ELN who were trained to attend to the organizers to those who did not receive such training, the researchers found that the strategy only benefitted the students when they were explicitly taught to make use of the organizer.

Advance organizers are good inclusion strategies because

- ♪ Organization of thought is promoted
- ♪ Confusion is avoided because students either get the big picture or connect the new learning to a concept with which they are familiar

What follows is an example of a preview-overview of a lesson on giving a persuasive speech.

Today you are going to learn how to turn your persuasive essay into a persuasive speech. Listen to answer these questions.

1. How can I capture and keep my audience's attention?

2. How can I adjust the tone of my speech to fit my audience?

3. How can I anticipate my audience's counterarguments?

⬤➤ Key 26: Provide a Plethora of Examples

Jones and Wilson (1997) noted that a critical task of teaching is selecting and organizing examples in order to direct student learning. Students learn from examples, and students with ELN need many more examples to learn a concept than do their nondisabled peers (Brigham & Snyder, 1986). Many teachers fail to provide enough examples for students who have ELN to master concepts (Silbert, Carnine, & Stein, 1990). Even otherwise good teachers may provide an inadequate number of examples for their students with ELN.

Not only do teachers need to provide many examples, but Jones and Wilson (1997) cautioned that teachers must provide a sufficient *range* of examples to adequately define the concept. They wrote, "If some instances of a concept are underrepresented in instruction or simply not included in instruction, students with LD will predictably fail to learn that concept adequately" (p. 152). A toddler who has a Labrador retriever may see other large dogs and thereby develop the concept of *dog*. Faced with a Chinese hairless, or even a yapping Yorkie, the child may think he has discovered an entirely new species. The error is concept undergeneralization, or failing to realize the category under which a specific exemplar resides. Students with ELN frequently undergeneralize.

Jones and Wilson (1997) explained that the number of examples required depends on four factors. First, the variations must be addressed. As in the case of the previously mentioned dogs, students will undergeneralize unless exposed to variations.

The second factor is whether nonessential attributes will be mistaken for essential attributes. In the case of the dog, the toddler mistook size as an essential attribute of *dog*.

The third factor that determines the number of examples required is the complexity of the concept. *Human rights* is a far more complex concept than is *volcano*, so it requires more exemplars.

The fourth factor is the number of ways that the concept may be applied. The word *work* can be applied in an enormous number of ways, far more than the word *microscope*—so *work* would require more examples in order for students with ELN to understand the concept.

Yoho (1985) compared teaching social studies concepts using critical attributes with using best examples and then having students contrast the best examples to other examples. He found that his concepts far better and retained the concepts longer when he used the best example technique as compared to the critical attributes technique. In addition, his male students who were poor readers performed far better with this strategy than with the critical attributes strategy; so in addition to soliciting examples from students' lives, we provide many more examples for them than we think they could possibly need.

Ranzijn (1991) examined the use of examples in teaching 50 Dutch secondary students. Ranzijn employed videotaped examples in his study. Ranzijn found that a wide variety of examples improved the students' understanding of the concepts taught.

Providing a plethora of examples promotes the learning of students with special needs because

- Motivation is heightened if at least one of the examples is related to the students' lives
- Attention is stronger if motivation is heightened
- Confusion is decreased when students have multiple representations provided by the multiple examples
- Memory is enhanced if students find an example among those given that already exists in their schema

⊶ Key 27: Provide Nonexamples

Whether teaching inductively or deductively, we all use examples when we teach new concepts. We either present examples and have the students induce the concept and its definition, or we supply the concept and its definition didactically and then provide examples to the students. However, few teachers include nonexamples (Lasley, Williams, & Hart, 1991) when they are teaching concepts, although nonexamples are critical to learning—especially for learners with ELN. Nonexamples highlight the critical attributes of the concept we are teaching.

In the early days of research on the use of examples and nonexamples in teaching, Tennyson, Merrill, and Woolley (1971) found that learners often overgeneralize, considering nonexemplars to be members of a class of which they are not members.

Two kinds of nonexamples have been identified: *intuitive nonexamples* and *nonintuitive nonexamples* (Tsamir, Tirosh, & Levenson, 2008). Intuitive nonexamples are those that most people discount as an example of the concept without being told: Even a toddler who does not have ELN knows that a hummingbird is not a dog. In contrast, nonintuitive nonexamples are nonmembers of a class that bear a striking resemblance to members of the class; they are therefore commonly mistaken for examples. Nonintuitive nonexamples can mislead an otherwise knowledgeable, intelligent person: Nonintuitive nonexamples of *continents* and *punishment* are *the Arctic* and *negative reinforcement*, respectively.

Researchers have stressed the importance of nonexamples in physics concept learning, in learning the geometric concept of semiregular polyhedra, and in the language learning of students with disabilities (Arons, 1984; Cohen & Carpenter, 1980; Cole, 1979).

Swanson (1972) examined the effects of positive and negative examples on students' learning of environmental concepts. He found that presenting examples and nonexamples in a rational teaching set promoted correct classification of newly encountered items and that omitting nonexamples resulted in students' overgeneralization of the concepts.

McMurray (1974) investigated the use of nonexamples with 64 middle school students with mild intellectual disabilities (formerly called *mental retardation*) who were learning geometric shapes. Presenting a wide variety of examples and nonexamples with matched pairs led to the students' best mastering of the geometric concepts without overgeneralization.

Nonexamples help students learn new concepts because

- ♪ Discrimination between the target concept and similar concepts is made more acute because the nonexamples help point out the critical attributes, and in addition, discrimination is increased when multiple nonrepresentations are provided
- ♪ Memory is supported when examples are contrasted with nonexamples

⚷ Key 28: Teach CSA/CRA

A number of researchers have recommended teaching new concepts by starting with *concrete examples,* moving through *semiconcrete* or *representational examples,* and only then on to *abstractions* (CSA/CRA) in teaching students with disabilities. For example, in their review of the literature on teaching algebra to learning disabled adolescents, Maccini, McNaughton, and Ruhl (1999) found empirical support for beginning with concrete examples before advancing to semiconcrete or representational examples and then finally to abstract examples.

Maccini and Hughes (2000) found strong positive results when using a CSA/CRA strategy with secondary students who had ELN. The six students were in a special education resource room for their Algebra I class; they were functioning more than two years below grade level in math. The students were taught computation and problem solving using integers. In the concrete stage, the students used concrete manipulatives. In the semiconcrete stage, the students translated the problem into pictorial form. In the third phase, the students used traditional mathematical symbols to solve the problems. After the students demonstrated mastery on two consecutive probes, they attempted one near- and one far-transfer generalization probe. The near-generalization probes were the same difficulty as those in the instructional procedure but had different story lines. The far-transfer probes were more complex than those in the instructional procedure and required more strategy use. The results demonstrated that CSA/CRA is a powerful tool for increasing the problem-solving skills of students who have ELN.

Cass, Cates, Jackson, and Smith (2002) used concrete manipulatives to teach three problem-solving skills involving calculating perimeter and area to secondary students who had ELN. Initially unable to solve perimeter and area problems, the students received 15 to 20 minutes of instruction on a geoboard for five to seven days. They reached performance criterion (80%) at that time, and three weekly maintenance checks indicated that they could solve all problems correctly with the geoboard. When they returned from Christmas vacation, the students were instructed to solve four perimeter and four area problems without the use of the geoboard, using only pencil and paper. All three students solved all eight problems correctly.

For concrete, Maria could tell about her experiences emigrating from Mexico. For representational, we could play "The Immigrating Game." Then we'll be ready for an abstract discussion!

We use a version of CSA/CRA in our teacher education classes through the use of videos and pictures as a concrete representation. For example, when teaching about human rights violations of persons with disabilities, we start with video clips and photographs before we move on to discussions of human rights in the abstract.

CSA/CRA helps support the learning of students who have ELN because

- ⚷ Motivation is increased when students see that they can succeed by working with the concrete examples
- ⚷ Attention is stronger when motivation is strong
- ⚷ Perception is increased by starting with the concrete examples
- ⚷ Memory is activated when the abstract learning is attached to the concrete representations
- ⚷ Confusion is avoided by working with the concrete examples first

⊶ Key 29: Role Play Difficult Content

Role playing is a powerful student-centered way to strengthen didactic instruction. Role play is especially valuable in teaching difficult content because it provides a way to make the invisible visible in a robust way.

While social studies teachers frequently use role playing in their classes, role playing is also a valuable tool in other disciplines. Resnick and Wilensky (1998) argued that role playing is a powerful tool in teaching both science and math—especially in the new science of complexity, which is the study of complex systems. Wyn and Stegink (2000) used role playing to teach secondary students the process of mitosis. Tyas and Cabot (1999) used role playing to help students understand the energy changes involved in an exothermic reaction by modeling how bond-breaking takes in energy, activates energy, causes a rise in temperature, and gives out energy. Batts (1999) successfully used role playing to help secondary students understand the abstract concept of color subtraction, Johnson (1999) used role playing to teach how the kidney functions, and Stencel and Barkoff (1993) used it to teach students about protein synthesis.

We have used the strategy to tutor students with ELN who were taking chemistry. We had them act out the chemical processes of single and double replacement reactions using the analogy of students losing their date to another person and the analogy of two double-dating students exchanging dates.

Role playing has been used extensively in foreign language classes, and skits have been used to help students develop a deeper understanding of vocabulary in their native language. We used skits to help students clarify the difference between *immigrate* and *emigrate.* A group of students stood together in one corner of the classroom. Another group stood in the opposite corner. Individual students moved from one group to the other, with each side holding up signs that stated either "She immigrated to us!" or "She emigrated away from us!"

Role playing is used extensively in colleges and in business. Medical schools frequently use role playing with physicians-in-training, seminaries use role playing in the preparation for providing pastoral care, and business colleges employ it with their students.

Maddrell (1994) noted that although role playing has been found to be effective in teaching geography, teachers seldom use the strategy because they lack confidence. He noted that students who are reluctant to speak in class often are more willing to speak when they are playing the role of another rather than transparently expressing their own views. He refers to role playing as an "empowering pedagogy."

Role Playing Difficult Content is a powerful strategy because

- ♪ Motivation is enhanced when students are physically involved and also when students are having fun
- ♪ Attention is heightened when motivation is enhanced
- ♪ Perception is stronger when the visual and kinesthetic senses are engaged
- ♪ Discrimination is more acute when contrasting concepts are role played
- ♪ Confusion is lessened when students have a physical experience of the concept
- ♪ Frustration is avoided when confusion is minimized
- ♪ Memory is activated when students deep process the information

Here is how one of our classes looked when we were teaching the concepts of *emigrate* and *immigrate.*

7

Increasing Learning by Using Note Taking Strategies

Note taking strategies are keys to help students who have exceptional learning needs (ELN) access the Knowledge and Comprehension domains. In general, note taking strategies help students by providing (1) an encoding function that causes them to process information deeply and (2) an external storage function that provides access to information that is not yet stored in long-term memory.

Note taking is surprisingly complex. Students must (1) sustain their attention, (2) comprehend what the teacher is saying, (3) discriminate between critical and irrelevant information, (4) paraphrase the information into a note format, (5) organize it in a coherent way, and (6) record it readably and quickly. No wonder so many students who have ELN are overwhelmed by note taking!

Although note taking is a difficult task, students with ELN *can* be taught to take notes more effectively. Because good note taking strategies impose structure, they are by nature good techniques for working with students who have ELN. If our students are to learn to take notes, we have to teach them explicitly how to conduct the note taking strategies we want them to use, and those strategies may vary by assignment types. We need to ensure that they receive substantial practice in the strategies we select, and we need to use good lecturing devices to ensure that they know what information should go into their notes.

Lecture is a major method of instruction in secondary schools and in college, so students must be prepared to learn from lectures. Note taking is the primary strategy used to learn the content from lectures, so secondary students must be taught to apply that strategy effectively. Preparing students who are going to college makes learning how to take notes even more critical because Anderson and Armbruster (1986) found that college students spend 80% of class time listening to lectures.

Note taking has both process and product functions. First, note taking allows students to encode new information—the process central to learning. Second, the notes become external storage—a product.

DiVesta and Gray (1972) noted that as an encoding function, note taking activates the student's attention and assists in the transfer of information to long-term memory. They explained that the student actively processes the information; he or she cognitively processes information by coding, integrating, and transforming the lecture content into meaningful notes. By these processes, the information becomes part of the student's schema.

DiVesta and Gray (1972) explained that note taking provided for external storage by preserving the content of the lecture. This preservation provided for later revision and review of the material. The revision and review allowed the student to organize and consolidate the materials more efficiently and elaborate upon them as needed.

Kobayashi (2006) conducted a meta-analysis of the effects of a variety of teacher interventions on having students take and review notes and the students' subsequent achievement. The interventions were of a wide variety, including telling the students to take notes, training the students on how to take notes, and so on. He compared three groups of participants: (1) students who took notes and then reviewed them, (2) students who were not allowed to take notes but were allowed to mentally review other people's notes, and (3) students who were neither allowed to take notes nor review others' notes. The effects of note taking and reviewing produced powerful results. The benefits for lower-performing students were greater than those for higher-performing students.

Taking notes in English is far more difficult for an English language learner than for a student whose native language is English. Piolat, Barbier, and Roussey (2008) examined the cognitive effort expended by French students taking lecture notes when the lecturer spoke in their native language as compared to in English. When the lecturer spoke in English, the students' cognitive effort expended in note taking was greater, they had more difficulty, and their writing speed was slower than when they took notes from a French lecturer.

A number of researchers have found that students who have ELN have difficulty taking notes. This is not surprising because note taking is complex; sustaining attention, comprehending, discriminating between critical and irrelevant information, paraphrasing the information into a note format, organizing it in a coherent way, and recording it readably and quickly (Hughes & Suritsky, 1993) are all essential to the process.

Englert, Mariage, and Okolo (2009) investigated how seventh-grade students with and without ELN took notes. Their participants were 121 students of whom 41 had ELN. The students who had ELN had more difficulty taking notes, but neither group were proficient note takers—no surprise to many seventh-grade teachers. The researchers called for content area teachers to support the development of their students by teaching note taking strategies.

Suritsky (1992) wanted to know what kinds of problems students who have ELN had with note taking, so he interviewed 31 college students who had ELN. He found that the students' most difficult note taking problem was not being able to write fast enough. Students also reported difficulty with sustaining attention, discriminating between essential and nonessential information, and interpreting their notes when using them to study later. Mortimore and Crozier (2006) found that the 26 British males they surveyed who had ELN also reported more problems with note taking than did their 74 nondisabled peers.

Malmquist (1999) noted that content area teachers must prompt their students who have ELN to use the note taking strategies they learned either in that teacher's class or in their special education classes. Malmquist worked with 42 seventh-grade students who have ELN, their 8 special education teachers, and their 13 general education history teachers. Half of the special education teachers taught note taking–study skills for four weeks, and the other half tutored the students in U.S. history content. Malmquist found that while the students learned the study skills, their general education teachers did not prompt them to use those skills in their history classes, so they did not use them. Not surprisingly, their achievement was not improved; content teachers must prompt students who have ELN to use strategies that they have learned.

In this chapter, we will address the following keys to help students with learning problems open the doors of Acquisition and Proficiency and Fluency to enter the rooms of Knowledge and Comprehension in our disciplines:

- Key 30: Teach Abbreviations
- Key 31: Teach Summarizing
- Key 32: Partial Graphic Organizer Notes
- Key 33: Guided Notes
- Key 34: Strategic Notes
- Key 35: Brick and Mortar Notes
- Key 36: Three-Column Personalized Notes
- Key 37: Newspaper Notes

☛ Key 30: Teach Abbreviations

Students who have ELN need to be taught explicitly to use abbreviations when they take notes. Suritsky (1992) interviewed 31 college students who had ELN about problems that they experienced with note taking. One of the main problems they listed was the inability to write fast enough, yet when asked whether they used abbreviations when taking notes, not one interviewee responded in the affirmative.

In a second study, Hughes and Suritsky (1993) asked 15 students with and 15 students without learning disabilities to view a 20-minute videotaped lecture and take notes. The notes demonstrated that the students without learning disabilities abbreviated twice as many words as did their peers with learning disabilities and used about twice as many abbreviations (some words being abbreviated several times).

Hughes and Suritsky (1994) then examined the notes of 60 college sophomores and juniors, half of whom had learning disabilities. First, the researchers created a 20-minute videotaped lecture on human memory in which the lecturer spoke at 108 words per minute. Then, the students viewed the lecture and took notes continuously. The students who had ELN used fewer abbreviations: 19 words compared to their peers' 34, and 11 different words abbreviated compared to 18. Finally, their writing was slower: 130 words per minute compared to 157 words per minute for their peers without ELN.

Hughes and Suritsky (1994) recommended teaching students who have ELN general abbreviation rules, such as using three or four letters for long words or word phrases such as *ant* for *antecedent, ex pow* for *executive powers,* or *conv* for *convection.* They also recommended teaching students initials for terms that will be frequently used during the lecture, such as CS for *cell specialization.*

Eighth-grade history teacher Carol Josel (1997) noted in the *Journal of Adolescent & Adult Literacy* that her eighth graders need to be explicitly taught how to abbreviate in their notes. They learned to code long and often-repeated words and place a key in the corner of the page; for example, *reconstruction* could be represented with an *R.* She cautioned that a key to the abbreviations in the corner of the paper is critical.

Piolat, Olive, and Kellogg (2005) noted that abbreviating may employ end truncation (writing *dis* for *disability*) and conservation of consonants (*stdnt* for *student*). Second, they suggested using symbols for syntax, such as dashes, arrows, or stars.

Students are so familiar with text messaging that consists almost exclusively of abbreviations that they should easily learn to use abbreviations in note taking.

Abbreviations			
And	&	*At*	@
With	w/	*For example*	e.g.
Without	w/o	*Government*	gvmt
That is	i.e.	*Causes*	→
Because	b/c	*Results from*	←
Why	?	*Less than*	<
		More than	>

Teaching students to abbreviate should help students improve their Acquisition and Proficiency and Fluency in Knowledge and Comprehension because

- ♪ Frustration is lowered because the abbreviation strategies help students write more quickly
- ♪ Memory is enhanced because students have a reliable document for study purposes

⚷ Key 31: Teach Summarizing

In a guide published by the Oregon Department of Education, titled *Essential Learning Skills Across the Curriculum,* Jacobson (1987) wrote the following:

> The purpose of summarizing is to have students think about what they have learned and begin to internalize it. Since this is part of the student's metacognitive development, it is necessary that they, not the teacher, do the summary. The teacher should guide them, however, by asking questions for students to answer in oral summaries and providing rules for written summaries. (p. 24)

How good are secondary students at summarizing? Researchers Mateos, Martin, Villaon, and Luna (2008) examined the cognitive and metacognitive activities of high school students who read expository texts and then engaged in writing activities. The students were asked to summarize a single text and to synthesize and summarize information from two texts. The researchers listened while the students talked aloud during the writing activities. The researchers concluded that secondary students lack the cognitive and metacognitive processes required to be strategic readers and writers and declared an urgent need for teachers to address this lack in the classroom.

We cover steps for teaching students to summarize in Key 60 in the chapter on improving expository writing (Chapter 12). Here we make the point that teaching students to summarize is a key to helping them learn to take notes proficiently. For example, when taking notes, students with ELN make poor choices about what goes into a summary. Although they know that a summary should include the important ideas from a text, they do not know what is important; such students tend to identify as important any information that they find personally interesting. In addition, they use the position of a sentence in the paragraph as an indicator of the importance of the sentence (Winograd, 1984).

A study of 56 college students in a remedial reading and study skills course compared three study strategies following a lecture. The first group of students was trained to generate questions to ask themselves and then to answer those questions. The second group of students was taught to summarize the lecture. The third group served as a control group and simply reviewed their notes. The summarizers remembered more lecture content than did the other groups on an immediate test. On a follow-up test, both the question-generators and the summarizers remembered more information than did the control group.

Teaching students to summarize in note taking is an important skill because

> *Summary of Summarizing*
>
> ○ *Teachers should teach students to summarize notes. The purpose of summarizing is to make students THINK about what they have learned and INTERNALIZE it.*
> ○ *Students, not teachers, should make the notes because it's part of METACOGNITIVE development. However, teachers should GUIDE students so they learn how to summarize correctly.*
> ○

- ♪ Discrimination is enhanced when students know what to include and what to exclude in their notes
- ♪ Memory is enhanced
- ♪ Frustration is decreased when students can keep up with the lecture
- ♪ Persistence is improved when students can finish their notes
- ♪ Motivation is increased when students see increases in their exam grades

⊶ Key 32: Partial Graphic Organizer Notes

Williams (2007) argued that students need to employ cognitive processes to facilitate learning and that graphic organizers (GOs) are one tactic that promotes such processes. However, research has revealed that some note taking strategies that employ GOs are more effective than others. Providing students with partial notes set in GOs consistently increases student achievement. Providing students who have ELN with a complete set of notes deprives them of the encoding advantage of note taking. Providing students with no notes at all increases the likelihood that they will take note of salient, rather than important, information. Providing partial notes in GOs provides exactly the right amount of scaffolding.

Katayama and Robinson (2000) assigned 117 undergraduate students to one of six conditions in order to assess the efficacy of six note taking strategies: (1) complete-note GOs, (2) partial-note GOs, (3) skeletal-note GOs, (4) complete-note outlines, (5) partial-note outlines, or (6) skeletal-note outlines. For the partial notes, one half of the notes from the complete-notes condition were systematically deleted. For the skeletal notes, only category and attributed headings were provided.

The students read an assignment on six types of sleep disorders. The students in the partial- and skeletal-notes groups completed the missing information in their notes. The students in the complete-notes condition were allowed to take extra notes if they chose.

Although the groups did not differ statistically on the factual recall test, the graphic organizer group that was supplied with partial notes outscored the other groups on an application test (i.e., the results of the study were statistically significant).

Robinson and colleagues (2006) conducted four experiments on partial graphic organizer notes in a classroom environment. In each experiment, they provided students either a partial or a complete GO to accompany a lesson. Across the four experiments, tests on the studied materials revealed that the students in the partial GO condition consistently outperformed their peers in the complete GO condition. In addition, many of the students changed their note taking style from linear to GO. The researchers concluded that GO partial notes may not only improve students' knowledge of course content but also increase their metacognitive skills.

Katayama and Crooks (2003) compared the effects of partial and complete notes on immediate and delayed testing on three kinds of performance: fact, structure, and application tests. All texts and notes were in electronic format. On the structure test, while the complete-notes condition yielded slightly higher scores, a week later the partial-notes condition slightly prevailed. On the application test, the students in the partial-notes condition slightly outperformed the students in the complete-notes condition immediately after instruction. However, the students in the partial-notes condition scored twice as high as those in the complete-notes condition on the delayed testing one week later.

Partial Notes Graphic Organizers are an effective inclusion strategy because

- Confusion is eliminated when students have a meaningful structure for understanding the relationships among concepts
- Memory is enhanced when students have a correct and complete GO to study
- Organization of concepts is ensured because the teacher has developed the GO
- Frustration is reduced because students can complete a meaningful GO
- Motivation is enhanced because students experience success

Partial Notes Graphic Organizer for Climate Types

	Arctic	Temperate	Subtropical	Tropical	Desert
Winter Temperature	Very cold		Cool to moderate	Hot	Hot in day, cold at night
Summer Temperature	Cool		Moderate to hot		
Humidity	Low	Higher summer, lower winter		High	
Precipitation	Low				
Cloud	Little	Ranges			Little
Day/Night Winter	Short daylight			Equal	
Day/Night Summer	Long daylight				

⚷ Key 33: Guided Notes

Developed by Lazarus (1988, 1991), Guided Notes are a skeleton outline of the main ideas and related concepts of a presentation with spaces left for students to insert supporting information. While lecturing, the teacher uses a completed guided notes overhead transparency so the students can see as well as hear and write the important notes.

Lazarus (1996) reported results of using Guided Notes with Review in a secondary science class; two students in the class had disabilities. The first student with disabilities scored between 10% and 25% without guided notes on the first five daily quizzes, between 60% and 70% on the first week of guided notes without review, and between 75% and 90% during the second week of guided notes with review.

The second student with disabilities scored between 20% and 35% on the quizzes during the baseline (No Guided Notes) condition, between 55% and 70% during the guided notes without review week, and between 80% and 95% during the week of guided notes with review. The students without disabilities increased in performance also, from approximately 75% on the baseline, to approximately 80% on the guided notes without review, to approximately 90% on the guided notes with review.

Lazarus (1991) also assessed the effectiveness of guided notes with and without daily review in two eleventh-grade history classes with a total of 45 nondisabled students and 5 students with ELN. Baseline chapter test scores for the students with ELN ranged from 25% to 40%. Under the guided note without review condition, the test scores of the students with ELN ranged from 59% to 65%, a respectable gain that had social significance because it raised a failing grade to a passing grade. However, when Guided Notes were paired with a daily review of the notes (ten minutes at the end of the class period), the average scores of the students with ELN ranged from 84% to 96%, which was a highly socially significant change. The guided notes provided explicitness and structure and the daily review provided repetition, the three keys to helping students with special needs succeed.

Anderson, Yilmaz, and Wasburn-Moses (2004) conducted a review of the literature on practical academic interventions that secondary and middle school content area teachers used with students who had ELN. They identified Guided Notes as one effective, practical intervention. They noted that Guided Notes reduce students' frustration, poor motivation, and off-task behaviors that are caused by poor note taking skills. They also noted that the Guided Notes provided students with accurate and complete notes and resulted in higher academic achievement.

Narjaikaew, Emarat, and Cowie (2009) investigated the efficacy of Guided Notes with 900 first-year college students. One third of the students were in a control group. The other 600 students were taught to use Guided Notes during their physics lecture on electromagnetism. The students who used guided notes outperformed their peers. In addition, the researchers stated that they considered guided notes to be a supportive tool that assisted them in concentrating on the lecture.

Guided notes, especially if paired with daily review, help students access Knowledge and Comprehension because

- ♪ Attention is increased because the students are actively engaged
- ♪ Perception is increased because three modalities are involved
- ♪ Discrimination between essential and nonessential information is increased because the teacher has guided the note taking process

♪ Confusion is decreased because the student is guided through the note taking process with three modalities involved

♪ Memory is increased if used with the daily review

Here is an example of a student's Guided Notes.

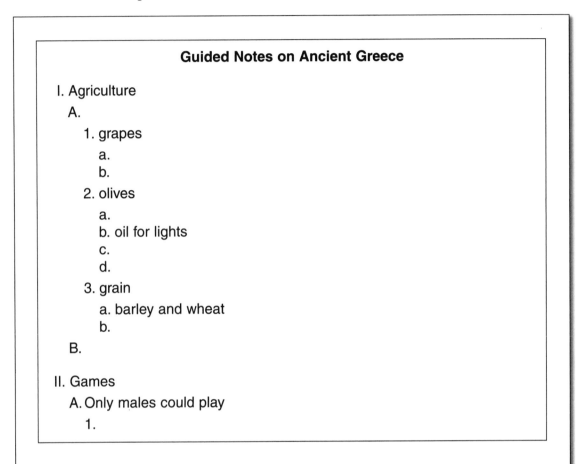

Guided Notes on Ancient Greece

I. Agriculture

  A.

     1. grapes

        a.

        b.

     2. olives

        a.

        b. oil for lights

        c.

        d.

     3. grain

        a. barley and wheat

        b.

  B.

II. Games

  A. Only males could play

     1.

🔑 Key 34: Strategic Notes

Boyle (1996) developed Strategic Notes with students in regular education; he later extended the research to include students with ELN. Strategic note taking is predicated upon the assumption that students can use metacognitive skills to become more strategic at note taking.

Students were given generic guides, as opposed to Lazarus's lecture-specific guides, with written cues to help them develop metacognitive skills during lectures. Boyle (1996) found that by using metacognitive skills, such as activating prior knowledge and organizing information, students became engaged in the lecture and improved their comprehension.

The first section of the strategic note taking guide directs students to identify the lecture topic and connect it to what they know about the topic. Next, the students are directed to cluster three to seven main points with details as the instructor lectures. At the bottom of each page, students summarize the information on that page.

The steps of clustering groups of new main points and summarizing them are repeated as necessary. Finally, as a review, the students write five main points presented in the lecture and describe each point. This step is intended to serve as a quick review of the lecture. Boyle (1996) noted that the typical 50-minute lecture will generate five to eight Strategic Notes pages.

Boyle and Weishaar (2001) investigated the effects of Strategic Note taking on the recall and comprehension of 26 high school students who had ELN. The students were members of a special education class in either science or English. Half of the students were in the control group, and the other half of the students were in the experimental group.

The experimental group of students was exposed to a videotaped lecture and taught to take Strategic Notes. Then both groups were exposed to a second lecture, with the experimental group using the new strategy; the control group took notes as they usually did.

The experimental group wrote seven times more notes during the lesson than did the control group. The experimental group also performed five times better than the control group on long-term recall of vocabulary terms and almost six times better on long-term number of words from the original notes remembered. The experimental group scored better than the control group in comprehension by about one third.

The use of Strategic Notes is a key that helps unlock the barriers to Acquisition and Proficiency and Fluency of Knowledge and Comprehension because

- Attention is enhanced because the students are actively engaged
- Memory is enhanced because students are required to activate prior knowledge and organize information and summarize it
- Confusion is reduced because of activating prior knowledge and organizing and summarizing strategies
- Organization is enhanced because the students' notes are in a meaningful format

The following figure shows how we used this strategy with secondary school students.

Strategic Notes

Topic: _____

What I already know about the topic:

_____

I._____

   A._____

   B._____

   C._____

2._____

   A._____

   B._____

   C._____

3._____

   A._____

   B._____

   C._____

Summary:

⚯ Key 35: Brick and Mortar Notes

Students can be taught to take notes effectively, and such instruction produces positive achievement. However, note taking instruction also produces behavioral improvement. Evans and his colleagues (1994–95) taught note taking strategies to adolescents with attention deficit hyperactivity disorder. The 30 teenagers were enrolled in a summer program and exhibited a passive learning style and disruptive behaviors. After the teens were taught a note taking strategy, they improved in both comprehension and in behavior.

Simbo (1988) compared three note taking strategies in a geography class: (1) students copying the teacher's complete notes on the board, (2) students making notes from the teacher's outline on the blackboard, and (3) students making their own notes without the teacher's outline. This Nigerian study involved 180 students and four teachers. The results revealed that the students who created their notes from the teachers' outlines produced the highest achievement on tested material.

One of the two important functions of notes is to provide a permanent record of information that can be reviewed at a later time (Carrier, Williams, & Dalgaard, 1988; Di Vesta & Gray, 1972). Brick and Mortar Notes facilitate review by allowing the student to move a blank sheet down the note page and see a question without seeing its answer. This allows the student to try to answer each question before reading the answer on the paper. This helps the student to process the information more deeply.

Brick and Mortar Notes are similar to Simbo's (1988) strategy of having students make notes from the teacher's outline on the board. Brick and Mortar Notes are intended for use when a teacher organizes a lecture into several questions and their answers. Students use notebook paper and draw a box around the space between two lines with a pencil. This is the mortar. The mortar box is drawn with a pencil. Then, the students draw a brick by drawing another box around the lines and spaces representing five or six lines of notebook paper. The brick is drawn with a red (or other colored) pen. The students continue down the page drawing bricks and mortar until the page is full.

Next, the students use a pencil to write the questions and a red (or other colored) pen to write the answers.

When a student is ready to study the notes, he or she covers the page of notes with a clean sheet of paper. The student then moves the paper down until he or she can see one question (the mortar). Then, the student tries to answer the question. Next, the student moves the paper down to expose the answer (the brick). The student continues down the page in this way until he or she has tried to answer all of the questions.

Brick and Mortar Notes are an effective inclusion strategy because

- Attention is increased because the student is actively engaged in the note taking process
- Comprehension is increased because of the deep processing involved in creating questions from the notes
- Memory is increased because of the deep processing and the judicious review

Here is an example from an English class in which the students were learning to develop an Idea Portfolio.

Brick and Mortar Notes on Creating My Idea Portfolio

What is an Idea Portfolio (IP)?

Collection v things I find that might gv me IDEA that I cld turn in2 a story, poem, etc. Cld Ncld photos, newspapr Rticles, stories I read/things I overhear Pple say. Don't have to have an idea at time.

How can an IP help me write a Found Poem?

Newspaper Rticle/story cld lead 2 a FP. FP is words, phrases/sentences frm a selection that R chosen & arranged to communicate essence v selection. IE, article on house fire: <u>devastation, homeless, destroyed</u> = FP.

How can an IP help me write a Character Sketch?

What is a good summary of what I have learned?

⚷ Key 36: Three-Column Personalized Notes

The importance of engaging students with the curriculum is addressed in hundreds of articles on education databases. In physical education, social studies, English, science, mathematics, and so on, researchers recommend finding ways to actively engage students. One way to engage students is through soliciting their personal connections to the curriculum as they take lecture or textbook notes.

Because most students, but especially students with learning problems, understand best when new ideas are directly related to their personal experiences, the Three-Column Personalized Notes strategy is designed to help students make that connection.

Placing notes in columnar format has been endorsed by a number of researchers. Horton, Lovitt, and Christensen (1991) investigated the use of columnar notes with 125 nondisabled high school students, 30 students who had ELN, and 43 students in remedial classes. The researchers found that the columnar note taking strategy increased achievement at the time of treatment, under near-transfer conditions, under far-transfer conditions, and under maintenance conditions.

Shambaugh (1994) recommended visual note taking strategies and included a three-column strategy with a column for personal reflections such as the Three-Column Personalized Notes strategy.

The first column, a narrow column, is for the chapter subheading or sub subheading. The second column, the widest of the three, is for the extended notes from that subchapter. The third column includes examples from the student's own life or personal thoughts. This connection not only helps comprehension and retention by explicitly connecting the new learning to our student's existing schema, it also increases motivation because our students are naturally interested in things that relate to themselves.

For example, in an economics class, several of our students had entries in their personal column on the tax loopholes their parents were able to use, many students had entries on the topic of minimum wage, and all had stories about scarcity.

We periodically have our students share their third-column entries with a partner or in a small group in order to provide multiple representations—which we know also increases comprehension and retention. Sometimes we have the entire group share, particularly if very few people have a personal story to relate to a topic. For example, when we studied public works, only one or two students in a class had a personal story about great-grandparents who worked on Works Progress Administration (WPA) or Civilian Conservation Corps (CCC) projects during the Great Depression, so we invited those students to share their stories with the entire class.

Three-Column Personalized Notes help unlock the doors to Knowledge and Comprehension because

- Motivation is increased when students can relate academic content to their own lives and share it with their classmates
- Attention is increased when students relate content to their own lives or hear stories about their classmates
- Confusion is decreased when real-life stories exemplify abstract concepts
- Memory is enhanced when abstract concepts are anchored to students' life experiences

Here we have an example from a history class in which students were studying Alexander the Great.

3-Column Notes for Alexander–Empire Builder		
Topic	Details	My Thoughts/Experiences
Phillip 2 builds Macedonia's power	Ms were tough people, lived mnts. Greeks looked down on them bt admired their kings.	Ms are like Goth kids. Preps look down on them
Phillip's Army 359 BC	Phillip (only 23!) became king & made Ms into unbeatable army.	I'm 16, and I wouldn't know where to start!
Conquest of Greece 338 BC	Ms Army took Greece's independence	When Mom took away my car, I lost my independence and was FURIOUS!
	Phillip 2 killed & son Alexander the Great becomes King at 20.	
Summary— Phillip 2 built great army of Macedonians & conquered Greece. When P2 died, son Alexander becomes king at age 20.		

⚷ Key 37: Newspaper Notes

Textbooks dating back to the 1800s show that teachers have been trying for at least that long to teach students how to summarize (Hood, 2008). Summarizing is a critical skill for secondary (Boling & Evans, 2008) and middle school students (Massey & Heafner, 2004), and one that is difficult (Mateos, Martin, Villalon, & Luna, 2008)—especially for students who have ELN or are English language learners (Honnert & Bozan, 2005). Being able to summarize is the equivalent of being able to comprehend, and it is not a skill that students automatically develop. In fact, Kelley and Clausen-Grace (2007) argued that summarization skills must be explicitly taught to students.

To *summarize* is to distill a text or lecture into its essence. Newspaper reporters are expert summarizers; they are taught to place all of the critical information in the first paragraph of an article. The rest of the article fleshes out the essentials that were presented in the first paragraph. Newspaper Notes is a strategy that we use that is not only a vehicle for note taking but also helps students learn to summarize as they take their notes.

Various learning tasks demand different graphic organizer note taking strategies (Makany, Kemp, & Dror, 2009), and Newspaper Notes are well-suited for use in literature, history, or current events classes. This strategy uses a graphic organizer that has columns in the form of a matrix, providing the requisite structure for supporting students who have ELN. This strategy is an adaptation of the 5 Ws and H of writing a news article: *who, what, when, where, why,* and *how,* with the addition of *to whom* and *effect.*

The first column is *When* in order to help students with sequencing. The next column is *Where* so that the context of time and place is established before we examine the actual event. The *Who* column comes next, followed by the *What* and *How* columns. The *To Whom* column follows, and the *Why* column is next. The last column is the *Effect* column.

Students who are reading a novel will find the Newspaper Notes tool helpful. Each row can summarize the major event of one chapter. The strategy can then assist students in writing a book report: The main events are all clearly identified.

When teachers carefully construct lectures to fit the Newspaper Notes format, history lectures can be well-represented by the GO. This works particularly well when the teacher wants to present events that are happening concurrently, such as various events taking place simultaneously during World War II.

The Newspaper Notes help students unlock access to Knowledge and Comprehension because

- Motivation is enhanced because identifying the Ws and H is less daunting than trying to process the material more globally
- Perception is enhanced by using all three modalities to process the material
- Discrimination is ensured by the highly explicit nature of the graphic organizer
- Sequencing the events correctly is ensured by the explicit method of recording the data
- Organization is enhanced by the very nature of the strategy and its graphic form
- Memory is enhanced by the explicit treatment of the material

Here is an example of the strategy that one of our students used in a history class.

Main Idea Reading Guide for

Main Idea #

Supporting Detail

Supporting Detail

Supporting Detail

Main Idea #

Supporting Detail

Supporting Detail

Supporting Detail

8

Promoting Students' Learning From the Textbook

Textbooks are ubiquitous in middle and high school, but they vary greatly in how friendly they are to readers. Some expository texts are better than others, and some are dreadful. But the strategies discussed in this chapter will help make all of them more effective in assisting students who have exceptional learning needs (ELN) to learn our disciplines. The strategies are inexpensive in terms of the amount of teacher time expended for the return received in student learning. Some of them, such as Highlighted Textbooks, do not have to be repeated after the initial effort; Universal Design for Learning digital environments do not even require that. What great keys to help our students enjoy the treasures of our disciplines!

The world of secondary students is one of immersion into expository texts. In fact, secondary students spend as much as 75% of classroom time and 90% of homework time interacting with textbooks. At each grade level, dependence upon textbooks increases—especially upon expository, as opposed to narrative, texts (Barton, 1997; Saenz & Fuchs, 2002; Woodward & Elliott, 1990). But in the *Harvard Education Letter*, Webb (1995) called the textbook industry "education's big dirty secret" because expository textbooks are "inconsiderate" texts and make comprehension unnecessarily difficult (p. 1). Writing for *The Circle of Information & Research on Civic Learning and Engagement*, Chambliss, Richardson, Torney-Purta, and Wildenfeld (2007) noted that textbook reviewers often find textbooks "turgid, poorly organized, and uninteresting" (p. 2). The problem is compounded by the fact that on the 2007 National Assessment of Educational Progress in Reading, only 31% of eighth graders scored at or above proficient. Even students who do not have ELN are ill equipped to learn from textbooks.

Resnick and Zurawsky (2007) argued that science textbooks frustrate teachers and prevent students from discovering the power of science because the books lack coherence and are replete with facts and short on connections. Catley and Novick (2008) examined

31 science textbooks and found that the diagrams were confusing, the textbooks failed to explicate the diagrams' structure and theoretical underpinnings, and that the books may even reinforce alternate views of evolution. Yager and Akcay (2008) compared a non-textbook approach with the use of textbooks in teaching science to middle school students. The two groups learned the concepts equally well, but the non-textbook group exceeded the textbook group in (1) application of the concepts, (2) attitudes toward science, (3) creativity, and (4) learning and using science at home and in the community.

Researchers in other disciplines found difficulties with textbooks as well. Herbel-Eisenmann (2007) noted that a mismatch may exist between mathematics textbooks and the goals of the National Council of Teachers of Mathematics standards. Yan (2007) compared the word-problem solving tasks in Chinese and American textbooks and the performance of the students who studied from those textbooks. The Chinese students outperformed the American students at an astonishing level, and Yan suggested that the difference in performance was due to the textbooks employed.

Dennis (2008) investigated history textbooks that are used in middle schools. She found that textbooks obstructed students' development of critical historical thinking. This occurred in part because history textbooks are generally written in an anonymous, authoritative style rather than in a manner that indicates that history is open to interpretation by multiple voices.

Jitendra and colleagues (2001) examined four middle school geography textbooks. The readability of the texts was at about a tenth-grade level, and the books were not supportive of students who had ELN. Among their recommendations was that when working with students who have ELN, teachers should develop textbook enhancements such as reading guides, graphic organizers (GOs), and carefully structured discussion questions. They noted that this was especially important for students who may have lacked prior knowledge.

The difficulties that students who have ELN have with making inferences from implicit text are compounded by their other difficulties: understanding relationships and connections in general, distinguishing between main ideas and insignificant details, and understanding the main idea of a passage. They have less awareness of the structure of a text and have poor recall of text ideas. In addition, the passive learning style of students who have ELN and their usual lack of processing skills and skills related to organizing written information makes their understanding of text difficult. Therefore, textbooks *must* make relationships among concepts explicit (Alexander, Schallert, & Hare, 1991; Bos & Vaughn, 1994; Kame' enui & Simmons, 1990; Lenz, Alley, & Schumaker, 1987; Oakhill & Patel, 1991; Torgesen, 1982).

Textbooks can be daunting for our students who have ELN; however, we can assist them in tackling the material by using these strategies.

- ⤙ Key 38: Use GOs to Make Relationships Explicit
- ⤙ Key 39: Explicitly Teach Text Structure
- ⤙ Key 40: Use Accessible Digital Textbooks
- ⤙ Key 41: Preteach Vocabulary

🔑 Key 38: Use GOs to Make Relationships Explicit

The National Institute for Literacy (2007) produced a report titled "What Content-Area Teachers Should Know About Adolescent Literacy," which is available online. The report identified GOs as one instructional strategy that can help adolescents increase text comprehension. The report stated that content area teachers should teach students how to use GOs to help organize concepts during and after reading. They noted that teachers can model the use of appropriate GOs and encourage students to use them as they read.

Writing in *American Secondary Education,* Anderson, Yilmaz, and Wasburn-Moses (2004) reviewed practical academic interventions for middle school and high school students with ELN. They identified GOs as one of the six most effective strategies. They concluded the following:

> GOs can be accepted as a successful teaching strategy to improve middle and high school students' conceptual understanding about concepts from different subject areas . . . For example, science teachers can use this approach to teach animals in the animal kingdom, cell organelles, or elements in the periodic table. Language teachers can use GOs to summarize a poem or novel. Mathematics teachers can use the same strategy to teach relationships among permutations, combinations, or probabilities. (p. 25)

DiCecco and Gleason (2002) created a well-controlled experiment in which they tested the impact of GOs on domain knowledge that was gleaned from a social studies text by 24 middle school students with ELN. Although the GOs did not increase factual recall (and were not expected to), they significantly increased students' relational knowledge as demonstrated by frequency of relational statements in essays.

The treatment in DiCecco and Gleason's (2002) study consisted of a type of explicit instruction following each section read in the history textbook used by both classes. The GO group received explicit instruction using GOs, and the No GO group received the same number of minutes of instruction using strategies traditionally used in social studies classes. After seven days of instruction, the GO group made 47 relational statements in an essay, as compared to 34 by the No GO group. At the end of 20 days of instruction, the GO group made 57 relational statements, as compared to only 27 by the No GO group. The authors argued not only that this provided support for explicit instruction using GOs in order to help students understand relational knowledge in textbooks, but also that a protracted period of instruction using GOs was a stronger intervention than a shorter period of instruction.

GOs make relationships within domain knowledge and discipline knowledge explicit. Using the strategy before students tackle the text is an effective inclusion strategy to help students comprehend text because

- 🎵 Confusion is conquered when students have visualized the relationships before they begin to read
- 🎵 Frustration is eliminated when confusion is conquered
- 🎵 Completion of the reading assignment is more likely when students comprehend the text
- 🎵 Reasoning is supported as students encounter the text because they have been introduced to the relationships before they have read about them

⚷ Key 39: Explicitly Teach Text Structure

Students' learning from textbooks can be improved by explicitly teaching text structure (Gorlewski, 2009). Sencibaugh (2007) conducted a meta-analysis of interventions that produced substantial benefits in reading comprehension for students with ELN. The results revealed that teaching text-structure yielded significant improvement in students' comprehension. Other researchers have found that English language learners in middle schools and high schools benefited from explicit teaching of text structures in the content areas (Meltzer & Hamann, 2006).

Downing, Bakken, and Whedon (2002) explained five types of expository text structure: (1) main idea, (2) list, (3) order, (4) compare-contrast, and (5) classification. They provided the following keys to identifying the type of text structure.

Main idea structure is characterized by a passage that focuses on a single idea. The other sentences in the passage provide details, extend support, clarify, or illustrate the main idea. Words that signal that the passage is a main idea text include *principles, laws,* and *definitions.* The authors suggested that the appropriate study strategy is to state the main idea and provide at least three supporting details.

Semicolons, numbers, or letters in parentheses signal that the text structure is a *list format.* This type of passage focuses on a general topic followed by a list of characteristics that describe the topic. The suggested study strategy is to state the topic and list at least four characteristics.

Order structure is the third text structure, and the signals for this type of structure are the words *first, second, stages, next,* and *then.* The order structure text focuses on a single topic and then consists of a series of ordered steps or events.

In *compare and contrast structure,* the text focuses on the relationship between two or among three or more things. Signals are phrases such as *in contrast to* or *in comparison.* Downing, Bakken, and Whedon (2002) suggested having students list the two or more items being compared and then having them list similarities in one column and differences in another column.

The authors explained that *classification structure* is the fifth structure and that the signals for this type of structure are phrases such as *two types of* and *can be classified as.* The classification structure explicates a scheme to be used later in classifying items. The suggested study strategy was to write down the topic and the related items in column form.

Smith (1986) investigated the effects of teaching text structure on the reading comprehension of 73 adolescents who had ELN. The students were randomly assigned to one of two groups. The experimental group was instructed on how to recognize and use an author's organizational structure while reading and taking notes on an expository passage. The control group was instructed on how to use a generic problem-solving model. The experimental group recalled more of the information in the selection both immediately and one week later and was able to recognize the specific text structure when they again encountered it. Smith and Friend (1986) reported the same findings with 27 more adolescents who had ELN.

Explicitly teaching text structure is a good inclusion strategy because

- ⚷ Confusion is decreased when students comprehend what the text is trying to communicate
- ⚷ Frustration is eliminated when confusion is decreased

- Organization is increased when the students are taught to recognize structure
- Metacognition is increased when students know that they know the structure of texts

<table>
<tr>
<td>

Compare and Contrast
Text Structure

Identifies a dimension and tells how each concept is alike and different (e.g., how the lives of early American men and women differed)

</td>
<td>

Signal Words for
Compare and Contrast

In comparison
In contrast
Unlike, like
Different from
Similar to
As opposed to
Whereas, although, yet, however

</td>
</tr>
</table>

⚷ Key 40: Use Accessible Digital Textbooks

Digital audio textbooks are one category of Accessible Textbooks as defined by the Center for Applied Special Technology's (CAST) Universal Design for Learning. Other Accessible Textbooks include digital large-print e-books for students with low vision and Braille textbooks for students who are blind and prefer that format to digital audio books. According to Chuck Hitchcock, Chief Officer of Policy and Technology for CAST and Director of NIMAS Technical Assistance Center, digital audio textbooks are not only for students who have visual impairments; they are also for students with dyslexia and students whose orthopedic impairments make holding a textbook and turning pages difficult.

Researchers at Johns Hopkins University investigated the effectiveness of audio books on content learning. The books were provided by the organization Reading for the Blind and Disabled (RFB&D), a national nonprofit organization. The participants in the study were 95 secondary students who had ELN and whose average IQ was between 77 and 79. The students, from self-contained special education classes at seven public high schools in Baltimore, used recorded copies of their American government textbooks for eight weeks in lieu of a printed version. Entire classes were randomly assigned to one of three treatment groups: (1) an experimental group that used the audio textbook for 15 to 20 minutes daily, (2) an experimental group that used the audio textbook but added a cued active listening strategy (cueing important text and integrating new with prior knowledge) in which they completed a worksheet as they listened, or (3) a control group that read the standard print textbook for the same amount of time. Each day, the teachers led a 5-minute drill, led discussion and instruction on the textbook material for 20 min-

utes, and required the students to engage with their recorded or print-based textbook for 20 minutes. The students completed a quiz each week, for a total of five quizzes. The students in both audio groups significantly outperformed their peers in the control group on content knowledge throughout the study. The cued active listening strategy did not significantly increase the power of the audio strategy alone. The researchers posited that they may have provided the students with insufficient training in the cued active listening strategy (Boyle et al., 2003).

The reauthorization of the Individuals with Disabilities Education Act (IDEA) in 2004 requires all state-adopted textbooks to be published in an accessible digital format. Every textbook is available for free to qualified students on www.bookshare.org because Bookshare is sponsored by the U.S. Department of Education and operates under an exception to U.S. copyright law. Audio books and e-books with large print can be downloaded directly to a qualified student's computer. The qualifying disability categories include dyslexia and orthopedic disabilities that make holding and turning a book impossible, as well as low vision and blindness.

Students with dyslexia or low vision may also access Reading for the Blind and Dyslexic at www.rfdb.org. For a fee of 35 dollars per year, an individual student can access both textbooks and other genres of books from that nonprofit organization, and districts can use the service for qualified students for a nominal fee.

Providing recorded textbooks is an excellent inclusion strategy because

- ♪ Perception is strengthened by providing the auditory input to a visual medium
- ♪ Comprehension is assured when the material is made accessible
- ♪ Confusion is eliminated when material is understood
- ♪ Frustration is avoided when confusion is eliminated
- ♪ Motivation is increased when material is understood
- ♪ Attention is stronger when motivation is increased

⌐ Key 41: Preteach Vocabulary

Vocabulary knowledge is the number one predictor of secondary students' reading comprehension of content area textbooks (Saenz & Fuchs, 2002). Good readers have extensive vocabularies; adolescents with ELN, however, typically have poor vocabularies. Hirsch (2003) noted that textbooks seldom provide legitimate opportunities for students who have ELN to learn the meanings of the words they encounter: The textbooks are too difficult, and the new vocabulary they present demands a degree of content-specific prior knowledge that students who have ELN typically lack. Such students fall farther and farther behind their academically successful peers (Stanovich, 1986).

The National Institute for Literacy (2007) recommended that secondary teachers preteach difficult vocabulary that students will encounter in their textbooks. The institute argued that teachers are setting students up for failure when they do not take the responsibility to ensure that students understand the meanings of the new words that they will encounter in an assignment. The institute's report stated that both specialized academic words and nonspecialized academic words should be pre-taught.

The institute cited Bryant, Goodwin, Bryant, and Higgins (2003) in recommending guidelines to assist teachers in determining the vocabulary to preteach. Those guidelines included

- The criticality of the word in understanding the text
- Students' prior knowledge of the concept
- The multiple meanings of the word

Multiple researchers recommended explicit instruction of vocabulary (Jitendra, Edwards, Sacks, & Jacobson, 2004; Taylor et al., 2009). Kim, Vaughn, Wanzek, and Wei (2004) recommended that direct preteaching of key vocabulary words include (1) simple definitions, (2) examples, (3) nonexamples, and (4) GOs. Providing repeated exposure to new words is critical; while students without disabilities need up to 12 exposures to understand a new word (McKeown, Beck, Omanson, & Pople, 1985), students who have ELN need many more encounters with the word before they reach a deep level of understanding. This is especially true of words that have multiple meanings.

When our intent is to get students prepared to master new content in a textbook chapter, we are best served by explicitly preteaching the vocabulary.

Preteaching vocabulary is a good strategy for helping special needs learners succeed because

- Confusion is diminished when students begin reading with the big picture in mind
- Frustration is prevented when confusion is not a problem
- Completion of the reading assignment is more likely when students are not frustrated

9

Increasing Learning Using Textbook Guides

As we noted in the last chapter, many textbooks actually create barriers to students' learning. Textbook study guides are keys to helping students with ELN access the Knowledge, Comprehension, and Analytical domains. In general, study guides help students by providing (1) an encoding function that causes them to process information deeply and (2) an external storage function that provides access to information that is not yet stored in long-term memory.

Study guides are explicit and structured cognitive frameworks that help motivate students to read textbooks and assist them in focusing their attention on what the teacher considers most important. Study guides can increase perception by providing for the multicoding of information. They also ensure that students discriminate between what we think is critical in a reading selection (or video) and what is less important. Study guides such as flowcharts can help students with sequencing and organization. Study guides can assist students in analytical thought by directing their attention to seeking evidence, comparing and contrasting, or seeking causes and effects. Finally, study guides assist in helping students retain information in long-term memory because they provide for increased depth of processing.

The use of textbooks is ubiquitous in secondary education. Students with ELN often experience difficulty learning from textbooks, and guides are excellent tools for use in this context. In addition, many teachers use videotapes in their instruction, and viewing guides can be important tools for increasing the learning of students with ELN with this medium.

Every teacher has heard this refrain a thousand times: *I studied the chapter! I just studied the wrong stuff!* Often students do study the wrong "stuff"; study guides are a solution because they provide an explicit and structured tool for learning from the book. In addition, few students understand that reading for information and studying are different things. Studying requires that students *do something* with the information that they have read; studying is not simply reading the information. Study guides provide students with a tool to do something with the information that they read.

Lovitt and Horton (1994), the gurus of study guide research, note that study guides are abstracts of important information from longer readings. They call teacher-created study guides *an adaptation of the textbook* and call for general education teachers, the content-area specialists, to make these study guides rather than depending on special education teachers, who are admittedly not content-area experts, to do so. They identify two primary reasons for creating study guides for students with ELN. First is that few students with ELN are able to read textbooks with the proficiency required to learn from them. The second reason is how inconsiderate the textbooks are with their (1) poor structure, (2) coherence, (3) appropriateness, and (4) unity. They argue that guides are one way to ameliorate these difficulties. Their guidelines for creating study guides include the following:

1. Modify only material that has proven difficult for students or that clearly lacks organization.

2. Collaborate with other teachers to create materials.

3. Co-teach with special education teachers and solicit their assistance in creating guides.

4. Computerize the study guides.

Boyle and Yeager (1997) argued that teachers can help students counteract their difficulty in learning from reading assignments by creating cognitive frameworks. Study guides provide such cognitive frameworks. Cognitive frameworks help students transfer and retain information; they help support students' learning by helping them organize information and link the various parts of that information together. Frameworks highlight important points and serve as guides for studying.

Wood, Lapp, and Flood (1992) explained that the use of a study guide differs from having students answer the questions at the end of the chapter in two critical ways. First, the teacher has control over the questions. Second, the students know what the teacher wants them to learn before they begin to read, rather than having to wait until they have finished reading—when it's often too late.

Fisher, Schumaker, and Deshler (1995) noted that like graphic organizers, study guides are characterized by flexibility of purpose and type; one-size-fits-all may apply to baseball caps, but it doesn't work with study guides. Study guides may be a teacher-prepared graphic organizer, a list of questions, or an outline given prior to students' reading a chapter or listening to a teacher presentation. They may be used to teach vocabulary terms or important main ideas in a unit of study. They may be used to promote higher-order thinking.

Wood (1988) argued that teachers should provide companion study guides when assigning textbook reading because textbooks are so often poorly organized and hard to understand. In their review of the literature on study guides, Wood, Lapp, and Flood (1992) noted that study guide questions interspersed throughout the text can make significant contributions to students' understanding.

We do not recommend the use of study guides that are available from textbook publishers; teachers know exactly what their students need and can target the needs of their curriculum with laser accuracy. Publishers' study guides are so broad and all-encompassing that students can't tell what is important and what is not. For example, Dickson, Miller, and Devoley (2005) employed textbook publisher study guides with 236 students in psychology classes. The learning objectives for each study guide ranged from 26 to 33, with vocabulary words in the guides ranging from 21 to 69. The guides had many exercises, including two full pages dedicated to the development of general language skills. At the end of the semester, the study guide group differed from the no-study-guide group by only three points: 75% to 78%. In addition, the students who completed 25% or less of the study guides did as well as students who completed 75% or more of the study guides.

While the difference was *statistically* significant due to the number of students, the difference was not *socially* significant; students' time can be put to better use. We argue that the difference would have been greater if the instructors themselves had created study guides targeted at what they wanted their students to know.

Wood (1995) identified guidelines to maximize the effective use of teacher-made study guides in guiding middle school students through textbooks. She argued that teachers should be creative when making the guides. She advocated allowing students to work in pairs or small groups, having them skim over the guide before reading the textbook, and not assigning grades for the guides.

Horton and Lovitt (1989) conducted a dual-experiment study to answer three questions: (1) Are study guides more effective than self-study for students with ELN, students identified as remedial, and general education students? (2) Are study guides effective for both science and social studies? For both middle and high school students? (3) Do teacher-directed study guides differ in effectiveness from student-directed study guides?

Horton and Lovitt (1989) asked students to read 1,500-word passages from textbooks while using study guides. They found that study guides are more effective than self-study for all types of students, that students in middle school and high school science and social studies scored higher on tests when they used study guides as opposed to self-study, and that both teacher-directed and student-directed study guides were effective.

In 1991, Horton, Lovitt, and Christensen investigated whether differentiated study guides for secondary and middle school students would be more effective than one-size-fits-all study guides. To that end, they created three different study guides for each text assignment. Students in the top group worked independently on questions with no referential cues. Students in the middle groups worked with peers on questions that included the page numbers where the answers to questions could be found. The students with ELN worked with the teacher on study guides that had the paragraph numbers as well as the page numbers where the answers could be found.

The results revealed that the method of matching students to study guides generally produced the best results among the lowest-performing students; the researchers also found that the teachers were able to successfully manage all three groups at the same time.

Lovitt and Horton (1994) offered these guidelines for creating differentiated study guides.

- Analyze the textbook material for content and difficulty.
- Select the most important content.
- Decide what processes students must use to learn the content.

- Consider students' literacy abilities; vary the guides by question type and format to promote generalization of learning.
- Avoid overcrowding print, and make the guides aesthetically pleasing.

When we first heard about how little students learn from videos without study guides, we were skeptical, so we tried an experiment with a video study guide. First, we showed a video from a series on human development to a group of 36 college juniors who were education majors and told them that they would be given a quiz at the end of the video. After the video, we gave the students a 15-question short answer quiz. The mean score of the group was 48%. We then asked ten randomly selected students to show us their notes. Seven of the students had not taken notes at all, and of the three who had taken notes, their sketchy notes had touched on both the important and unimportant information, demonstrating that they could not discriminate between the two.

The following week, we showed a video from the same series on a different topic; the material was of a difficulty level equivalent to that of the first video. This time, however, we gave the students a video study guide and instructed them to study the guide for five minutes before viewing the video. They completed the study guide as they viewed the second video; after completing the video and study guide, we gave a posttest with a difficulty level equivalent to that given in the control condition. The mean posttest score for the video condition was 92%. We were sold!

In this chapter, we will address the following keys to help students with ELN open the doors of Acquisition and Proficiency and Fluency to enter the rooms of Knowledge and Comprehension in our disciplines:

- Key 42: Main Idea Text Structure Study Guide
- Key 43: List Text Structure Study Guide
- Key 44: Order Text Structure Study Guide
- Key 45: Compare and Contrast Text Structure Study Guide
- Key 46: Cause and Effect Text Structure Study Guide
- Key 47: Problem Solution Study Guide
- Key 48: Analogy Study Guide

⛌ Key 42: Main Idea Text Structure Study Guide

Downing, Bakken, and Whedon (2002) explained that one type of expository text structure is the *main idea structure.* Main idea structure is characterized by a passage that focuses on a single idea. The other sentences in the passage provide details that extend support, clarify, or illustrate the main idea. Words that signal that the passage is a main idea text include *principles, laws,* and *definitions.* The best study strategy is to state the main idea and provide three or more supporting details.

Lovitt, Rudsit, Jenkins, Pious, and Benedetti (1985) investigated the use of a main-idea study guide with 166 seventh-grade science students who were high-, middle-, and low-achieving students, a number of whom had ELN. The researchers found significant gains for all groups who used the main idea study guide, including those students with ELN.

Main idea study guides can be effective whether they are teacher-directed or student-directed. Horton and Lovitt (1989) compared the effects of using a teacher-directed study guide to self-study for 121 high school students in science and social studies classes, of whom 8 had ELN. The study guide consisted of 15 short-answer questions on main ideas taken from throughout the textbook assignment. The teacher instructed the students on how to use the study guide. The students were divided into two groups; in the first part of the experiment, Group A used the study guide while Group B used self-study. In the second part of the experiment, the groups switched interventions. The results were statistically significant. The average test score of the students with ELN during the self-study condition was 49%; their average test score on the study guide condition was 68%. Of the students without ELN, the self-study mean score was 80%, and the study guide mean score was 93%.

Horton and Lovitt (1989) repeated their experiment with a student-directed (as opposed to teacher-directed) study guide condition as compared to the self-study condition on recall of main ideas from a reading assignment. In this experiment, the students with ELN had a mean score of 43% on the self-study condition and a mean score of 77% on the student-directed study guide condition. The students without ELN scored 55% on the self-study condition and 87% on the self-directed study guide condition.

The results of the treatment on the students with ELN are especially encouraging because any treatment that moves a student with a failing score into the range in which the score is passing is known as *socially significant.*

Study guides are effective tools for students with ELN because they employ explicitness and structure. They assist in acquisition of knowledge because

- ⛌ Frustration is decreased because the student knows exactly what the teacher considers most important in the chapter
- ⛌ Perception is enhanced because of the use of three modalities
- ⛌ Discrimination is ensured because the student does not have to try to discriminate between essential and nonessential information in the text
- ⛌ Confusion is decreased because the important information is clearly delineated in the guide

This guide directs students through a chapter on the judicial branch of the government.

Main Idea Reading Guide *for Judicial Branch of Government*

Main Idea 1:

> *Judicial branch balances the Executive Branch and the Legislative Branch of U.S. government by interpreting the laws.*

Supporting Detail

> *Insulated from political pressures b/c appointed until death unless impeached & convicted (rare); this allows to apply law w/o political pressure.*

Supporting Detail

> *Has sole power to interpret law, determine constitutionality & apply to individual cases.*

Supporting Detail

> *Congress cannot strip Supreme Court of its jurisdiction*

Main Idea:

Supporting Detail

Supporting Detail

Supporting Detail

⚷ Key 43: List Text Structure Study Guide

In secondary and middle schools, the language of textbooks is expository rather than narrative. As compared to narrative text, expository text is (1) more formal, (2) less familiar, (3) more logical, (4) less engaging, and (5) more difficult. In addition, the purpose of expository text is to cause the reader to change her or his knowledge about the world; such a proposition is effortful and often unsuccessful (Schallert & Tierney, 1980).

Kamalski, Sanders, and Lentz (2008) explained that *understanding a text* means constructing an accurate mental representation of the text. The representation must be coherent, with the elements in the discourse related to each other. Making the relationship explicit by text markers makes the relationship easier to understand.

Downing, Bakken, and Whedon (2002) noted that semicolons, numbers, or letters in parentheses are text markers that signal that the text structure is a list format. List formats focus on a general topic that is followed by a list of characteristics that describe the topic.

List text structure is the most difficult of the structure types. Sanders and Noordman (2000) compared readers' speed, comprehension, and memory for two types of text structure: problem-solution and list. A team of linguists carefully constructed noncontroversial texts from newspaper articles. The constructed texts varied from 5 to 15 sentences. Each text started with an introduction and concluded with a closing sentence. A target sentence within comparison texts was in an identical location: For example, the fifth sentences in both a list text and a problem-solution pair of texts were the target sentences. Half of the list texts and half of the problem-solution texts contained cue words such as *because* or *in addition.* The participants were 68 Dutch students from Utrecht University in the Netherlands. They read 12 texts, three in each of the four experimental conditions. Their reading speed was calculated to the millisecond, and they were tested immediately afterward. After a brief break, the participants read 12 more texts. List-structured readings took students longer to read than problem-solution-structured readings, and uncued readings took students longer to read than did cued readings. Although list-structured readings took longer to read, participants recalled less information in the list-structure than they did in the problem-solution condition. As hypothesized, the participants were able to read the sections that included cue words more quickly than those without cue words; likewise, they recalled more information from texts with cue words than those without such linguistic aids.

Study guides are effective tools for students with ELN because they employ explicitness and structure. They assist in the acquisition of knowledge because

- ♪ Frustration is decreased because students know exactly what the teacher considers most important in the chapter
- ♪ Perception is enhanced because of the use of three modalities
- ♪ Discrimination is ensured because the student does not have to try to discriminate between essential and nonessential information in the text
- ♪ Confusion is decreased because the important information is clearly delineated in the guide

The following list text structure guide was developed for a secondary school class on the novel.

List Study Guide on: Types of Novels

Introduction: *As opposed to nonfiction, which is based on reality, novels are fiction, i.e., not real.*

1. *Allegory- symbolic story with 2 meanings*

2. *Satire- criticizes contemporary society; often comedic*

3. *Ironic- satire w/ excessive use of narrative technique*

4. *Picaresque- satirizes corrupt society; low SES roguish hero survives in corrupt society*

5. *Epistolary- series of letters or other documents*

6.

7.

8.

⚷➞ Key 44: Order Text Structure Study Guide

Steele (2007) noted that high school textbooks are difficult for students with ELN and that social studies textbooks are generally different from and even more complex than the textbooks of other disciplines. Brittain (1981) investigated the readability of a sixth-grade social studies text. The readability of six samples from the 11-page chapter averaged at the eighth-grade level and ranged from Grades 6.2 to Grade 11. Forty participants—graduate students who were practicing teachers and undergraduate teacher-education majors—completed Cloze exercises on the 11-page chapter in order to assess their comprehension of the material. The scores ranged from 39% to 70% for the undergraduates and from 44% to 75% for the experienced teachers, yet sixth graders were required to learn social studies from the material.

So what is a teacher to do with difficult, inconsiderate texts adopted by the district? One of the thousands of decisions a teacher makes each day involves the selection of alternate teaching strategies. This type of decision involves determining (1) which strategy best communicates the target information, (2) why to use it, (3) how to use it, (4) when and where to use it, and (5) how to evaluate its effectiveness (Winograd & Hare, 1988). Teachers who don't have a wide variety of strategies at their disposal may use less-than-ideal strategies or even inappropriate strategies. After all, as our old department chair used to say, *If the only tool you have is a hammer, everything looks like a nail.* Fortunately, teacher-made study guides are a strategy that can be created for various types of text structures to assist in communicating target information.

Steele (2007) argued that using easier textbooks, historical fiction, and information from the Internet can be more productive for students with ELN than using textbooks. However, she noted that when textbooks are used with students with ELN who are enrolled in general education history classes, study guides can ameliorate the difficulty that such textbooks cause; she especially recommended them for students with low reading skill levels. She cautions that teachers should explain the purpose of guides, model their use, and provide assistance while students work on the guides.

Many variations of study guides have been proposed and a number have been subjected to empirical research. In her review of study guides, Wood (1989) noted that the wide variation of study guides fall into three categories: (1) those targeted at improving reading skills, (2) those targeted at the acquisition of content, and (3) those that fall somewhere in between the other two. The text structure study guides such as the Order Text Structure Study Guide are examples of the latter. They not only assist students in learning content, they also help students improve their reading skills by teaching them to identify text structure.

This study guide assists students in Acquisition of Knowledge and Comprehension because

- ♪ Frustration is decreased because students know exactly what the teacher considers most important in the chapter
- ♪ Perception is enhanced because of the use of three modalities
- ♪ Discrimination is ensured because the student does not have to try to discriminate between essential and nonessential information in the text
- ♪ Confusion is decreased because the important information is clearly delineated in the guide

Order Study Guide for: Hurricanes

Introduction: Hurricanes evolve through a life cycle from birth to death. Hurricanes often live for as long as two to three weeks. They start over tropical ocean waters and can be 600 miles across. Can reach 200 mph. Gather heat and energy from warm H20. Rotate counter-clockwise around calm "eye."

First: Tropical wave: lack closed circulation; winds < 25 mph

Second: Tropical depression - Closed circulation in storm; sustained winds 25 mph; disorganized

Third: Tropical storm - when sustained winds are 39-73 mph; more organized and circular

Fourth: Hurricane: Sustained winds reach 74 mph; pronounced rotation around central core

Fifth:

Sixth:

Seventh:

⚷ Key 45: Compare and Contrast Text Structure Study Guide

Comparing and contrasting is a common text structure, and this study guide will assist students in their navigation of textbook selections in which comparing and contrasting is the structure. Students can learn to recognize cue words in text that signal that the structure is compare and contrast: *compared to, in contrast, as opposed to, similarly.*

Wylie and McGuinness (2004) hypothesized that high levels of prior knowledge of content would ameliorate the difficulties caused by poor text structure. The participants in their study were 195 college students studying psychology at Queen's University in Belfast, Northern Ireland. The students were grouped as having high or low prior knowledge on the topic passages: memory and cognition. Passages were rated by the researchers as being well or poorly structured. Contrary to the researchers' hypothesis, high prior knowledge did not ameliorate poor text structure. Poor text structure hurts everyone. However, good study guides can help readers cope with poor text structure.

Wyatt and Hayes (1991) compared two types of compare and contrast study guide approaches in teaching an obscure religion to 87 undergraduate college students. In the first condition, the students read a selection about a religion that was similar to the target religion. They compared and contrasted the two similar religions. In the second condition, the students read a passage about a religion that was quite different from the target religion and then read the passage about the target religion. They then compared and contrasted the two dissimilar religions.

When the students were asked to list the facts they remembered about the target text, they made many more correct responses about the target text when they had studied dissimilar texts. When they had studied similar texts, they made many more wrong responses about the target text, instead making statements that referred to the similar religion instead of the target religion. Therefore, one criterion for deciding to use a Compare and Contrast Study Guide is that our concepts should be highly dissimilar.

Teachers may wish to computerize study guides, as recommended by Lovitt and Horton (1994). Horton, Lovitt, Givens, and Nelson (1989) investigated the use of study guides on the computer. The study involved 31 freshman students, of whom 13 had ELN and 18 were identified as remedial; the students were all enrolled in a low-track world geography class.

The students with ELN scored an average of 76% when they studied a chapter using the computerized study guide, compared to an average of 42% when they independently took notes. The remedial students scored an average of 77% on the study guide condition compared to 58% on the note taking condition.

Study guides such as the Compare and Contrast Text Structure Study Guide are good inclusion strategies because

- ♪ Attention is captured because the student is actively engaged
- ♪ Discrimination is enhanced because the student explicitly discriminates between the target concept and another concept; discrimination between critical and less important information is assured because the student is directed to seek the analogous information only
- ♪ Memory is strengthened because of the level of processing
- ♪ Reasoning is supported because the student must identify the target concept's analogous information from the text

Here is our example from a class that was comparing the Age of Reason to the Age of Romanticism, two very different concepts.

Compare and Contrast Study Guide for The Age of Enlightenment v. Romanticism

Introduction: Complicated artistic, literary, & intellectual movement. Charles Baudelaire wrote, "Romanticism is precisely situated neither in choice or subject nor exact truth, but in the way of feeling."

Dimension	Concept 1 Age of Reason/Enlightenment	Concept 2 Age of Romanticism
When & where?	1750s in France	Second half of 18th C in Western Europe
Who were initiators?	Scientists	
Emphasis:	Reason and logic are the source of all knowing.	
How can world improve?	People can improve themselves & the world by careful study & rigorous thinking.	
What contributed to movement?	Galileo's telescope: showed the Universe as an orderly place.	
Why?	Newton's Law of Gravity showed that the world followed rules that could be learned through study.	

Summary:

⬤⟶ Key 46: Cause and Effect Text Structure Study Guide

Ciardiello (2002) noted that middle school students were on their own when reading social studies textbooks, although researchers have noted that social studies texts are not designed for independent reading. This is compounded by the fact that middle school social studies teachers identify textbooks as their preferred instructional materials (Schug, Western, & Enochs, 1997).

Ciardiello (2002) argued that cause and effect structures are particularly difficult. This pattern is a dominant feature of social studies texts. Causes and events may mirror the domino effect, in which one event causes a second, which in turn causes a third. In contrast, multiple disparate events may culminate to cause an event. Or both the domino effect and the multiple disparate events may work together to cause a target event.

Not only are cause and effect structures difficult, they are often understandable only with inferences made by the reader, and background knowledge may be essential for a student to be able to make those inferences (Escoe, 1981). For example, the sentence "I scared the blue jays away from the feeder because the finches were hungry" requires the reader to know that blue jays are aggressive birds that won't allow other birds to come near birdfeeders. Escoe wrote, "Even when cause-and-effect relations are stated by means of markers . . . [such as *because* in the example above], readers must be able to recognize the causal marker, know its function in the particular context, and identify its referents in order to understand the relations expressed by the statement" (p. 54).

However, markers are often absent in middle school expository texts, and that makes the inference even more complex, such as: "The finches were hungry, and I scared away the blue jays." Escoe (1981) noted that *suspended causality rules,* propositions that specify the types of events that often cause other events, are the basis for inference.

McCrudden, Schraw, and Lehman (2009) examined making cause and effect relationships explicit with graphic organizers. In their experiment, participants read a selection and then either (1) reread the text, (2) studied a list, or (3) studied a causal graphic organizer. The participants who studied the graphic organizer demonstrated greater recall of the causal sequences, answered more questions about the transitive relationships between the causes and effects correctly, and answered more problem-solving questions correctly than the other groups. The researchers attributed the difference to the visual aid's explicitness in representing the cause and effect relationship.

Cause and Effect Study Guides are powerful tools to help students with ELN succeed because

- ♪ Attention is captured because the student is actively engaged
- ♪ Discrimination is enhanced because the student explicitly discriminates between the target concept and another concept; discrimination between critical and less important information is assured because the student is directed to seek the analogous information only
- ♪ Memory is strengthened because of the level of processing
- ♪ Reasoning is supported because the student must identify the target concept's analogous information from the text

Cause and Effect Study Guide for

Irish Immigration to America

Early 19th C: dominant industry of Ireland is agriculture. English own land which is rented to small Irish farmers. Tools and methods are backward.

Terrible poverty. Irish farm laborers earn only 1/5 of what they could make in U.S.

Poor people start thinking of immigrating to U.S. In 1816, some do. They are recruited to build canals for good money. Friends and family back in Ireland hear the good news. More follow.

1845: Irish Famine results from potato blight. Typhus follows. 1 million die. Famine stimulates desire to move to U.S. for better life. By 1855, 2 million have emigrated to America.

⚷ Key 47: Problem Solution Study Guide

Harniss, Dickson, Kinder, and Hollenbeck (2001) wrote, "The textbook *is* the curriculum for most content area courses . . . 75% to 90% of classroom instruction is organized around textbooks" (p. 129). We should not be surprised, then, by students' low performance on the National Education Assessment Program's most recent report cards in history and science. In 2005, only 29% of eighth graders and 18% of seniors scored proficient or above in science; in 2006, only 17% of eighth graders and 13% of seniors scored proficient or above in history.

The *macrostructure* of a text represents its meaning organized into a coherent whole. Armbruster, Anderson, and Ostertag (1986) conducted a National Institute of Education–sponsored study on teaching expository text macrostructure. The researchers examined how explicit instruction on expository test structure affects fifth graders' ability to learn from problem-solution social studies text. The participants were 82 students, of whom half received direct instruction in recognizing problem-solution text structure. The control students read and discussed answers to questions about the social studies selections. The experimental group recalled 50% more of the macrostructure ideas as assessed by writing an essay than did their control peers, wrote summaries that contained more main ideas than did their peers, and wrote better-organized summaries. The groups did not differ on a short-answer test of information that was not part of the macrostructure.

Explicitly teaching text structure may be especially critical when students are English language learners. Talbot (1997) explicitly taught half of 244 Chinese students the macrostructure of comparison-contrast, cause-effect, and problem-solution texts. The students who were taught about the text structure significantly outperformed the students who were not, and the medium- and low-proficiency students gained the most from the intervention. The students were able to transfer their learning to new tasks. Then the researchers interviewed 26 of the students, and those interviews revealed that the students had greater metacognitive awareness of text structure.

Hague (1989) demonstrated that understanding text structure is an important strategy for our students who are learning another language. Hague's participants were 62 native-English-speaking high school students who were taking their fourth year of Spanish. She tested knowledge of text structure as a predictor of their ability to read expository text in their second language. Participants who used text structure recalled more information than students who did not. In addition, students were more aware of causation and comparison text structure than of descriptive and problem-solution text structure. She concluded that knowledge of text structures is an important reading strategy for students who are learning a language. Teachers who have English language learners in their classes will find that teaching them text structure is requisite for supporting academic success.

Problem Solution Study Guides can help students learn from the text because

- ♪ Attention is captured because the student is actively engaged
- ♪ Discrimination is enhanced because the student explicitly discriminates between the target concept and another concept; discrimination between critical and less important information is assured because the student is directed to seek the analogous information only
- ♪ Memory is strengthened because of the level of processing
- ♪ Reasoning is supported because the student must identify the target concept's analogous information from the text

Problem Solution Study Guide for Building the Transcontinental Railroad

Problem: California became a state in 1850 after Gold Rush, but was isolated by distance from the rest of the United States. Commerce difficult, natural resources difficult to exploit, communication difficult.
Promise of new riches for wealthy, hope for landless poor.

Rejected Solution
Take a boat to Panama, cross Central America by land, take another boat up Pacific coast. Costly, dangerous, takes months.

Rejected Solution
Cross the U.S. by wagon train. Costly, dangerous, takes months.

Selected Solution
Build Transcontinental Railroad. Already 9,000 miles of track east of Mississippi. U.S. economy in East thriving from easy transportation. President Lincoln signs Pacific Railroad Act. Govt. (1) makes low-interest loans and (2) huge land grants to railroads (Union Pacific to build track from Omaha head west and Central Pacific to build track from Sacramento and head east). Completed 1869 at Promontory, Utah.

⚸┓ Key 48: Analogy Study Guide

Bean, Singer, and Cowan (1985) explained that an Analogy Study Guide is especially helpful in assisting students to understand complex or unfamiliar material. The strategy allows them to connect the foreign material to concepts that are well-known and comfortable to them. The strategy also helps the students engage in higher-order thinking because they must analyze both the lecture material and the referent to which they are comparing the material.

Bean, Singer, and Cowen (1985) wrote that when we construct an Analogy Study Guide, we should think *only* about the critical concepts and eliminate the rest of the material in the chapter; we should only have our students read the critical material. This will help reinforce to our students that the textbook is a learning resource, and reading a textbook is not an end unto itself.

Hayes (1986) conducted an Analogy Study Guide experiment with 52 eleventh-grade students. The students were divided into four groups and were assigned to read a selection about the game of cricket. All four groups were given study guides. Two of the study guides included diagrams, and two of the study guides included analogies to baseball. Both interventions were highly effective on a 20-question posttest, but the analogy groups scored higher than the diagram groups on a follow-up test at a later date on both understanding and retention. Hayes recommended visual tools for assisting students to learn new material initially, but analogies to help students retain the information longer.

Bean, Searles, Singer, and Cowen (1990) tested the hypothesis that combining a pictorial analogy with a written analogy study guide would produce greater understanding of concepts in biology than would a written analogical study guide alone. Their participants were 111 high school students whose classes were randomly assigned to either treatment or control conditions. The first treatment condition was listening to a lecture on cell parts and functions accompanied by a pictorial and written analogy study guide comparing the cell with a factory. The second treatment condition was the same lecture with the written analogical guide without the pictorial dimension. The third condition was the written guide without teacher explanation. The control condition was independent reading in a text with analogies to a factory. An essay test produced the following mean scores: text reading alone, 3.63; adding analogical guide, 6.10; adding lecture, 7.75; adding picture, 16.32. The researchers concluded the following:

> Supplementing text analogies with explicit guide material in the form of an analogical study guide will further assist students' understanding of difficult concepts. Taking the additional step of supplying a pictorial representation of the analogy will significantly advance students' comprehension beyond the level that might be supplied with use of an analogical guide alone. (p. 236)

The Analogy Study Guide helps students unlock the barriers to Acquisition and Proficiency and Fluency in Acquisition and Comprehension because

- ♪ Frustration is decreased because the new material is compared to something the student knows well
- ♪ Perception is enhanced because of the use of three modalities
- ♪ Sequencing is ensured if the material involves seriation because of the comparison to a well-understood sequence of steps
- ♪ Confusion is decreased because the new information is compared to well-known information
- ♪ Memory is assured because of the connection of the new material to the known material

Here is our completed study guide for a biology lesson.

Analogy Study Guide for *The Immune System*

Element of the Immune System	Function	Element of Medieval City
Skin and Mucous Membranes (Guard Nasal Passages, Lungs, Reproductive Tract, Digestive System, etc.)	First Line of Defense: Blocks Entry	City's Outer Walls
Secretions of Sweat and Oil Glands and Mucous	Weapons That Protect External Surfaces	Boiling Oil Poured Down Water in Moat Surrounding
Microbes	Enemy	Nomadic Invaders From Outside City
Cells That Kill Invading Microbes	Second Line of Defense: Counter Attacks	Armed Guards Inside City
1. Macrophages (Type of White Blood Cell)	Kill Invaders One at a Time by Eating Them	Cannibal Guards
2. Neutrophils (Type of White Blood Cell)	Kill Invaders by Poisoning Them and Simultaneously Sacrifice Themselves	Suicide Guards
3. Natural Killer Cells	1. Kill Cells Infected by Microbes 2. Immune Surveillance	1. Executioner 2. Police Guards

Drawing:

10

Promoting Factual Mastery Through Mnemonic Devices

Mnemonic strategies are the single most powerful inclusion strategy (Kavale & Forness, 1999), with an astonishing effect size of 1.62. In addition, the playful nature of keyword and musical mnemonic strategies motivates students and captures their attention.

Because students must master discipline-specific Knowledge level information before they can engage in higher-order thinking in that discipline, as craftspeople must gather rough gems before they can process them and create beautiful jewelry, mnemonic devices are valuable tools for working with students with memory problems. The fact that they are fun is a delightful bonus.

As middle and secondary school teachers, we love to teach higher-order thinking skills. But in the same way that craftspeople must gather rough gems before they can grade and sort, cut and polish, analyze for use, create and design, and appraise and set a value on their finished products of precious stones, we must teach knowledge level information first. Our students must first know the basic facts of our disciplines. While scoffing at knowledge-level teaching de rigueur, the knowledgeable teacher knows that Bloom's Taxonomy defines Knowledge as

- A discipline's terminology
- Specifics
- The ways and means of dealing with those specific (1) conventions, (2) trends and sequences, (3) classifications and categories, (4) criteria, and (5) methodology
- Universals and abstractions: (1) principles and generalizations and (2) theories and structures

Knowledge is significant, and Knowledge is a prerequisite for higher levels of thinking.

> An important key to teaching knowledge to students with disabilities is mnemonic instruction. . . In a mega-analysis of meta-analyses, Kavale and Forness (1999) revealed, in their classic monograph *Efficacy of Special Education and Related Services,* that the single most effective teaching strategy with students receiving special education services was mnemonic instruction. The effect size was 1.62. Students in special education . . . who receive mnemonic instruction would be better off than 98% of students not receiving such instruction and would gain over $1\frac{1}{2}$ years of credit on an achievement measure. (p. 81)

In "Mega-Analysis of Meta-Analyses: What Works in Special Education and Related Services," Forness, Kavale, Blum, and Lloyd (1997) explained that a meta-analysis aggregates research findings on a subject by converting the findings to an effect size (ES). The ES is calculated by subtracting the mean of the control group from the mean of the experimental group and dividing the difference by the standard deviation of the control group or a similar measure of variance. When no control group is used, alternate statistical strategies are employed.

In the monograph, Kavale and Forness (1999) noted,

> Mastropieri and Scruggs (1989) synthesized the experimental literature investigating the effectiveness of mnemonic instruction with special education students using meta-analytic procedures. Across 19 studies and 983 subjects, the ES was 1.62, indicating that the average special education students receiving instruction would be better off than 95% of students not receiving such instruction. The expected 45 percentile-rank gain on an outcome assessment means that special education students may almost double their original scores when instructed mnemonically. The associated standard deviation (.79) is also noteworthy because it indicates the presence of no negative effects (i.e., control subjects outperforming experimental subjects). The uniformly positive effects (range = .68 to 3.42) for mnemonic instruction suggest that it represents an effective means for enhancing the academic performance of special education students. (p. 74)

Scruggs and Mastropieri (1990a) wrote that the foundations of mnemonic instruction are meaningfulness, concreteness, and elaboration. We learn information that is meaningful to us more easily than that which is not meaningful; concreteness, as opposed to abstractness, promotes retention. The more we elaborate on concepts, the more fully we encode them for later retrieval.

The strategies we discuss in this chapter include the following:

- Key 49: Keyword Mnemonics With Narrative Chains
- Key 50: Musical Mnemonics

⌇→ Key 49: Keyword Mnemonics With Narrative Chains

Keyword Mnemonics (discussed in Key 14) are memory strategies in which a key word sounds like a target word and is matched to a visual image that connects the target and key word. For example, to remember that President Jimmy Carter established a national energy policy, a student could picture the president parking his car (*Car*-ter) and walking instead of driving. When we add narrative chaining, we create a story that places several keywords in an order to help us remember multiple items, especially when they need to be remembered in chronological order.

Wolgemuth, Cobb, and Alwell (2008) conducted a systematic review of rigorous research on mnemonic devices employed with secondary students. The studies they reviewed all employed the keyword method, or variations thereof. The researchers found an effect size of 1.38, making their evaluation of keyword mnemonics with secondary students "overwhelmingly positive" (p. 9).

Because secondary students with ELN in Virginia scored so poorly on their state end-of-course World History I test (59% of students with ELN passed, compared to 82% of students without ELN), Fontana, Scruggs, and Mastropieri (2007) investigated the use of mnemonics in assisting such students. The researchers attributed the poor scores to difficulties internal to students with learning disabilities as well as to external factors. They cited poor reading skills, memory problems, poor metacognitive skills, and poor frustration tolerance as internal problems. They identified multiple external problems: (1) teachers' assumptions that all students had enough prior knowledge, (2) inconsiderate textbooks, (3) teachers' lecture techniques, and (4) overwhelming long-term assignments.

Mastropieri and Scruggs, the undisputed gurus of mnemonic research, defined mnemonic strategies as "specific reconstruction of target content intended to tie new information more closely to the learners' existing knowledge base and, therefore, facilitate retrieval" (Scruggs & Mastropieri, 1990a, pp. 271–272).

Terrill, Scruggs, and Mastropieri (2004) reported on a study in which one female and seven male tenth graders with learning disabilities received instruction on SAT vocabulary from a special education teacher for six weeks. Each week, the students were presented 10 new words. The method of instruction varied every other week between mnemonic instruction and traditional workbook instruction. The vocabulary included words such as *altruistic, diffident,* and *virulent.* The assessment was a multiple choice test. Under the mnemonic condition, the mean score was 92%; under the traditional condition, the mean score was 49%. These results were both highly statistically significant and socially significant; a finding is considered *socially significant* in special education if the control intervention does not result in a passing grade while the experimental intervention does result in a passing grade. In this case, the social significance was not merely the difference between an F and a D, but between an F and an A.

The Keyword Mnemonics strategy works for students with special needs because

♪ Memory is enhanced when material is presented auditorily and visually and because the information requires students to elaborate on material that is made concrete and meaningful

♪ Motivation is elevated by the playful nature of the strategies

♪ Attention is increased when motivation is elevated

In the following example, we present a mnemonic keyword strategy combined with a narrative chain to remember the four Noble Gases.

🔑 Key 50: Musical Mnemonics

Musical mnemonics can be powerful tools. Several researchers provide evidence that supports the use of musical mnemonics.

Researchers at the Center for Biomedical Research in Music, Molecular, Cellular, and Integrative Neuroscience Programs at Colorado State University investigated how the brain responds to musical mnemonics. In healthy adults, the musical mnemonic condition produced significantly more activity in alpha and gamma brainwaves than did the spoken condition. In a similar study, adults with multiple sclerosis demonstrated superior learning and memory in the musical mnemonic condition and produced significant power increase in low-alpha brainwaves. The researchers posited that musical mnemonics may access compensatory pathways that strengthen learning and memory (Thaut, Peterson, & McIntosh, 2005).

Chazin and Neuschatz (1990) compared the effects of a mnemonic song to those of a traditional lecture in geology. The participants were of disparate ages: 20 students were of ages between 18 and 21, and 26 students were age 8. The participants were divided into four groups according to age and treatment condition. The students in the mnemonic song conditions were taught information about minerals to the tune of "Mary Had a Little Lamb." The control groups listened to a lecture covering the same information. When the experimental groups listened to the song the second and third time, they were asked to sing along. Afterward, the participants wrote down everything they could recall about minerals. The participants in the musical mnemonic groups outperformed the participants in the lecture group.

VanVoorhis (2002) investigated the effects of musical mnemonics on teaching statistics to two sections of undergraduate students taking Psychological Measurements. Students in one section learned and sang the definitions of three statistics in jingles. Their peers in the second section read the definitions aloud. When the students attempted application tests using the statistics, the jingle group significantly outperformed the read-aloud group. In addition, the students' self-ratings of how well they knew the definitions were correlated with their test scores: the musical mnemonic group knew that they knew the definitions well, and the read-aloud group knew that they did not.

Gfeller (1983) investigated the effects of musical mnemonics with boys. Her participants were 30 boys who had learning disabilities and 30 boys who did not. The boys ranged from 9 to 11.9 years of age. The participants tried to memorize multiplication facts either through standard verbal rehearsal or through chanting to a simple tune. After the first trial, all of the boys without disabilities significantly outperformed all the boys with learning disabilities. However, by the end of the fifth trial, both the boys with and without learning disabilities who used the musical mnemonic significantly outperformed all of the boys—with or without learning disabilities—who used the standard procedure. Gfeller (1986) noted that familiar and liked melodies produced better results than unfamiliar melodies. She also stressed the importance of cueing students about how and when to employ a mnemonic strategy.

> *"Big Ideas in Science Song"*
> *Sung to the tune of "Jingle Bells"!*
>
> *Systems, models, change and stability,*
> *Evolution and scale, what this means to me*
> *Is*
> *The Big Ideas in Science*
> *Will help you and me*
> *Make this world, this big blue world*
> *A better place to be!*

Musical Mnemonics is a good memory strategy for students with disabilities because

- ♪ Memory is supported when the words are linked together with a melody
- ♪ Motivation is elevated by the playful nature of the strategies
- ♪ Attention is increased when motivation is elevated

11

Improving Higher-Order Thinking Skills

We often think that we are teaching students to use higher-order thinking skills when what we are actually doing is giving them problems that require such skills without teaching them the skills required to tackle the problems. General education students may develop workable strategies without our help, but students who have ELN almost certainly will not. However, teaching students strategies and heuristics for analyzing, synthesizing, and evaluating is possible. In fact, it is not difficult at all. By explicitly teaching these strategies, not only will our students who have ELN increase their academic achievement in our classes, they will also transfer the skills to new settings if we encourage them to do so.

In this chapter, we will address strategies to help students analyze and evaluate. In the following chapter, we will discuss ways to help students with the synthesis skills involved in expository writing.

Teaching that involves higher-order thinking skills (HOTS) is what most teachers love to do best, but we sometimes wish we knew more effective strategies for doing it. These strategies will help all of our students use HOTS more effectively, but they are especially important if we are to help our students who have ELN develop those crucial HOTS.

Ivie (1998) argued that three criteria exist for defining HOTS. First is the use of abstract structures for thinking, and we have already explained that structure is one of the keys to special education. He wrote, "If we wish to think in abstract terms, we must necessarily come to grips with the structure of knowledge" (p. 35). This implies that we must master the basic facts of a discipline, which we may then construct into hierarchies and manipulate with HOTS.

Ivie's (1998) second criterion is the organization of knowledge into an integrated system. Poor learners and effective learners differ in their conceptualization of knowledge. Students with ELN see only an unrelated conglomeration of facts; effective learners see classes, systems, relationships, and analogies. This implies that we must make instruction explicit and structured.

Ivie's (1998) third criterion is the application of sound rules of logic. Logic is a structure for thinking. We must explicitly teach structures of logic in order for students with special needs to be able to learn them. Ivie also argued that logic is metacognition: thinking about thinking.

Order Thinking Skills in Vocational Education (accessible at www.eric.ed.gov), written by Sandra Kerka (1992), stated the following:

> Thomas (1992) identifies three types of cognitive theories upon which teaching strategies can be based. Information processing theory explains how the mind takes in information. Knowledge structure theories depict how knowledge is represented and organized in the mind. Social history theory explains the vital role of cultural context in the development of individual thinking. Together, these three perspectives offer a comprehensive view of cognition. In this view, learning is characterized as an active process in which the learner constructs knowledge as a result of interaction with the physical and social environment. Learning is moving from basic skills and pure facts to linking new information with prior knowledge; from relying on a single authority to recognizing multiple sources of knowledge; from novice-like to expert-like problem solving. (pp. 2–3)

The article further identified five general principles for teaching HOTS that were outlined by Johnson and Thomas (1992). The first principle was to help students organize what they know, and the authors noted that use of graphic organizers (GOs) helps students structure their knowledge. They explained that GOs help ease the cognitive load and free up working memory for higher-order tasks. Their second principle was to build on what students already know. Again, they supported the use of GOs for this principle.

The third principle was to facilitate information processing through explicit modeling of problem solving, including selection of strategies. (This explicit modeling is explained in the fifth principle.) The fourth principle was to facilitate thinking through elaboration. Their fifth principle was for teachers to make their thinking processes explicit, a strategy that Vygotsky (1962) called Cognitive Apprenticeship. Teachers can also use GOs to implement these final three principles for teaching students HOTS.

Most secondary students with special needs are concrete thinkers; in fact, Collea (1981) stated that the typical college freshman functions at the concrete level of intelligence. *Teaching Problem Solving—Secondary School Science* (Blosser, 1988) cited research by Powers (1984) that stated that 50% of all college chemistry students were concrete thinkers and have not reached the level of abstract operations.

HOTS can be taught to students with ELN, as evidenced by increased performance among secondary students studying Spanish as a second language, Chapter I students, seventh- and eighth-grade poor readers, and sixth-grade mathematics and reading students. In addition to increased thinking ability, mastery of HOTS results in higher self-esteem and increased confidence in the ability to solve problems (DeWispelaere & Kossack, 1996; Eisenman & Payne, 1997; Jackson, 2000).

GOs are effective at helping us teach HOTS. DeWispelaere and Kossack (1996) used GOs to teach the HOTS of sequencing, classifying, and comparing and contrasting. Their participants were secondary students who were studying Spanish as a second language. Appropriate GOs were used for instruction in course content and for testing, and the students were provided with feedback. Students also made their own GOs. Increased performance was demonstrated in written tests, organization of projects, and behavior.

GOs are excellent tools for teaching HOTS to students with learning problems. They work because they help make highly abstract and usually verbal information into a representational form.

In this chapter, we will address the following HOTS strategies:

- Key 51: Storyboards Type I
- Key 52: Storyboards Type II
- Key 53: Flowcharts
- Key 54: Venn-Euler Diagram
- Key 55: Compare and Contrast Matrix
- Key 56: Campfire Metaphor for Cause and Effect
- Key 57: Evaluation by Elimination by Aspects Matrix
- Key 58: Evaluation by Addition Matrix
- Key 59: Reasoning by Metaphor and Analogy

⚷ Key 51: Storyboards Type I

Storyboards (what we call *Storyboards Type I*) are planning strategies that are used in a variety of professions. For example, storyboards have been recommended in professions in such diverse contexts as planning stream management, surveyor training, advertising, and snow removal. They have also been used by school faculties for developing school-wide Quality Improvement Plans. Teaching students how to use storyboards will not only meet a teacher's immediate instructional goal, it will also provide a strategy for use beyond the classroom.

Denison (1995) explained that storyboarding is a strategy for project planning that begins with a problem. She employs storyboarding with groups of six to eight students who form a planning team and meet for a brainstorming session. The brainstorming session is followed by a critical thinking session in which ideas are evaluated for viability and either adopted or discarded. She noted that the visual display allows students to see how the ideas are related, to rearrange them, and to "hitchhike" on them.

Denison (1995) uses three sets of index cards: (1) a few blue 5" × 8" *Topic Cards* that state the topic and are placed at the top of each storyboard, (2) a number of 4" × 6" salmon *Header Cards* that head each major subdivision of ideas, and (3) many 3" × 5" yellow *Subber Cards* that list each creative idea. She notes that every member of the team needs at least 20 Subber Cards. She recommends at least 200 pushpins for each team.

Sakurai, Dohi, and Tsuruta, of Tokyo Denki University in Japan, and their research colleague Knauf, of the University of Ilmenau in Germany (2009), recommend dynamic storyboarding with university students. They explained that dynamic storyboarding "is based on the idea of semi-formally representing, processing, evaluating, and refining didactic knowledge" (p. 307). They found that dynamic storyboarding clearly and easily represented didactic knowledge.

Preddy (2003) used collaboration with a library media specialist and a classroom teacher to teach an inquiry approach to the research process. The students created storyboards as part of their research plan.

Type I Storyboards are good tools for inclusion because

- ♪ Sequencing can be made explicit
- ♪ Confusion is eliminated when everything is made explicit
- ♪ Reasoning is facilitated by the discussion paired with the visual tool
- ♪ Metacognition is supported as students are taught the process

Storyboard on How to Plan a Settlement

To Ensure Safety	To Provide Food	To Provide Homes

To Ensure Safety

Spoue dnnwoj noerni	f oie n njer zxOsiohg
Weoj mn ipes	Fepoun nreopwne rniOw
Kw n ; ewuor njkl;	Oje nwOei erei n
f eokl;n njjn	

To Provide Food

Deryeu hn ne nreui sne'	Feon tgoieng
Per twr-rjelkjn njkeson g	Vuor nj jere j o;wkl;
Spaved dnnwoj	

To Provide Homes

Fepoun nreopwne rniOw	Villane doint erei
fBobble njjn doien f	Millie o;wkl;
Cu nakfepso liw er	Pifflen toen erei

⚷➔ Key 52: Storyboards Type II

Whereas Denison's type of storyboarding (Storyboards Type I), which was used by Sakurai and colleagues (2009), involves text, a second type of storyboarding (Storyboards Type II) involves graphics. This type of storyboarding requires students to draw a series of sketches or cartoon frames. Rubman and Waters (2000) found that this second type of storyboard enhanced the integration of text propositions and helped students discover inconsistencies in text. The researchers had third and sixth graders read stories that contained inconsistencies. Half of the students constructed storyboards, and half did not. As compared to the control condition, the storyboard construction scaffolded the readers—particularly the less skilled readers—in detecting the inconsistencies in the stories as well as in enhancing the integration of the text's propositions. The experimental condition also produced significant effects on recall of the critical propositions.

MacGregor (2007) recommended the use of storyboards to keep track of multiple points of view in literature, and Lee (2003) used *kamishibai* storyboards, a Japanese form of folk art storyboarding, to teach middle school students about Egyptian history.

As part of a larger study on using GOs to teach HOTS, DeWispelaere and Kossack (1996) used cartoon frames as storyboards to help students who were learning Spanish as a foreign language develop HOTS. The strategy increased the students' sequencing skills, and the overall treatment improved not only performance on examinations but also the organization of their projects and eventually their behavior.

Harrington (1994) recommended using storyboarding as a prewriting strategy, especially with students with ELN. She noted that students who were attempting to write fiction wrote without direction or destination. She explicitly taught storyboarding to middle school students and noted evidence that students were empowered by the process and that their written products were improved. Of even greater import was the student-generated transfer of the skill.

Storyboards help students visualize what they read (see Schur, 1980), thereby helping them to understand sequences, which in turn increases comprehension and analysis skills. Students with ELN are often nonlinear thinkers who need help in conceptualizing in a linear fashion. This graphic tool helps them develop linear thinking and can be extended to as many cartoon frames as required. We even used cartoon frames to help adult students increase their ability to follow a convoluted legal case; as the students read aloud, we stopped periodically and drew cartoon frames that depicted each event. Not only did the process help students better comprehend the material, they also reported that the strategy helped them understand the cause and effect relationships of the events as each event led to the next. That is the reason for our great attraction to sequencing strategies: They help our students learn cause and effect.

Storyboards are effective strategies for helping students who have ELN learn cause and effect relationships and thereby acquire analytical skills because

⚷ Confusion is eliminated because the causes and effects of events are made explicit

⚷ Reasoning is developed as the cause and effect nature of events is demonstrated

⚷ Key 53: Flowcharts

We all know what flowcharts are, but we tend to underutilize them in the classroom. When we are teaching a process that involves several steps, we use a flowchart. A flowchart can represent a simple, straightforward, one-way process, such as a simple science experiment or mathematical process, or it can represent a more complex scientific, mathematical, or other process with loops and decision-making points.

In research, flowcharts have been reported to be effective in such diverse contexts as providing jury instructions, training parents to parent more effectively, and cutting the cost of surgery.

Writing in the *Journal of Baltic Science Education,* Cizková and Ctrnáctová (2003) conducted an experiment that demonstrated that flowcharts are effective tools for teaching chemistry and biology to students from elementary through high school. The use of flowcharts has been recommended in teaching in such diverse science contexts as secondary chemistry (Wagner, 2001), middle school robotics (Norton, McRobbie, & Ginns, 2007), and college molecular biology (Wilterdung & Luckie, 2002).

In language arts, Swartz (2003) recommended using flow charts to teach students how to write how-to writing. Jacobucci, Richert, Ronan, and Tanis (2002) found that flowcharts were effective for increasing reading comprehension through teaching sequence of events to low academic achieving middle and elementary school students, and Ollman (1989) argued that flowcharts can show multiple cause and effect relationships in the literature read by secondary students.

Flowcharts can also be used to help teach the analytical skills involved in identifying cause and effect in history, current events, and the behavioral sciences. Flowcharts are excellent tools for analytical thinking because they help students see how Event B is both an effect of Event A and a cause of Event C (Moon, 1992; Ollmann, 1989).

Cooke (1995) recommended the use of flowcharts to assist students in understanding a teacher's instructions and expectations. He noted that the flowchart visually maps all of the steps, activities, events, or tasks in a process. The chart describes process and ensures mutual understanding and agreement in the process steps. The chart also provides an opportunity to improve a process through simplifying or redesigning it. In his work on the Quality Classroom, Cooke (1995) declared flowcharts to be a quality tool.

Flowcharts are good tools for helping students acquire the analytical skill of cause and effect because

♪ Confusion is eliminated when causes and effects are made explicit in a visual form
♪ Reasoning is developed when the relationships between events and their causes and effects are elucidated

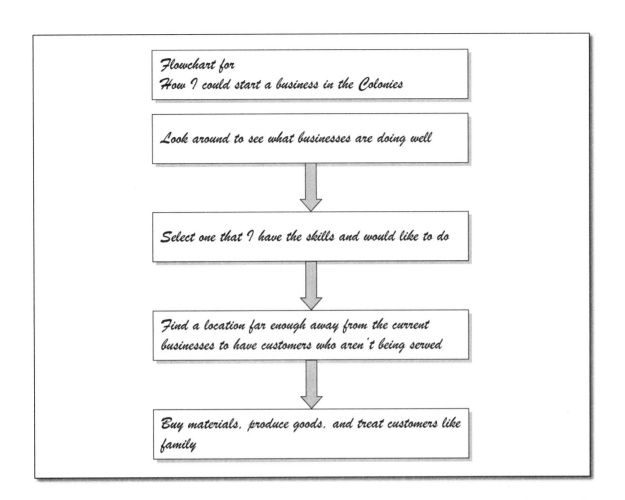

⚷→ Key 54: Venn-Euler Diagram

The Venn-Euler Diagram was first described by the eighteenth-century mathematician-logician Euler and made famous by the nineteenth-century cleric Venn. When using the Venn-Euler Diagram, we draw circles that may or may not overlap to show relationships among classes. To compare and contrast, a different purpose from that for which the strategy was originally developed, we overlap the circles.

As we use the diagram, each circle represents one concept, and the overlapping area represents the commonalities among the concepts. The commonalities are written in the overlapping area. The differences that discriminate one concept from the other are written in the nonoverlapping areas.

In the social studies, teacher-researchers have recommended using Venn-Euler Diagrams in history classes to teach students to compare and contrast Roosevelt and Churchill; in world culture classes to teach students to compare and contrast the Qur'an and the Old Testament; and in American Government classes to teach federalism as a source of conflict and cooperation. In the language arts, Yopp and Yopp (1996) recommended their use in teaching literature; others have recommended their use in teaching developmental college students to compare and contrast in writing and in teaching English to secondary ESL students (Gray, 2000; Hartman & Stewart, 2001; Michalak, 2000).

Boyle (2000) used Venn-Euler Diagrams to improve the reading comprehension of 26 high school students who had mild disabilities and were poor readers. The students who were taught the strategy demonstrated gains in both literal and relational comprehension.

While the Venn-Euler Diagram is an excellent tool for comparing and contrasting, its original function was to assist in developing logic through examining class membership; instead of only having overlapping circles, this application has circles within circles, circles outside of circles, overlapping circles, and combinations thereof.

VanDyke (1995) recommended teaching secondary mathematics students to use logic with the aid of Venn Diagrams. They have also been recommended for teaching deductive reasoning to secondary students and developing cognitive processes in adult students. Still other teacher-researchers have recommended teaching them as life-long learning strategies beginning in middle school and continuing on through high school.

Using Venn-Euler Diagrams, the student can make 16 statements such as "Every A is a B," "No A is a B," "Some As are Bs," "Some As are not Bs," and so forth. By using this strategy, teachers not only help their students gain a deeper understanding of their content area, they also help students develop logic—an area that is problematic for many students with learning problems. The following diagram shows a Venn-Euler Diagram used in an English composition class by a teacher who was concerned because his students' written arguments were illogical.

Using Venn-Euler Diagrams to help students develop analytical ability in inclusion classes is a good strategy because

- ⚷ Reasoning is supported when the invisible is made visible
- ⚷ Frustration is reduced when relationships are explicit

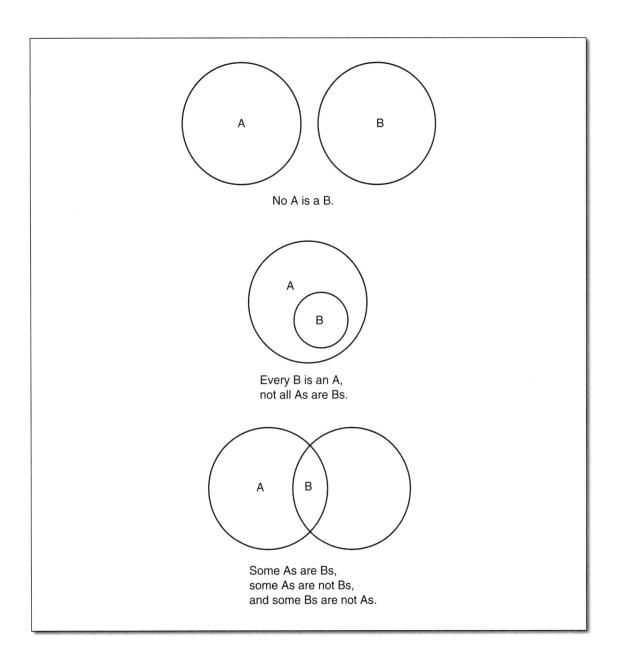

No A is a B.

Every B is an A,
not all As are Bs.

Some As are Bs,
some As are not Bs,
and some Bs are not As.

☞ Key 55: Compare and Contrast Matrix

Graphic organizers such as the Compare and Contrast Matrix are tools that scaffold students' critical thinking.

Collier, Guenther, and Veerman (2002) documented a deficit in students' critical thinking and problem solving skills through teacher checklists, student journals, and surveys of the students, their parents, and teachers. The researchers posited that the students were not consistently called upon to use thinking skills in the classroom. The researchers implemented an 11-week thinking skill program through a variety of instructional activities that included the use of GOs. Most of the students demonstrated improvement in problem solving activities.

Instruction on teaching students to use GOs to compare and contrast has been found to transfer to new settings. For example, Weisberg and Balajthy (1989) taught 16 below-average high school readers to summarize material and construct graphic organizers to compare and contrast material in social studies selections. A control group of 16 students was provided with alternate instruction. One month after the instruction, the students were given a high-prior-knowledge selection on nuclear power plant disasters and a low-prior-knowledge selection on the death penalty. Transfer of the summarization and compare and contrast graphic organizer skills occurred on both the high-prior-knowledge and low-prior-knowledge selections. When the researchers tested the strategy with college freshmen who were required to take a developmental reading course, they found that those students also transferred the knowledge to other contexts.

MacKinnon (2006) investigated critical thinking approaches in a science classroom in Canada. Using the concept of evolution versus creationism as a contentious issue, 68 students used compare and contrast and other electronic graphic organizers to engage in critical thinking. The students reported that the graphic organizers improved their ability to formulate arguments. MacKinnon posited that such tools are generic and can be used across content domains.

The Compare and Contrast Matrix is an effective tool for helping students who have ELN increase their analytical skills because

- ♪ Reasoning is supported when the invisible is made visible
- ♪ Confusion is reduced when reasoning is supported
- ♪ Discrimination between confusing concepts is ensured

Here is an example that compares ancient Rome and Greece.

How did ancient Greeks' and Romans' geography make their nutrition different?

	Ancient Greece	Ancient Rome
Where were the countries in relation to water?	City-states all near water	Inland on side of Tiber River
Where did people live?	Most people lived along coast where soil was good for farming	People lived in hilly countryside and in towns
What did people eat?	Sea fish, squid, octopus, small birds, occasional lamb; wheat, barley, olives, grapes	Chicken, pork, rabbit; wheat, turnips, apples, olives, grapes

Conclusion: Because they lived along the ocean, the Greeks lived on ocean fish as their source of protein. They did not have to use any crops to feed livestock. Because they lived inland, the Romans' protein was livestock that they had to raise. They had to use some crops to feed the livestock, so had less to eat themselves. Both groups grew olives and grapes. Olives have healthy fats and red wine has healthy antioxidants.

⚷ Key 56: Campfire Metaphor for Cause and Effect

Meyrowitz (1980) noted that the use of metaphor for developing critical thinking skills is a particularly useful and powerful strategy, in part because it helps students to begin to think metacognitively. Visual metaphors and analogies add additional dimensions to the strength of a metaphor because the combination of verbal and visual provides for dual coding (ChanLin & Chan, 1996). For example, in the ERIC abstract of *Scientific Thinking Is in the Mind's Eye*, Ganguly (1995) wrote the following:

> It is important to incorporate visual thinking into science instruction. Imagination and perception play vital roles in scientific inquiry. Metaphors, like perceptions, are drawn from common experiences and are a means to anchor scientists' thought processes in generating a pattern that bridges the gap between the seen and the unseen.

Using a graphic metaphor renders the metaphor even more effective; when McKay (1999) compared the use of text with textual organizer to text with graphic organizer, she found that the 37 adults in the study increased their understanding of difficult content significantly in the graphic metaphor treatment.

ChanLin and Chan (1996) developed six versions of an instructional packet on the dimensions of including or excluding metaphors, including or excluding static graphics, and including or excluding animated graphics. While the animated graphics with metaphors produced the highest academic gains, the static graphics with metaphors also produced greater gains than metaphors without graphics or any of the nonmetaphor conditions.

The Campfire strategy is for helping students understand multiple causality and the multiple effects of an event. First, the students write the name of the event and a description of it in the middle of a page; then, the students draw a fire around it. Next, as the students discover the proximal cause, they write it next to the campfire and draw a match around the cause. As they discover each of the other causes, they draw a log under the fire and write their notes about the cause on the log. They stack the logs (down) until all of the distal causes have been identified.

The effects of the event are symbolized by the smoke from the campfire: The more far-reaching the effect, the larger the cloud of smoke. A spark can even drop down out of a cloud to start another fire.

The Campfire strategy is a good strategy to help students understand because

- ♪ Reasoning is supported when the unfamiliar is made familiar and when the invisible is made visible
- ♪ Attention is garnered when information is presented or manipulated in a creative way
- ♪ Synthesis skills are developed as students begin thinking metaphorically about other topics

⊶ Key 57: Evaluation by Elimination by Aspects Matrix

The Evaluation by Elimination by Aspects Matrix teaches students a strategy for evaluation by external criteria. Bloom's taxonomy lists evaluation as the highest level of thinking and identifies only two types of evaluation: evaluation by external criteria and evaluation by examination of internal consistency. We will discuss two ways to conduct evaluations by external criteria.

Evaluation by Elimination by Aspects, formally called Elimination by Aspects (Tversky, 1972), is a heuristic for helping us make decisions when the greatest number of criteria for making a decision must be met. We eliminate each alternate solution as it fails to meet a criterion and continue until only one solution is left. Tversky and Sattath (1979) explained that the process of choosing between several alternatives is a tree structure: Each time a person eliminates an aspect of an alternative, he or she has eliminated all the potential future decisions along that branch. We can think of the decision as a binary in which once a zero is scored, the alternative on which the zero was scored is eliminated.

Hogarth, of The Universitat Pompea Fabra of Barcelona, Spain, and her colleague Karelaia, of the Universite de Lausanne of Switzerland (2005), explained that the elimination by aspects decision-making model is highly effective in a range of contexts. They noted that while they cannot claim to know how frequently people's choices involve binary attributes, they contend that the frequency of such attributes is substantial: presence versus absence, sweet versus bitter, and so on.

In order to help students who have ELN learn this evaluation model, we first help them identify the criteria on which their decision is to be made. Because they have difficulty learning inductively, we need to explicitly teach what criteria are appropriate for making a particular decision. Then, we help the students prioritize the criteria or teach them a strategy for prioritizing the criteria themselves. Next, we help students select options upon which to test their criteria. We have them enter the criteria and the options into a rubric matrix and determine whether each option meets each criterion. Each option is eliminated when it fails to meet a criterion. The last option standing is selected.

We have taught students to use this strategy with great success. In our classes, they used the strategy to select the best site for establishing a frontier town given factors such as the availability of water, game, and so forth. They also selected a menu for a picnic given such factors as the temperature and accessibility, and they even explored the ethical issues involved in stem cell research and cloning.

The Evaluation by Elimination by Aspects Matrix is effective because

- ♪ Motivation is increased when what seems like an undoable task is made doable
- ♪ Attention is secured when students are asked to make judgments
- ♪ Frustration is prevented when a difficult task is made achievable
- ♪ Discrimination among alternatives is clarified
- ♪ Organization is assured by the very nature of the strategy

Evaluation by Elimination by Aspects

Compare each alternative on each criterion. List the criteria in order of importance. The first dimension to fail to meet a criterion is eliminated.

	Alternative I **Establish colony at** **Location A**	**Alternative 2** **Establish colony at** **Location B**
Criterion 1 Water is available.	+	+
Criterion 2 Game is available.	+	+
Criterion 3 Land is arable.	–	+
Criterion 4 Weather supports agriculture.		
Criterion 5 Region is safe.		

Decision:

The better location for establishing a colony is Location B. While both locations have water and game, only Location B has arable land. Land must be arable in order to sustain the colony.

⚷ Key 58: Evaluation by Addition Matrix

The strategy that we use for Evaluation by Addition Matrix is a simplified version of Multiattribute Utility Theory (MAUT). Baron (1994) noted that MAUT, like the Evaluation by Elimination Matrix, is predicated upon the motto "Divide and conquer." By this, he meant that the alternative solutions are divided into psychologically independent attributes. MAUT is used by the US Air Force to make decisions, as well as in a range of international public decision-making endeavors such as nuclear emergency management, telecommunications policy-making, and environmental planning.

Whereas in the Evaluation by Elimination Matrix each alternative solution is compared to each criterion in an all-or-nothing approach, in the Evaluation by Addition Matrix, each alternative solution is examined and given a weighted rating. A solution might fail to meet one or more criterion and still be selected because it scored higher than the other alternatives overall.

The most difficult aspect of this strategy is determining how much weight to accord each alternative. Edwards and Newman (1982) identified several procedures for weighting. One of those uses the following steps:

1. List attributes in rank order of importance, from least to most important.

2. Assign the least important attribute a value of 100.

3. The next-least-important attribute is assigned a value relative to the least important attribute (i.e., if the next-least-important attribute is half again as important, it would be weighted 100 + 50, or 150).

4. Each next-least-important attribute is rated relative to the least important.

5. Initial importance weights are calculated by dividing each attribute's weight by the total of all the weights.

We have used Evaluation by Addition on the same kinds of topics that we used the Evaluation by Elimination Matrix, but for our students with ELN, we usually rated the least important attributes as 1, with the most important attributes as 3, and those between as 2.

This strategy tends to engender spirited disagreement and excitement among the students. Everyone gets involved. Specifically, we have used this strategy with current events to decide the best location for a nuclear power plant and a nuclear waste facility, we have used it in literature classes to determine the best solution to a character's problem, and we have used it in government to select the best solution to a civic problem.

Like the Evaluation by Elimination Matrix, students tell us that they use the strategy at home and teach it to their family members. One family used it to decide on a family vacation, another used it to decide how to spend a small but unexpected inheritance, and another used it to decide what breed of dog would best fit their family.

The Evaluation by Addition Matrix is a good strategy for including students with special needs because

- ♪ Motivation is greater when a difficult task is made doable
- ♪ Frustration is prevented when a difficult task is made doable
- ♪ Attention is captured when students are asked to make judgments
- ♪ Discrimination among alternative solutions is clarified
- ♪ Organization is assured by the very nature of the strategy

Here is a classroom example.

Evaluation by Addition

Compare each alternative on each criterion. List the criteria in order of importance with the least important criterion listed first. Give this criterion a weight of 10. Increase the value of each subsequent criterion in comparison to the first criterion. For example, a criterion half again as important would be weighted as 15. After weighting all criteria, score each alternative on each criterion. The alternative with the higher score is the better alternative.

	Alternative I Establish colony at Location A	Alternative 2 Establish colony at Location B
Criterion 1 Game is available. 10	8	10
Criterion 2 Weather supports agriculture. 15	10	12
Criterion 3 Land is arable. 15	15	10
Criterion 4 Region is safe. 20	20	15
Criterion 5 Water is available. 25	25	25
Total	78	72

Decision:

The better location for establishing a colony is Location A. While both locations have water and game, Location A has better land and is safer. Land must be arable in order to sustain the colony, and if people aren't safe, they may not survive.

Key 59: Reasoning by Metaphor and Analogy

Metaphor influences a reader's ability to assimilate new concepts into existing conceptual schema and to accommodate new concepts by creating new conceptual schema for formal thinkers. Metaphors can be used to clarify and elaborate on ideas and to help students move from the concrete and the familiar to the abstract and strange (Flynn, Dagostino, & Carifio, 1995).

In a collaborative interdisciplinary project, Barrell and Oxman (1984) and their colleagues had secondary students explore the meaning of metaphors in everyday language, analyze more formal metaphors from various subject areas, create their own metaphors moving from familiar concepts to more abstract concepts, create metaphors for subject-related concepts, and evaluate the final metaphors in general classroom discussions. From their successful experiment, Barrell and Oxman and their fellow teachers concluded that metaphoric thinking is especially useful in developing critical thinking skills.

Writing in *History and Philosophy of Logic,* Gasser (2000) wrote that "the pervasiveness of figurative language is to be counted among the features that characterize logic and distinguish it from other sciences. This characteristic feature reflects the creativity that is inherent in logic and indeed has been demonstrated to be a necessary part of logic" (p. 227). Worsley (1988) explained that metaphors are effective because they help

students visualize information. For the last two decades, many researchers have agreed that one subject in which metaphors are particularly useful is mathematics, and Burton (1986) especially recommended the use of metaphors in teaching mathematics to students in remedial programs.

Chiu (1994) explored the use of metaphor in mathematics with 12 middle school novice mathematics students and explained that metaphors helped the students understand mathematics for several reasons. First, metaphors intuitively justify mathematical operations. Second, they help students integrate mathematical knowledge into their knowledge structures. Third, metaphors enhance the students' computational environment; and fourth, metaphors assist students' recall. For example, Chiu explained adding a negative and a positive number as combining holes (negative numbers) and marbles (positive numbers). When the number of holes was greater than the number of marbles, empty holes were left (i.e., the number was negative). In a later study, Chiu (2001) found that her participants employed the use of metaphors when they had difficulty solving a problem; she therefore determined that metaphors were scaffolds.

Metaphors and analogies support learning of students with ELN because

- ♪ Comprehension is increased when the abstract is made concrete and the strange is made familiar
- ♪ Analytic reasoning skills are developed as students begin to see that wholes can be analyzed by examining their parts
- ♪ Synthetic thinking skills are developed as students are encouraged to begin thinking about ways they can use metaphors
- ♪ Attention is garnered when information is presented or manipulated in creative ways

12

Improving the Quality of Expository Writing

Writing is a complex process that involves most of the thinking skills and certainly the analysis, synthesis, and evaluation skills. First, our students must acquire knowledge through reading, listening, viewing, or doing; in addition, they must understand well the knowledge they collect. Then, they must analyze that knowledge to determine what is relevant to the paper they are to write. Often, they must also analyze cause and effect, break something down into its parts, or compare and contrast two or more things. Then, they have to synthesize that knowledge. Finally, they must use an evaluation tool to evaluate and edit their written product.

Such a complex task is difficult for most students with learning problems, but the skills a student needs in order to write competently can be taught. The job of teaching them falls to us.

We can only write clearly if we understand clearly, and this is one reason that writing assignments are especially difficult for students who have ELN. But understanding clearly is only one prerequisite for being able to write well. Like narrative writing, expository writing is a synthesis-level skill, and knowing what kinds of data to collect, collecting those data, clearly and completely understanding those data, organizing them, and getting them down on paper can be overwhelming.

Fortunately, however, we can teach our students to be better writers in our content domains. Speaking at a National Center for Learning Disabilities conference, Gersten and Baker (1999) noted that teachers can help students significantly improve their writing through explicit instruction, teacher demonstration, and teacher or peer feedback. Speaking at the same conference, Swanson (1999) reported on a meta-analysis of 58 interventions and demonstrated that strategy instruction and direct instruction were the most effective approaches for teaching students with learning problems how to write well.

The National Institute for Literacy's (2007) *What Content-Area Teachers Should Know About Adolescent Literacy* identifies several research-supported strategies.

- Employing explicit, systematic writing instruction
- Teaching the importance of prewriting
- Providing supportive instruction
- Using rubrics
- Addressing diverse needs

The report explains that GOs are one of the most common types of prewriting strategies. Brainstorming GOs can help students generate thoughts as a first step in the writing process. Other types of GOs can help students take their amorphous plethora of thoughts about a topic and assemble them into a meaningful whole. These GOs can help students understand the connections between the various ideas and can serve as a visual structure to inform and guide their writing.

The Institute (2007) also encourages the use of rubrics. Rubrics clarify the teacher's expectations and provide guidelines for students before they begin to write. Rubrics also provide a checklist that can be used as the writing progresses; they then help students assess their own work and allow peers to also provide useful assessment data. When the teacher uses the rubric to assess students, the rubric makes the feedback much more meaningful than does a simple letter grade: Students know exactly what they need to improve on the next assignment.

Each content area has its own specific genre, so students should be taught genre-specific strategies. The instructional focus varies depending on the discipline. Wong (2000) wrote that for the opinion genre, teachers should focus on students' (1) clarity, (2) organization, and (3) cogency of arguments. For compare and contrast, she recommended that teachers focus students' attention on (1) clarity, (2) aptness of ideas, and (3) organization. Regardless of the genre, she recommended that teachers train students to use the following stages in the writing process: (1) collaborative planning, (2) independent writing, (3) peer and teacher conferencing, (4) independent revision, and (5) touch-up.

The strategies provide explicit instruction that helps students improve their writing in the content areas. The strategies are not only explicit, they also provide the much-needed structure that helps students with learning problems meet their academic goals. The strategies this chapter addresses include the following:

- Key 60: Teach Summarizing
- Key 61: Teach Text Structure
- Key 62: Writing Frames
- Key 63: Rubrics for Writing
- Key 64: Data Retrieval Charts
- Key 65: Adapted Evaluation Matrices
- Key 66: Graphic Organizers for Expository Writing

⌐ Key 60: Teach Summarizing

Inefficient readers tend to focus on the meaning of individual words or one to two sentences at a time (microstructure), rather than processing the global meaning (macrostructure) of a text. Explicit teaching of summary writing may assist readers in attending to the global meaning. Summarization is more than simple recall; summarization demands explicit and coherent expression of the macrostructure, directing the reader-writer's attention to the information that is essential to include. Included information depends upon generalities in order to create a concise representation of the original document (Kintsch, 2002).

Kintsch (1990) investigated the summarization skills of 96 students. Sixth graders, tenth graders, and college students each comprised exactly one third of the group. All participants were native English speakers and most were in the high average range in reading assessments. All students read two sixth-grade-level passages of compare and contrast text about developing countries; Indonesia was compared to Korea, and Peru was compared to Argentina on geography, economy, and culture. While all ages of students produced the same number of macrostructures (topic sentences), the sixth graders did not include second and third level macrostructures. (Second level macrostructures were inferred generalizations about geography, economy, and culture. Third level macrostructures about geography were land, vegetation, etc.) Instead of macrostructures, after the topic sentence, the sixth graders wrote sentences about individual details; in contrast, the older students subsumed groups of details together under generalizations (i.e., macrostructures).

The good news is that we can teach students to summarize using explicit instruction.

Taylor and Frye (1992) investigated the effects of strategy instruction on teaching students to summarize. Their participants were intermediate grade students in a social studies class. The results revealed that strategy instruction was effective in teaching summarization skills; the students in the experimental group outperformed their peers in the control group.

Several researchers have identified similar lists of rules for summarizing. Block and Pressley (2003) listed these rules for summarizing: (1) delete unnecessary details, (2) combine similar ideas, (3) condense the main ideas, and (4) combine the major themes into concise statements. We combine and borrow from Brown and Day (1983) and Block and Pressley (2003) to recommend these rules for use with students with ELN:

- Select a topic sentence
- Invent a topic sentence if necessary
- Delete all examples and unimportant details
- Delete repetitive material
- Substitute a superordinate concept for a group of items or actions
- Condense main ideas
- Combine similar main ideas

Explicitly teaching summarizing is a key to unlocking the doors to production because

- Discrimination is supported as students are taught to recognize important and unimportant information
- Reasoning is supported when students are taught to condense and combine ideas

🎵 Metacognition is developed when students are taught to think about their thinking

🎵 Frustration is reduced when students can use summarization for note taking

🎵 Motivation is increased when explicit instruction helps students know exactly what to do

🎵 Production is increased when students see that they are making progress

---

Rules for Summarizing

1. Select a topic sentence

2. Invent a topic sentence if necessary

3. Delete all examples and unimportant details

4. Delete repetitive material

5. Substitute a superordinate concept for a group of items or actions

6. Condense main ideas

7. Combine similar main ideas

Commercial Fishing

~~Commercial fishermen throughout the world harvest many types of sea creatures: tuna, cod, salmon, shrimp, krill, lobster, clams, squid, and crab. They capture these creatures for commercial profit,~~ ~~mostly~~ from wild fisheries. The commercial fishing industry provides ~~a~~ ~~large quantity of~~ food ~~to people around the world, from the Asia to the United States and everywhere between.~~

~~Commercial fishing~~ methods vary according to ~~the~~ region, ~~the~~ type of fish ~~being hunted~~, and ~~the~~ technology ~~that the fishermen have~~ available ~~to them. The methods vary from a single person with a small boat and a dozen pots or a few hand-cast nets to an enormous fleet of trawlers that employ hundreds of fishermen and bring in tons of fish each day~~.

Summary of Commercial Fishing

The commercial fishing industry provides food from wild fisheries. Methods vary according to region, type of fish, and technology available.

⚷ Key 61: Teach Text Structure

Wong (2000) wrote that students with ELN appear not to have any notion of the structure of a paragraph. They do not realize that a paragraph consists of a main idea and sentences that support that idea. In addition, they do not appear cognizant of the fact that they need to organize the sentences within a paragraph logically when they write. They consistently have difficulty with organization in their writing.

We know that teaching text structure not only helps students improve their reading comprehension and note-taking ability, it also helps students who have ELN learn to write in our various disciplines. Our disciplines seek truth in different ways, and they express the truth they find in different writing styles (Wong, 2000). Teachers of basic English composition classes teach students to write in a variety of genres, but they cannot be expected to teach students to write in the lexicon and style of every discipline. Colomb (1988) noted the following:

> A mistake is made when writing is taught as though what students learn in one discipline (usually English) can simply be carried forward unchanged to any number of different writing situations and tasks . . . grammar changes from discipline to discipline. These variations occur at every level of text structure, from syntax through global discourse structure, and they occur in ways that are miscellaneous and unpredictable. The dominant grammatical feature of student-produced texts is that these texts make points, but where and how points can be made, and even what counts as a point worth making, changes from discipline to discipline. (p. 1)

Because students with learning problems have difficulty both ascertaining text structure in their reading and using it in their writing (Englert & Thomas, 1987), they, even more than their peers, need instruction on identifying and using text structure in their writing. Our small time investment in teaching them to do so can help them become more competent writers in various subject matter areas.

Kirkpatrick and Klein (2009) investigated the effectiveness of teaching compare and contrast text structure to improve writing skills. Their participants were 83 seventh- and eighth-grade students. The researchers required students to memorize and use a table to structure their reports. The intervention produced a large effect size: The students in the experimental group far outpaced their peers in the control group in the holistic and structural quality of their reports.

Teaching text structure is both explicit and structured, so it uses two of the critical keys to successful special education. The key helps students improve their writing and is an excellent strategy because

- ⚷ Production is increased when an assignment is seen as achievable
- ⚷ Confusion is avoided when students have a pattern to follow
- ⚷ Frustration is avoided when confusion is circumnavigated
- ⚷ Organization is supported by the pattern structure

We created and posted the following Text Structure Chart on the walls of one of our classrooms. Students used the chart to structure their writing when using the Evaluative Matrices. We think the improvement that resulted from the chart was commendable.

Writing _Compare and_ _Contrast Text_	_Words to Use_
Identify a dimension and tell how each concept is alike and different	In comparison In contrast Unlike, like Different from Similar to As opposed to Whereas, although, yet, however, both, also

⚷ Key 62: Writing Frames

Three professors from the University of Cambridge in England investigated the use of writing frames. Warwick, Stephenson, and Webster (2003) explained that curriculum initiatives in the United Kingdom called for increased emphasis on having students write in a variety of genres for a variety of purposes. They cited Wray and Lewis (1997), who argued that writing frames can scaffold students' understanding of how to write expository text. The researchers explained that oral language is scaffolded by spoken prompts, gestures, references to visible objects, and the common usage of incomplete sentences and informal language. Writing frames are an attempt to provide such scaffolding for the student writer. Writing frames consist of a template of "starters, connectives and sentence modifiers which gives children a structure within which they can concentrate on communicating what they want to say whilst scaffolding them in the use of a particular generic form" (Wray & Lewis, 1997, p. 122, cited in Warwick, Stephenson, & Webster, 2003, p. 174).

Warwick, Stephenson, and Webster (2003) conducted case studies of two boys and two girls from each of three schools in England: a primary, a middle, and a secondary school. Science teachers at each school implemented the study: the elementary generalist who coordinated science in the school, a science specialist at the middle school laboratory, and a science department teacher at the high school laboratory. After participating in science experiments and activities, the students wrote about the experiment using a frame. The experiment the students conducted was to determine the fat content of crisps (potato chips). The high school teacher, who was focused on whether the students could reflect on the accuracy and reliability of their findings, provided this writing frame and scaffolded the students with dialogue as they worked in collaborative groups:

- ♪ I can check the accuracy of my test by . . .
- ♪ There may be some errors in the results I collected because . . .
- ♪ I would like to do this test again, but this time I would . . .
- ♪ My results are accurate and reliable because . . .

The researchers compared the students' oral and written responses. They found high levels of understanding of the concepts of evidence in both the oral and written summaries. The researchers concluded that writing frames are a powerful tool. However, they added this caveat: Writing frames are not to be used as worksheets that a teacher gives out after an introduction and then expects students to complete alone. The frames are dependent upon how the teacher facilitates discussion and collaboration based upon the frame's prompts.

Writing frames scaffold students with ELN as they attempt the writing process because

- ♪ Sequencing of the paper is clarified and supported
- ♪ Confusion is eliminated as the frame is an explicit scaffold
- ♪ Organization is ensured because of the frame's structure
- ♪ Motivation increases as students experience success
- ♪ Persistence/production is increased when students experience success

Writing Frame for Comparing and Contrasting Two Types of X

Experts identify two types of X: A and B.
These two X are similar in some ways and different in others.
First, A and B are alike in that F. For example, A is F and B is F.
Second, A and B are alike in that G. For example, A is G and B is G.

Experts say that A and B are different in several ways.
First, A and B are different in that M. For example, A is M and B is not M.
Second, A and B are different in that Z. For example, A is Z1 and B is Z2.
In summary, A and B are both alike and different. They are (more alike than different or more different than alike) because _____.

Comparing and Contrasting Two Types of Islands

Experts identify two types of islands: continental and oceanic. These two types of islands are similar in some ways and different in others.

First, continental and oceanic islands are alike in that they are completely surrounded by water. For example, both Greenland and Hawaii are completely surrounded by water. Second, continental and oceanic islands are alike in that they are smaller than continents. For example, Greenland and the Galapagos Islands are both smaller than North America and Africa.

Continental and oceanic islands are different in several ways. First, continental islands have the same flora and fauna as their close continents, and oceanic islands have unique species. For example, the blue footed boobie can only be found in the Galapagos Islands.

Second, continental and oceanic islands are different in that they are formed differently. Continental islands are either on the shallow water margin of a continent, so a drop in sea level would make these islands part of the nearby continent, or they are pieces of land that broke away from their nearby continent. In contrast, oceanic islands are the result of volcanic activity.

In summary, continental and oceanic islands are both alike and different. They are more different than alike because continental islands are similar to their continents, and oceanic islands are unique.

⌗ Key 63: Rubrics for Writing

A rubric provides a guide that shows students exactly what they must do in order to do well on an assignment. Andrade (2000) wrote in *Educational Leadership* that rubrics

- ♪ Are teacher-friendly and student-friendly
- ♪ Make teacher expectations explicit
- ♪ Provide constructive feedback to students
- ♪ Support students' learning, skill development, understanding, and thinking

Writing in *Scoring Rubrics Part I: What and When,* Moskal (2000) noted that writing rubrics have been used successfully from kindergarten through college. She also noted that several categories of rubrics exist, beginning with holistic versus analytic rubrics. Writing in *Teaching Exceptional Children,* Schirmer and Bailey (2000) stated that rubrics for writing assignments may be generic or content specific; however, Smagorinsky (2000) and others have argued that every writing assignment should be accompanied by a rubric specific to that assignment because good writing in one context is bad writing in another.

Wong (2000) wrote that a writing-checklist rubric provided to students who have ELN fosters self-regulation as they self-monitor and self-check. She recommended that students tape their checklist to a folder for handy reference. The students could then tape a pocket on the folder to hold their writing computer disk; in that way, the rubric and the disk would always be together.

Sadler and Andrade (2004) affirmed that rubrics help students become self-regulated learners. They argued that while rubrics are good assessment tools, they are more important as teaching tools. They note that good, self-regulated writers love rubrics, but that rubrics are even more valuable to poor writers because they help those writers develop self-regulation.

Duke (2004) investigated the use of rubrics with and without cognitive strategy instruction. His 164 participants were high school students. The results of instruction revealed that cognitive strategy instruction paired with rubrics yielded significant results on self-regulation, the amount of time spent writing, and the number of content revisions made. Duke cautioned against simply handing students a rubric and expecting major changes.

When we used rubrics to guide students' writing for several consecutive assignments and then failed to provide a rubric for a writing assignment, the students complained. They argued that having the rubric reduced their anxiety about our expectations and that they liked being able to ensure that their work would receive a good grade.

Rubrics provide explicitness because of their nature: The criteria are explicitly identified. They also provide structure by their graphic structure.

Rubrics are good inclusionary strategies because

- ♪ Motivation is increased when students understand exactly what to expect and exactly what they must do in order to earn a good grade
- ♪ Attention is elevated when motivation is increased
- ♪ Organization is supported if the rubric includes organizational information

Here is a rubric we used in a class on writing in Current Events.

Rubric for Current Events Term Report

	20 points	*15 points*	*10 points*
1. *Relevance of topic to course*	Timely and important	Within last 10 years and important	More than 10 years old or not important
2. *References used*	5 or more valid references	4 valid references	3 valid references
3. *Perspectives presented*	Multiple perspectives presented	A few perspectives presented	Only 1 perspective presented
4. *Evidence presented*	3 or more kinds of evidence presented for each perspective	2 types of evidence presented for each perspective	1 type of evidence presented
5. *Writing style*	Well-organized with well-developed paragraphs with main idea and supporting details	Organization competent with well-developed paragraphs with main idea and supporting details	Organization difficult to follow; paragraphs include main idea and supporting details

⚷ Key 64: Data Retrieval Charts

The venerable social studies scion Hilda Taba first discussed the Data Retrieval Chart (DRC) over 50 years ago as part of an inductive learning strategy. However, the chart is also a powerful tool for helping students with learning problems to improve their writing skills. We use this strategy when we ask students to learn from multiple sources and synthesize that information into a report. The strategy is good for inclusion because it explicitly identifies the information that the student seeks, and it provides structure in the form of a graphic organizer. The GO not only provides visual structure, it also creates a structure by which the student approaches the problem of data gathering and synthesis.

While a search of the relevant databases yielded no research on Taba's Data Retrieval Chart, Hoffman's (1992) I-Chart (Information Chart) did yield research. Hoffman's I-Chart is essentially Taba's chart with the addition of a column for information that the student already knows. We prefer Taba's chart because the I-Chart allows students to include information that they "already know," and may be spurious, without the responsibility of citing sources.

Viscovich (2002) compared three organizational strategies on the writing abilities of fifth graders. Her participants were 127 students in intact classes; each class was assigned to one of three conditions for writing a research paper. The first group was taught to use an outline; the second group was taught to use a type of graphic organizer; the third group was taught to use an I-Chart, a tool similar to Taba's Data Retrieval Matrix. After six weeks, a team of practitioners evaluated the research papers and determined that, with the exception of mechanics, the I-Chart was more effective at assisting the students in writing their research papers than were either the outline process or the other type of graphic organizer.

To use Taba's DRC, we first have our students construct a matrix. We then help them identify three or four questions to guide their data search. We have the students write these questions in the boxes in the first column. Second, we help the students identify three or four relevant sources. We might include an encyclopedia, a textbook, a nonfiction book, and a reputable Web site. Then, we have the students search each source for the answer to the questions they identified.

We have our students write the information that answers each question in the box at the intersection of the row headed by that question and the column headed by the data source. They can then construct a summary of the information on each row, with that information providing the material for one well-developed paragraph or for several paragraphs in a longer paper. Finally, the students then construct both an introductory and a conclusion paragraph based on what they learned in their search.

The Data Retrieval Chart is a powerful strategy for helping students synthesize material into a written report because

- ♪ Motivation is enhanced when a daunting task becomes manageable
- ♪ Attention is focused when motivation is enhanced
- ♪ Discrimination between essential and nonessential information is supported because the student is looking for the answers to specific questions
- ♪ Organization is provided by the nature of the strategy itself

Here is an example of a Data Retrieval Chart for a report in a science class.

Data Retrieval Matrix for *Plutonium Report*

	Encyclopedia Online	Textbook	Library Book	Website.edu	Summary
What is plutonium?	Transuranium element; traces found naturally, most human made; half-life of 24,360 yrs!	P239 made from bombarding U238 w/neutrons	Dull silver, 2X as heavy as lead		P exists in traces in nature, but most is human made. It is . . .
What is plutonium used for?	Nuclear reactors/weapons/power equipment on the moon "extremely"	Satellites/ nuclear weapons	Power plants/ Long-range space missions/ smoke detectors		
How dangerous is plutonium?		Dose, duration, route, etc. determine danger; in dog experiments, cancer, immune problems, from 1 day exposure	Not very.	1 minute within 1 m of single, glassified waste brick is fatal! Government doesn't want us to know!	
How is waste handled?				Discharged into air, ground, sea, glass bricks to be buried	

⚷ Key 65: Adapted Evaluation Matrices

The 2007 National Assessment of Educational Progress (NAEP) assessment of writing instructed high school seniors to write a persuasive essay on such topics as whether large twentieth-century inventions (such as computers or televisions) or small inventions (such as ballpoint pens or headphones) played a larger role in the student's daily life. The findings were troublesome. Only 5% of the students scored in the *proficient* range on their assessment; only another 21% scored in the *skilled* range. The study found that *three quarters of our graduating seniors can't write well.* Finding ways to improve students' ability to master persuasive writing is critical.

One useful tool is Evaluation by Addition (see Key 59). Evaluation by Addition is based upon Utility Theory, which posits that the best choice is the choice that brings the greatest amount of happiness to the greatest number of people. Evaluation by Addition is used by governments and businesses to make decisions.

Our Adapted Evaluation (by Addition) Matrix helps students improve their ability to justify and defend their decisions, and the tool can assist them in improving their writing about such decisions. We have adapted the tool to make it a more powerful scaffold for students' writing.

Two major types of argumentation are *Aristotelian,* or *adversarial, argumentation* and *Rogerian,* or *consensus, argumentation.* The former seeks to prove the opponent wrong. The latter attempts to see all sides of the argument and come up with a gentle compromise that will satisfy everyone. Our Adapted Evaluation Matrix can be used to advance either type of argument.

Noting that argumentative writing is more cognitively demanding than other types of writing, Crowhurst (1988) argued that such writing can be taught. She further contended that all students, not only older and brighter students, should be taught to write and be expected to write evaluative papers.

Applebee, Langer, Mullis, Latham, and Gentile (1994) assessed samples of writing from 30,000 students in Grades 4, 8, and 12. They found that overall, when provided with enough information about a subject, students wrote acceptable narrative and descriptive papers. However, all groups experienced difficulty in writing assignments that required them to present evidence and create an argument. Little writing instruction was dedicated to the persuasive essay; we think that is because teachers do not know what great tools the Evaluation Matrices are for not only teaching students to evaluate but also for helping them to write good arguments.

We have been consistently pleased with the results we have received when we have taught students to use the Evaluation Matrices to write persuasive essays. Even college students have told us that the strategy has had a powerful effect on their writing skills.

Evaluation Matrices explicitly identify the evidence for an argument, and they structure the evidence both conceptually and graphically. Evaluation Matrices are excellent tools for inclusion because

- Motivation can result when students see a task in manageable steps
- Attention results when motivation is engaged
- Discrimination between essential and nonessential is ensured
- Frustration is diminished when the cognitive load is eased
- Organization is supported by the structure of the tool

♪ Reasoning is strengthened when the invisible is made visible and has a structure imposed upon it

♪ Production problems are assuaged when a difficult task becomes manageable

Included is an example of an Evaluation Matrix that a student used to write an argument.

Adapted Evaluation by Addition for Argumentation

Compare each alternative on each criterion. List the criteria in order of importance with the least important criterion listed first. Give this criterion a weight of 10. Increase the value of each subsequent criterion in comparison to the first criterion. For example, a criterion half again as important would be weighted as 15. After weighting all criteria, score each alternative on each criterion. The alternative with the higher score is the better alternative.

	Alternative I Establish colony at Location A	Alternative 2 Establish colony at Location B
Criterion 1 Game is available. 10	8 Enough deer	10 Deer abundant
Criterion 2 Weather supports agriculture. 15	10 Sunny, some rain	12 Sunny, more rain
Criterion 3 Land is arable. 15	15 Dark rich loam	10 More rocks and clay
Criterion 4 Region is safe. 20	20 No people near	15 Periodic roving bandits
Criterion 5 Water is available. 25	25 Good river	25 Good river
Total	78	72

Decision:

While A and B are both good locations for establishing a colony, A is the better location.

Both locations have excellent, fresh water. A is located on River X, and B is located on River Z. Both have plenty of game; too many deer will affect the crop production, and B has far more deer than A. B has more rain than A, but A's soil is so superior to that of B's that it more than makes up for the slightly less rain. Finally, A is significantly safer than B; A has no people living near, whereas roving bandits periodically travel through B. The bandits would result in loss of goods, and might result in loss of life. Therefore, A is the better choice for locating a colony.

⚷ Key 66: Graphic Organizers for Expository Writing

The Graphic Organizers (GOs) that are guides for helping students learn from expository text are Keys 42 through 47: Main Idea, List, Order, Compare and Contrast, Cause and Effect, and Problem Solution. Not only do these GOs improve students' ability to learn from text, they also provide strong supports for writing.

A number of researchers have found that GOs scaffold students' writing. Cleaves (2008) found that GOs combined with metaphors and analogies increased the writing and reading test scores of fourth-grade students. Nussbaum (2008) investigated the effects of GOs as compared to criteria instruction in the written argumentation skills of college undergraduates. He found that each of the strategies provided unique advantages, activating different argumentation schema.

Sanchez and Perez (2007), of the Universidad de Leon in Spain, investigated the effects of GOs on the writing of Spanish students. His participants were 326 middle and high school students. Their results showed that the graphic organizer condition produced better results in both the process of writing and in the products that they produced.

Troyer (1994) compared the use of GOs to mental modeling on students' comprehension and writing in three expository text structures: attribution, collection, and comparison. The participants were fourth-, fifth-, and sixth-grade students. The participants were randomly assigned to one of the two experimental groups or a control group that read and answered questions about the text. The six-week intervention revealed that the most powerful strategy was the use of GOs, but both mental modeling and GOs were effective in increasing students' writing skill.

Multiple researchers have supported the use of GOs in teaching writing in a variety of disciplines, in a variety of contexts, for a variety of students, and in a variety of genres. For example, researchers have recommended using GOs to teach secondary students with behavioral and learning problems, migrant students, late-arriving immigrant students, middle school Chinese-speaking English language learners, and other English language learners K through 12, to name a few (Alberta Education, 2007; Huang, 2008; Salinas, Fránquiz, & Reidel, 2008; Sundeen, 2007; Vocke, 2007). GOs have been recommended for teaching writing in mathematics, chemistry, history, and geography, as well as other disciplines (Litteral, 1998; McCarthy, 2008; Reagan, 2008; Salinas, Fránquiz, & Reidel, 2008).

In their review of the effects of GOs in the teaching of writing, Lee, Bopry, and Hedberg (2007) found that different GOs serve different purposes in writing. We therefore recommend using the various expository text structure organizers in Chapter 7, Keys 45 through 47, as GOs to guide students' writing.

Using GOs in the various expository genres is a powerful tool to scaffold students with ELN because

- Discrimination between essential and nonessential information is ensured
- Frustration is diminished when the cognitive load is eased
- Organization is supported by the structure of the tool
- Reasoning is strengthened when the invisible is made visible and has a structure imposed upon it
- Production problems are assuaged when a difficult task becomes manageable

Every expository text structure guide should be used to support students' writing in that particular genre. Here is one example.

Cause and Effect Study Guide for

Irish Immigration to America

Early 19th C: dominant industry of Ireland is agriculture. English own land, which is rented to small Irish farmers. Tools and methods are backward.

Terrible poverty. Irish farm laborers earn only 1/5 of what they could make in United States

Poor people start thinking of immigrating to United States. In 1816, some do. They are recruited to build canals for good money. Friends and family back in Ireland hear the good news. More follow.

1845: Irish Famine results from potato blight. Typhus follows. 1 million die. Famine stimulates desire to move to United States for better life. By 1855, 2 million have emigrated to America.

13

Future Keys

Teachers have at their disposal a number of research-supported and teacher-approved strategies that will assist middle school and secondary students with ELN to succeed in general education classes. However, the future holds the potential for many new keys.

We think that many of the future keys will come from the field of technology. For example, they might include the following:

- fMRI–Supported Learning Strategies
- Virtual reality
- Video podcasts
- Videogame-based learning
- Videoconference tutoring

Future Key 1: fMRI-Supported Learning Strategies

fMRI, or *functional magnetic resonance imaging,* studies the blood flow in the brain while a person completes some sort of mental activity. Only in 2000 did fMRI technology reach the stage at which practical applications began to be feasible; before 2000, the education database ERIC indexed only one article using fMRI findings: a study on hearing.

In 2000, however, two articles were indexed: one that described fMRI, and another that examined working memory in children. In 2001, two more articles were added: another that explained how fMRIs works, and one that investigated the brains of adults engaged in an inspection-time task. No articles were added in 2002 or 2003.

However, 2004 brought an explosion of fMRI studies in education-related fields: 24 new fMRI articles were added to the ERIC database. These included studies in such diverse areas as attention, memory, reasoning, and language.

While the use of fMRIs waxed and waned during the next three years (2005: 14 articles; 2006: 32 articles; 2007: 18 articles), 2008 produced exciting results: 41 new articles were catalogued, but that was only the beginning. As of this date, July 22, 2009, 41 new studies have been catalogued in 2009, as many studies in the last six months as in all of 2008. That means that almost one quarter of the 175 articles indexed in ERIC have been indexed in six months before this writing.

Therefore, we posit that the findings of neuroscience will lead to the development of new keys that will assist all students, but especially students with ELN.

Future Key 2: Virtual Reality

We think that virtual reality is a possible future key, and one that holds great promise, but a key that may not come to fruition for another decade or two. An ERIC search of "virtual reality" yielded only 25 results, and some of the results were only tangentially related to virtual reality, such as an article on censorship. The first virtual reality (VR) study was added to the ERIC database in 1990; that study called VR in education an *emerging trend.* Unfortunately, 20 years later we are still waiting for virtual reality to become a reality in schools.

That first report was followed by one or two per year until 1997, when four papers were added—but none of those papers reported the actual use of VR in a classroom. The papers continued to trickle in to ERIC, for a total of 25 by mid-2009. However, not a single paper reported on the actual use of VR in a classroom and its effect on achievement.

The lack of work on VR in education is surprising when one considers the popularity of Second Life and other virtual reality worlds. We anticipate reading exciting research in this field within the next five years.

Future Key 3: Podcasting

Podcasts and video podcasts are evolving at an astonishing rate, and podcasting is an emerging trend in education (Rosell-Aguilar, 2007). Lectures can be recorded as podcasts or video podcasts so students can listen to or watch them multiple times at will. Research shows that students enjoy podcasts and tend to listen to them at home on their PCs instead of while on-the-move with MP3 players. The podcast allows students to listen several times to part of a lecture that they failed to understand the first time (Hew, 2009).

Like VR, podcasting entries in ERIC are surprisingly few: only 49. However, unlike the first VR report, the first podcasting entry was published in 2005. The trend is beginning to catch on: Nine of the reports were added in the first six months of 2009. Some of the additions have been on research, and the research is encouraging.

For example, McKinney, Dyck, and Luber (2009) compared the effectiveness of a podcast with PowerPoint handouts to typical college instruction in an undergraduate psychology class. The students in the podcast condition scored significantly higher on an assessment than did the students in the traditional condition.

We think that video podcasts of secondary teachers' lectures and podcasts created by students in lieu of traditional written products are a key that will develop fully within the next two or three years.

Future Key 4: Videogame-Based Learning

The first ERIC article about videogame-based learning was published in 1979 by the U.S. Army. The next ERIC article was not added until 24 years later. As of this date, a total of 29 articles are indexed, and 12 of those have been indexed since January 2008.

The articles that present research have employed college students, children, and secondary students as their participants. With the exception of one study in which the performance of the videogame group was consistent with that of the control group, every study showed that the use of videogames was a far more effective strategy than the control method.

For example, fourth- and fifth-grade students in Turkey studied geography in a videogame format. They made significant learning gains, demonstrated statistically significant higher intrinsic motivation, decreased focus on earning grades, and increased independence (Tuzun, Yilmaz-Soylu, Karakus, Inal, & Kizilkaya, 2009) as compared to the traditional condition.

Greek high school students used videogames for learning computer memory concepts. The experimental condition was both more effective than the traditional instructional condition and more highly motivating. Girls were as highly motivated as boys in playing the game (Papasterqiou, 2009).

Future Key 5: Videoconference Tutoring

Many districts offer free telephone tutoring in the evenings. These districts pay teachers of various disciplines to be available by phone one or two evenings a week to work with students who call for help with homework. Now, videoconference tutoring can be employed to improve upon the old telephone-tutoring strategy. Students and tutors can view each other's terminals and see each other in real time. The potential for improving students' academic performance through this electronic resource is enormous.

We all know of students who come from homes in which parents work in the evenings, are too exhausted to help with homework, or simply lack the skills to help their students with assignments. Videoconference tutoring can provide students with the extra help they need with homework. The problem will be to ensure that students in lower-income families have access to a computer at home. However, one state has addressed the problem.

In 2000, Maine supplied every seventh- and eighth-grade student with a free laptop computer. State writing scores improved as a result of the technology. As of fall 2009, all of Maine's high school and middle school students will have school-supplied laptops, at a cost of about $242 per computer per year through a four-year lease with Apple. The state sees great advantages beyond those of the classroom. Governor John Baldacci said in his State of the State address, "Every night when students in seventh through twelfth grade bring those computers home, they'll connect the whole family to new opportunities and new resources."

THE LAST WORD

Every public middle school and high school classroom in the world has students with ELN, and the numbers of students with needs seems to be growing daily. Those students will fail without teachers who care deeply about their success. But we have good news: The world is full of smart, dedicated, hardworking middle school and secondary school teachers who want to make a difference in the lives of students with ELN. Research-supported keys can help those teachers unlock the locks on the doors of learning that impede the success of their students with ELN. And more keys are right around the corner: The field of technology is expanding exponentially, and many technological tools have classroom applications.

The keys to the locks are in our pockets. The future is bright.

Appendix

APPENDIX A: MAIN IDEA
TEXT STRUCTURE STUDY GUIDE

Main Idea Reading Guide for

Main Idea

Supporting Detail | Supporting Detail | Supporting Detail

Main Idea

Supporting Detail | Supporting Detail | Supporting Detail

APPENDIX B: LIST TEXT STRUCTURE STUDY GUIDE

List Study Guide on:

Introduction:

1.

2.

3.

4.

5.

6.

7.

8.

APPENDIX C: ORDER TEXT STRUCTURE STUDY GUIDE

Order Study Guide for

Introduction:

First:

Second:

Third:

Fourth:

Fifth:

Sixth:

Seventh:

APPENDIX D: COMPARE AND CONTRAST TEXT STRUCTURE STUDY GUIDE

Compare and Contrast Study Guide for

Introduction:

Summary:

APPENDIX E: CAUSE AND EFFECT TEXT STRUCTURE STUDY GUIDE

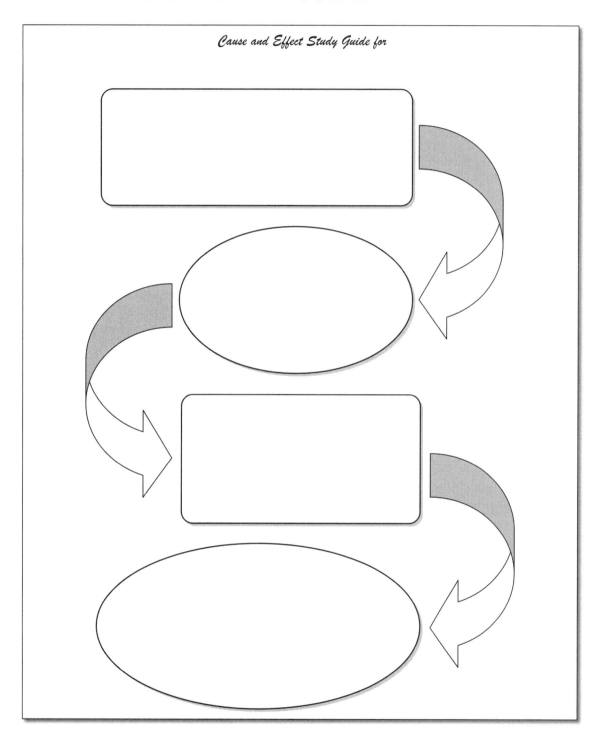

Cause and Effect Study Guide for

APPENDIX F: PROBLEM SOLUTION STUDY GUIDE

Problem Solution Study Guide for

Problem

Rejected Solution

Rejected Solution

Selected Solution

APPENDIX G: ANALOGY STUDY GUIDE

Analogy Study Guide for

	Is Like	

Drawing:

APPENDIX H: FLOWCHART

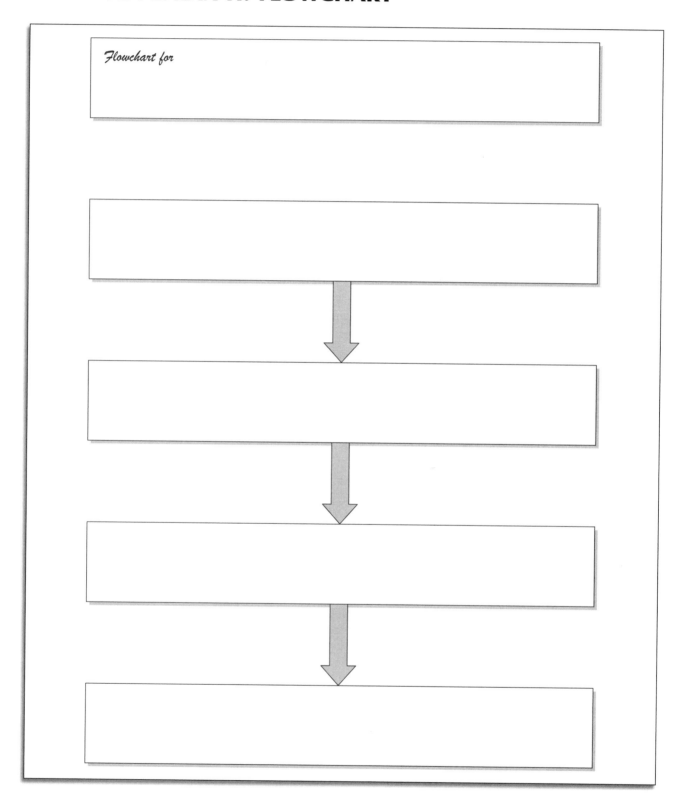

Flowchart for

APPENDIX I: COMPARE AND CONTRAST OF HIGHER-ORDER THINKING QUESTION

Compare and Contrast of Higher-Order Thinking

Question:

Conclusion:

APPENDIX J: EVALUATION BY ELIMINATION BY ASPECTS MATRIX

Evaluation by Elimination by Aspects

Compare each alternative on each criterion. List the criteria in order of importance. The first alternative to fail to meet a criterion is eliminated.

	Alternative I	Alternative 2
Criterion 1		
Criterion 2		
Criterion 3		
Criterion 4		
Criterion 5		

Decision:

APPENDIX K: EVALUATION BY ADDITION MATRIX

Evaluation by Addition

Compare each alternative on each criterion. List the criteria in order of importance with the least important criterion listed first. Give this criterion a weight of 10. Increase the value of each subsequent criterion in comparison to the first criterion. For example, a criterion half again as important would be weighted as 15. After weighting all criteria, score each alternative on each criterion. The alternative with the higher score is the better alternative.

	Alternative I	Alternative 2
Criterion 1		
Criterion 2		
Criterion 3		
Criterion 4		
Criterion 5		
Total		

Decision:

Resources

Abbitt, J., & Ophus, J. (2008). What we know about the impacts of WebQuests: A review of research. *AACE Journal, 16*(4), 441–456.

Abrams, J. C. (1984). Interaction of neurological and emotional factors in learning disability. *Learning Disabilities: An Interdisciplinary Journal, 3*(3), 27–37.

Adams, R. (1971). A sociological approach to classroom research. In J. Westbury & A. Bellack (Eds.), *Research in classroom processes: Recent developments and next steps* (pp. 101–117). New York: Columbia University, Teachers College Bureau of Publications.

Adank, P., Evans, B. G., Stuart-Smith, J., & Scott, S. K. (2009). Familiarity with a regional accent facilitates comprehension of that accent in noise. *Journal of Experimental Psychology: Human Perception and Performance, 35*(2), 520–529.

Adelman, H. S., & Taylor, L. (1983a). Classifying students by inferred motivation to learn. *Learning Disability Quarterly, 6,* 201–206.

Adelman, H. S., & Taylor, L. (1983b). Enhancing motivation for overcoming learning and behavior problems. *Journal of Learning Disabilities, 16,* 384–392.

Adelman, H. S., & Taylor, L. (1990). Intrinsic motivation and school misbehavior: Some intervention implications. *Journal of Learning Disabilities, 23,* 541–550.

Ajayi, L. (2008). Meaning-making, multimodal representation, and transformative pedagogy: An exploration of meaning construction instructional practices in an ESL high school classroom. *Journal of Language, Identity, and Education, 7*(3–4), 206–229.

Alberta Education. (2007). *English as a second language: Guide to implementation. Kindergarten to Grade 9.* Edmonton, Alberta, Canada: Author. (ERIC Document Reproduction Service No.ED502914)

Alexander, A. A., Schallert, D. L., & Hare, C. H. (1991). Coming to terms: How researchers in learning and literacy talk about knowledge. *Review of Educational Research, 61,* 315–343.

Al-Hilawani, Y. A., & Poteet, J. A. (1995). *Cognitive processing in mild disabilities.* (ERIC Document Reproduction Service No. ED383143)

Allsopp, D. H. (1999). Using modeling, manipulatives, and mnemonics with eighth-grade math students. *Teaching Exceptional Children, 32*(2), 74–81.

Alvermann, D. (1981, April). *The compensatory effect of graphic organizer instruction on text structure.* Paper presented at the annual meeting of the American Educational Research Association, Los Angeles, CA. (ERIC Document Reproduction Service No. ED208019)

American Association for the Advancement of Science. (1989). *Science for all Americans.* Retrieved November 21, 2002, from http://www.project2061. org/tools/sfaaol.chap11.htm

Anday-Porter, S., Henne, K., & Horan, S. (2000). *Improving student organizational skills through the use of organizational skills in the curriculum.* Master's Research Project, Saint Xavier University and SkyLight Professional Development. (ERIC Document Reproduction Service No. ED442139)

Anders, P. L., Bos, C. S., & Filip, D. (1984). The effect of semantic feature analysis on the reading comprehension of learning disabled students. *National Reading Conference Yearbook, 33,* pp. 162–166.

Anderson, S., Yilmaz, O., & Washburn-Moses, L. (2004). Middle and high school students with learning disabilities: Practical academic interventions for general education teachers—A review of the literature. *American Secondary Education, 32*(2), 19–38.

Anderson, T. H., & Armbruster, B. B. (1986). *The value of taking notes* (Reading Education Report No. 374). Champaign: University of Illinois at Urbana-Champaign, Center for the Study of Reading. (ERIC Document Reproduction Service No. ED277996)

Andrade, H. G. (2000). Using rubrics to promote thinking and learning. *Educational Leadership, 57*(5), 13–18.

Annis, L. F., & Annis, D. B. (1987, April). Does *practice make perfect? The effects of repetition on student learning.* Paper presented at the annual meeting of the American Educational Research Association, Washington, DC. (ERIC Document Reproduction Service No. ED281861)

Applebee, A. N., Langer, J. A., Mullis, I. V. S., Latham, A. S., & Gentile, C. A. (1994). *NAEP 1992 writing report card.* Washington, DC: U.S. Department of Education, Office of Educational Research and Improvement, National Center for Education Statistics. (ERIC Document Reproduction Service No. ED370119)

Armbruster, B. B., & Anderson, T. H. (1988). On selecting "considerate" content area textbooks. *Remedial and Special Education, 9,* 47–52.

Armbruster, B. B., Anderson, T., & Ostertag, J. (1986). *Does text structure/summarization instruction facilitate learning from expository text?* (Technical report No. 394). (ERIC Document Reproduction Service No. ED281185)

Arons, A. B. (1984). Student patterns of thinking and reasoning: Part two of three parts. *Physics Teacher, 22,* 21–26.

Asher, J. (1981). *Learning another language through actions: The complete teacher's guidebook.* Los Gatos, CA: Sky Oaks. (ERIC Document Reproduction Service No. ED191314)

Asher, J. J. (1969). The total physical response technique of learning. *Journal of Special Education, 3*(3), 253–262.

Asher, J. J. (1977). Children learning another language: A developmental hypothesis. *Child Development, 48,*1040–1048.

Atkinson, R. C. (1975). Mnemotechnics in second language learning. *American Psychologist, 30,* 821–828.

Ausubel, D. P. (1963). Cognitive structure and the facilitation of meaningful verbal learning. *Journal of Teacher Education, 14,* 217–222.

Ausubel, D. P. (1968). *Educational psychology: A cognitive view.* New York: Holt, Rinehart & Winston.

Ayres, R., Cooley, E., & Dunn, C. (1990). Self-concept, attribution, and persistence in learning-disabled students [Abstract]. *Journal of School Psychology, 28*(2), 153–163.

Baba, K. (2007). Dimensions of lexical proficiency in writing summaries for an English as a foreign language test. *Dissertation Abstracts International Section A: Humanities and Social Sciences, 68*(6-A), 2288.

Balajthy, E., & Weisberg, R. (1988, December). *Effects of transfer to real-world subject area materials from training in graphic organizers and summarizing on developmental college readers' comprehension of the compare/contrast text structure in science expository text.* Paper presented at the 38th annual meeting of the National Reading Conference, Tucson, AZ. (ERIC Document Reproduction Service No. ED300771)

Baldwin, J. D., & Baldwin, J. I. (1999). The value of everyday examples in the teaching of learning: A comment prompted by Machado and Silva (1998). *Journal of the Experimental Analysis of Behavior, 72*(2), 269–272.

Banai, K., Nicol, T., Zecker, S. G., & Kraus, N. (2005). Brainstem timing: Implications for cortical processing and literacy. *Journal of Neuroscience, 25*(43), 9850–9857. Retrieved from Academic Search Complete database. (AN 18748227)

Barbetta, P. M., Heron, T. E., & Heward, W. L. (1993). Effects of active student response during error correction on the acquisition, maintenance, and generalization of sight words by students with developmental disabilities. *Journal of Applied Behavior Analysis, 26,* 111–119.

Barkin, B., Gardner, E., Kass, L., & Polo, M. (1981). *Activities, ideas, definition, strategies (AIDS). Learning disabilities: A book of resources for the classroom teacher.* New Rochelle, NY: City School District of New Rochelle. (ERIC Document Reproduction Service No. ED214358)

Baron, J. (1994). *Thinking and deciding* (2nd ed.). Cambridge, England: Cambridge University.

Barrell, J., & Oxman, W. G. (1984, April). *"Hi heels and walking shadows": Metaphoric thinking in schools.* Paper presented at the annual meeting of the American Educational Research Association, New Orleans, LA.

Barsch, R. H., & Bryant, N. D. (1966, April). *Symposium on the education of children with learning disabilities.* New Brunswick, NJ: Rutgers State University. (ERIC Document Reproduction Service No. ED014176)

Barton, M. L. (1997). Addressing the literacy crisis: Teaching reading in the content areas. *NASSP Bulletin, 81*(587), 22–30.

Batts, G. R. (1999). Learning about color subtraction by role-play. *School Science Review, 80*(292), 99–100.

Bean, T. W., Searles, D., Singer, H., & Cowen, S. (1990). Learning concepts from biology text through pictorial analogies and an analogical study guide. *Journal of Educational Research, 83*(4), 233–237.

Bean, T. W., Singer, H., & Cowen, S. (1985). Analogical study guides: Improving comprehension in science. *Journal of Reading, 29,* 246–250.

Beck, I. L., & McKeown, M. (1991). Conditions of vocabulary acquisition. In R. Barr, M. L. Kamil, P. B. Mosenthal, & D. P. Pearson (Eds.), *Handbook of reading research* (Vol. 2, pp. 789–814). Mahwah, NJ: Erlbaum.

Beck, I. L., McKeown, M. G., & Gromoll, E. W. (1989). Learning from social studies texts. *Cognition and Instruction, 6,* 99–158.

Beck, I. L., McKeown, M. G., & Kucan, L. (2002). *Bringing words to life: Robust vocabulary instruction.* New York: Guilford Press.

Becker, L., & Morrison, G. (1978). *The effects of levels of organization on clustering and recall in normal, learning disabled, and educable mentally retarded children. Final Report.* (ERIC Document Reproduction Service No. ED1 80147)

Beckman, K. R. (1968, January). *Characteristics of the child with learning disabilities.* Paper presented at the workshop on Learning Disabilities—Identification and Remediation, Chicago, IL. (ERIC Document Reproduction Service No. ED060578)

Belfiore, P. J., Skinner, C. H., & Ferkis, M. A. (1995). Effects of response and trial repetition on sight-word training for students with learning disabilities. *Journal of Applied Behavior Analysis, 28*(3), 347–348.

Bellgrove, M. A., & Mattingley, J. B. (2008). Molecular genetics of attention. *Annals of the New York Academy of Sciences, 1129,* 200–212. Retrieved July 1, 2009, from Academic Search Premier database. (AN 32659556)

Bergert, S. (2000). *The warning signs of learning disabilities* (ERIC Digest E603). (ERIC Document Reproduction Service No. ED449633)

Billingsley, B. S., & Wildman, T. M. (1988). The effects of prereading activities on the comprehension monitoring of learning disabled adolescents. *Learning Disabilities Research, 4,* 36–44.

Birnbaum, B. W. (1989). *Increasing organizational skills and homework productivity with ninth grade emotionally handicapped and regular students.* Ed.D. Practicum, Nova University, Fort Lauderdale, FL. (ERIC Document Reproduction Service No. ED321428)

Blabock, J. W. (1982). Persistent auditory language deficits in adults with learning disabilities. *Journal of Learning Disabilities, 15,* 604–609.

Blake, C. R. L., & Garner, P. (2000, April). *"We may give advice but we can never prompt behavior": Lessons from Britain in teaching students whose behavior causes concern.* Paper presented at the annual meeting of the American Educational Research Association, New Orleans, LA. (ERIC Document Reproduction Service No. ED442209)

Blankenship, T. (1982). Is anyone listening? *Science Teacher, 49*(9), 40–41.

Bligh, D. (2000). *What's the use of lectures?* San Francisco: Jossey-Bass.

Block, C. C., & Pressley, M. (2003). Best practices in comprehension instruction. In L. M. Morrow, L. B. Gambrell, & M. Pressley (Eds.), *Best practices in literacy instruction* (2nd ed., pp. 111–126). New York: Guilford Press.

Bloom, B. S. (Ed.). (1956). *Taxonomy of educational objectives: The classification of educational goals. Handbook 1: Cognitive domain.* New York: McKay.

Blosser, P. E. (1988). *Teaching problem solving—secondary school science* (ERIC/SMEAC Science Education Digest No. 2). (ERIC Document Reproduction Service No. ED309049)

Boden, C., & Brodeur, D. A. (1999). Visual processing of verbal and nonverbal stimuli in adolescents with reading disabilities. *Journal of Learning Disabilities, 32,* 58–71.

Boling, C. J., & Evans, W. H. (2008). Reading success in the secondary classroom. *Preventing School Failure, 52* (2), 59–66.

Bos, C. S., Anders, P. L., Filip, D., & Jaffe, L. E. (1989). The effects of an interactive instructional strategy for enhancing reading comprehension and content area learning for students with learning disabilities. *Journal of Learning Disabilities, 22*(6), 384–390.

Bos, C. S., & Vaughn, S. (1994). *Strategies for teaching students with learning and behavior problems.* Boston: Allyn & Bacon.

Boudah, D. J., & Weiss, M. P. (2002). *Learning disabilities overview: Update 2002* (ERIC Digest E624). (ERIC Document Reproduction Service No. ED462808)

Bowman, L. A., Carpenter, J., & Paone, R. A. (1998). *Using graphic organizers, cooperative learning groups, and higher order thinking skills to improve reading comprehension.* Master's Action Research Project, Saint Xavier University. (ERIC Document Reproduction Service No. ED420842)

Boyle, E. A., Rosenberg, M. S., Connelly, V. J., Brinckerhoff, L. C., & Banerjee, M. (2003). Effects of audio texts on the acquisition of secondary-level content by students with mild disabilities. *Learning Disability Quarterly, 26*(3), 203–214.

Boyle, J. (1996). Thinking while notetaking: Teaching college students to use notetaking during lectures. In B. G. Grown (Ed.), *Innovative learning strategies: Twelfth yearbook* (pp. 9–18). Newark, DE: International Reading Association.

Boyle, J. R. (2000). The effects of a Venn diagram strategy on the literal, inferential, and relational comprehension of students with mild disabilities. *Learning Disabilities: A Multidisciplinary Journal, 10*(1), 5–13.

Boyle, J. R., & Weishaar, M. (2001). The effects of strategic notetaking on the recall and comprehension of lecture information for high school students with learning disabilities. *Learning Disabilities: Research & Practice, 16*(3), 133–141.

Boyle, J. R., & Yeager, N. (1997). Blueprints for learning: Using cognitive frameworks for understanding. *Teaching Exceptional Children, 29*(4), 26–31.

Brahler, C. J., & Walker, D. (2008). Learning scientific and medical terminology with a mnemonic strategy using an illogical association technique. *Advances in Physiology Education, 32,* 219–224.

Brand, A. G. (1998). *Writing in the majors: A guide for disciplinary faculty.* New York: SUNY College at Brockport. (ERIC Document Reproduction Service No. ED421723)

Brandhorst, A., & Splittgerber, R. (1984, March). *Teaching thinking skills using the concept time.* Paper presented at the National Council for the Social Studies Southeast Regional Conference, New Orleans, LA. (ERIC Document Reproduction Service No. ED247159)

Brenner, M. E., Mayer, R. E., Moseley, B., Brar, T., Duran, R., Reed, B. S., & Webb, D. (1980). Learning by understanding: The role of multiple representations in learning algebra. *American Educational Research Journal, 34*(4), 663–689.

Brigham, F. J. (1993, April). *Places, spaces and memory traces: Showing students with learning disabilities ways to remember locations and events on maps.* Paper presented at the 71st annual conference of the Council for Exceptional Children, San Antonio, TX. (ERIC Document Reproduction Service No. ED357558)

Brigham, F. J., & Scruggs, T. E. (1995). Elaborative maps for enhanced learning of historical information: Uniting spatial, verbal, and imaginal information. *Journal of Special Education, 28*(4), 440–460. Retrieved January 4, 2003, from Academic Search Premier database.

Brigham, F. J., & Snyder, J. (1986). *Developing application-oriented examples in language arts for students with mild handicaps.* (ERIC Document Reproduction Service No. ED 278184)

Brittain, M. M. (1981). *Teacher awareness of cognitive complexities in social studies materials.* Paper presented at the annual meeting of the College Reading Association, Louisville, KY. (ERIC Document Reproduction Service No. ED 211930)

Brock, H. B., & Kowitz, G. T. (1980, October). *Learned helplessness in exceptional children.* Paper presented at the annual conference of the Rocky Mountain Educational Research Association, Holy Cross, NM. (ERIC Document Reproduction Service No. ED060578)

Brophy, J. (1988). Research linking teacher behavior to student achievement: Potential implications for instruction of Chapter 1 students. *Educational Psychologist, 23*, 235–286.

Brown, A. I. (1975). The development of memory: Knowing, knowing about knowing, and knowing how to know. In W. H. Reece (Ed.), *Advances in child development and behavior* (Vol. 10, pp. 103–152). New York: Academic Press.

Brown, A. I. (1978). Knowing when, where, and how to remember: A problem of metacognition. In R. Glaser (Ed.), *Advances in instructional psychology.* Hillsdale, NJ: Erlbaum.

Brown, A. I. (1979). Metacognitive development and reading. In R. J. Spiro, B. Bruce, & W. R. Brewer (Eds.), *Theoretical issues in reading comprehension.* Hillsdale, NJ: Erlbaum.

Brown, A. L., & Barclay, C. R. (1976). The effects of training specific mnemonics on the metamnemonic efficacy of retarded children. *Child Development, 47*, 71–80.

Brown, A. L., & Day, J. D. (1983). Macrorules for summarizing texts: The development of expertise. *Journal of Verbal Learning and Verbal Behavior, 22*, 1–14.

Brown, A. L., & Palincsar, A. S. (1982). Inducing strategic learning from texts by means of informed self-control training. *Topics in Learning and Learning Disabilities, 2*, 1–17.

Brown, G. A., & Bakhtar, M. (1987). Styles of lecturing: A study and its implications. *Research Papers in Education, 3*, 131–153.

Brown, G., & Manogue, M. (2001). AMEE medical education guide 22: Refreshing lecturing: A guide for lecturers. *Medical Teacher, 23*(3), 231–244.

Brown, S. A., Dunne, J. D., & Cooper, J. O. (1996). Immediate retelling's effect on student retention. *Education & Treatment of Children, 19*(4), 387–407.

Brown-Chidsey, R., & Boscardin, M. L. (1999). *Computers as accessibility tools for students with and without learning disabilities.* (ERIC Document Reproduction Service No. ED433671)

Brozo, W. G., & Simpson, M. L. (2007). *Content literacy for today's adolescents: Honoring diversity and building competence.* Upper Saddle River, NJ: Merrill/Prentice Hall.

Brunn, M. (2002). The four-square strategy. *Reading Teacher, 55*(6), 522–525.

Brunye, T. T., Taylor, H. A., & Rapp, D. N. (2008). Repetition and dual coding in procedural multimedia presentations. *Applied Cognitive Psychology, 22*(7), 877–895. Retrieved June 28, 2009, from Academic Search Complete database. (AN 34962191)

Bryant, D. P., Goodwin, M., Bryant, B. R., & Higgins, K. (2003). Vocabulary instruction for students with learning disabilities: A review of the research. *Learning Disability Quarterly, 26*(2), 117–128.

Buchholz, J., & Davies, A. A. (2008). Adults with dyslexia demonstrate attentional orienting deficits. *Dyslexia, 14*(4). 247–270. Retrieved January 1, 2009, from Academic Search Complete database. (AN 34978129)

Buehl, D. (2001). *Classroom strategies for interactive learning* (2nd ed.). Newark, DE: International Reading Association.

Bull, B. L., & Wittrock, M. C. (1973). Imagery in the learning of verbal definitions. *British Journal of Educational Psychology, 43*, 289–293.

Bull, K. S., Montgomery, D., Hyle, A., & Salyer, K. (1991, March). Administrator's perceptions of special education dropouts: A comparison of priorities by school location. In M. H. Lee (Ed.), *Reaching our potential: Rural education in the 90s. Conference Proceedings* (pp. 1–12). Nashville, TN: Rural Education Symposium. (ERIC Document Reproduction Service No. ED342550)

Bullock, J. O. (1994). Literacy in the language of mathematics. *American Mathematical Monthly, 101,* 735–743.

Burton, G. M. (1986). Using neurolinguistic programming: Some suggestions for the remedial teacher. *Focus on Learning Problems in Mathematics, 8*(2), 41–49.

Byrne, E. X. (1981). Acquisition of physics principles. *Physics Teacher, 19*(2), 122–123.

Cade, T., & Gunter, P. L. (2002). Teaching students with severe emotional or behavioral disorders to use a musical mnemonic technique to solve basic division calculations. *Behavioral Disorders, 27*(3), 208–214.

Cahnmann, M. (2000). Rhythm and resource: Repetition as a linguistic style in an urban elementary classroom. *Working Papers in Educational Linguistics, 16,* 39–52. (ERIC Document Reproduction Service No. ED446431)

Cajete, G. A. (1999). *Igniting the sparkle: An indigenous science education model.* Skyland, NC: Kivaki.

Calfee, R., & Chambliss, M. (1988). Beyond decoding: Pictures of expository prose. *Annals of Dyslexia, 38,* 243–257.

Calhoun, M. L., & Beattie, J. (1987). School competence needs of mildly handicapped adolescents. *Adolescence, 22,* 555–563.

Canino, F. J. (1981). Learned-helplessness theory: Implications for research in learning disabilities. *Journal of Special Education, 15,* 471–484.

Capretz, K., Ricker, B., & Sasak, A. (2003). *Improving organizational skills through the use of graphic organizers.* (ERIC Document Reproduction Service No. ED473056)

Carlisle, J. (1993). Selecting approaches to vocabulary instruction for the reading disabled. *Learning Disabilities Research & Practice, 8,* 97–105.

Carney, J. J., Anderson, D., Blackburn, C., & Blessing, D. (1984). Preteaching vocabulary and the comprehension of social studies materials by elementary school children. *Social Education, 48,*195–196.

Carnine, D. (1994). The big accommodation program. *Educational Leadership, 51*(6), 87.

Carnine, D. W. (1994). Introduction to the mini-series: Educational tools for diverse learners. *School Psychology Review, 23,* 341–350.

Carr, E., & Wixson, K. K. (1986). Guidelines for evaluating vocabulary instruction. *Journal of Reading, 29,* 588–595.

Carrier, C. (1983). Notetaking research. *Journal of Instructional Development, 6*(3), 19–26.

Carrier, C. A., Williams, M. D., & Dalgaard, B. R. (1988). College students' perceptions of notetaking and their relationship to selected learner characteristics and course achievement. *Research in Higher Education, 28,* 223–239.

Carroll, J. B. (Ed.). (1956). *Language, thought, and reality: Selected writings of Benjamin Lee Whorf.* New York: Technology Press of Massachusetts Institute of Technology, John Wiley.

Cass, M., Cates, D., Jackson, C. W., & Smith, M. (2002, March). Facilitating adolescents with disabilities understanding of area and perimeter concepts via manipulative instruction. In *No Child Left Behind: The vital role of rural schools.* 22nd annual national conference proceedings of the American Council on Rural Special Education, Reno, NV. (ERIC Document Reproduction Service No. ED463113)

Catley, K. M., & Novick, L. R. (2008). Seeing the wood for the trees: An analysis of evolutionary diagrams in biology textbooks. *BioScience, 58,* 976–987.

Catrambone, R. (1988). *Specific versus general procedures in instructions.* Unpublished doctoral dissertation, The University of Michigan.

Chalfant, J. C., & Scheffelin, M. A. (1969). *Central processing dysfunctions in children: A review of research.* (ERIC Document Reproduction Service No. ED040546)

Chall, J. S. (1987). Two vocabularies for reading: Recognition and meaning. In M. G. McKeown & M. E. Curtis (Eds.), *The nature of vocabulary acquisition* (pp. 7–17). Hillsdale, NJ: Erlbaum.

Chalmers, L. (1995). Mediating content area learning through the use of flip-flop study guides. *LD Forum, 20*(4), 37–38.

Chambliss, M., Richardson, W., Torney-Purta, J., & Wildenfeld, B. (2007). Improving textbooks as a way to foster civic understanding and engagement. CIRCLE Working Paper 54. College Park, MD: Center for Information and Research on Civic Learning and Engagement. (ERIC Document Reproduction No. ED497604)

Chang, K.-E., Sung, Y.-T., & Chen, I.-D. (2002). Effect of concept mapping to enhance text comprehension and summarization. *Journal of Experimental Education, 71*(1), 5–26.

ChanLin, L.-J., & Chan, K.-C. (1996, February). *Computer graphics and metaphorical elaboration for learning science concepts.* Paper presented at the annual meeting of the Association for Educational Communication and Technology, Indianapolis, IN. (ERIC Document Reproduction Service No. ED392390)

Chard, D. J., & Kame' enui, E. J. (1995). Mathematics instruction for students with diverse learning needs: Heeding the message of the Cheshire Cat. *Focus on Learning Problems in Mathematics, 17*(2), 24–38.

Charuhas, M. S. (1983). *A curriculum for logical thinking. NAAESC Occasional Papers, Volume 1, Number 4.* (ERIC Document Reproduction Service No. ED256908)

Chazin, S., & Neuschatz, J. S. (1990). Using a mnemonic to aid in the recall of unfamiliar information. *Perceptual and Motor Skills, 71*(3), 1067–1071.

Cherkes-Julkowski, M., & Stolzenberg, J. (1991, October). *Reading comprehension, extended processing and attention dysfunction.* Paper presented at the meeting of the National Council on Learning Disabilities, Minneapolis, MN. (ERIC Document Reproduction Service No. ED340194)

Chiu, M. M. (1994, April). *Metaphorical reasoning in mathematics: Experts and novices solving negative number problems.* Paper presented at the annual meeting of the American Educational Research Association, New Orleans, LA. (ERIC Document Reproduction Service No. ED374988)

Chiu, M. M. (2001). Using metaphors to understand and solve arithmetic problems: Novices and experts working with negative numbers. *Mathematical Thinking & Learning, 3* (2-3), 93–124. Retrieved July 5, 2009, from Academic Search Complete database. (AN 5707049)

Chiu, M. M., Chow, B. W-Y., & Mcbride-Chang, C. (2007). Universals and specifics in learning strategies: Explaining adolescent mathematics, science, and reading achievement across 34 countries. *Learning & Individual Differences, 17*(4), 344–365.

Christidou, V., Koulaidis, V., & Christidis, T. (1997). Children's use of metaphors in relation to their mental models: The case of the ozone layer and its depletion. *Research in Science Education, 27,* 541–552.

Chuang, T.-Y., & Chen, W.-F. (2009). Effect of computer-based video games on children: An experimental study. *Educational Technology & Society, 12*(2), 1–10. (ERIC Document Reproduction Service No. EJ836287)

Chyczij, M. A. (1993). Self-report measures of perceived difficulty and strategies used in dichotic listening. *Canadian Journal of Special Education, 9,*160–170.

Ciardiello, A. V. (1998). Did you ask a good question today? Alternative cognitive and metacognitive strategies. *Journal of Adolescent & Adult Literacy, 42*(3). Retrieved December 19, 2002, from Academic Search Premier database.

Ciardiello, A. V. (2002). Helping adolescents understand cause/effect text structure in social studies. *Social Studies, 93*(1). Retrieved January 14, 2003, from Academic Search Premier database.

Cízková, V., & Ctrnáctová, H. (2003). Development of logical thinking in science subjects teaching. *Journal of Baltic Science Education, 4,* 12–20. Retrieved from Academic Search Complete database. (AN 11418806)

Clark, J. M., & Paivio, A. (1991). Dual coding theory and education. *Educational Psychology Review, 3*(3), 149–210.

Cleaves, G. R. (2008). The effects of using metaphors, analogies, and graphic organizers in vocabulary development and comprehension on fourth-grade students' reading and writing scores. *Dissertation Abstracts International Section A: Humanities and Social Sciences, 68*(11-A), 4648.

Cocking, R. R., & Mestre, J. P. (1989). *Cognitive Science.* (ERIC Documentation Service No. ED 307104)

Cohen, L., Spruill, J., & Herns, V. (1982, April). *The relationship between language disorders, learning disabilities, verbal and performance IQ discrepancies and measures of language abilities.* Paper presented at the annual international convention of the Council for Exceptional Children, Houston, TX. (ERIC Document Reproduction Service No. ED223011)

Cohen, M. P., & Carpenter, J. (1980). The effects of nonexamples in geometrical concept acquisition. *International Journal of Mathematical Education in Science and Technology, 11,* 259–263.

Cohen, M. W. (1986). Intrinsic motivation in the special education classroom. *Journal of Learning Disabilities, 19,* 258–261.

Cole, C. L., Gardner, W. I., & Karan, O. C. (1983). *Self-management training of mentally retarded adults with chronic conduct difficulties.* A part of the series in Rehabilitation of the Developmentally Disabled: Issues, Research and Practices. (ERIC Document Reproduction Service No. ED271937)

Cole, M. (1979, April). *Language training for the nonverbal or language delayed child.* Paper presented at the 57th annual international convention of the Council for Exceptional Children, Dallas, TX. (ERIC Document Reproduction Service No. ED171022)

Collea, E. P. (1981). *Intellectual development of college science students.* California State University at Fullerton, Development of Reasoning in Science Project. (ERIC Document Reproduction Service No. ED226620)

Collier, K., Guenther, T., & Veerman, C. (2002). *Developing critical thinking skills through a variety of instructional strategies.* (ERIC Document Reproduction Service No. ED469416)

Colomb, G. G. (1988, March). *Where should students start writing in the disciplines?* Paper presented at the 39th Annual Meeting of the Conference on College Composition and Communication, St. Louis, MO.

Conderman, G., & Bresnahan, V. (2008). Teaching big ideas in diverse middle school classrooms. *Kappa Delta Pi Record, 44*(4), 176–180.

Cook, G. (1994). Repetition and learning by heart: An aspect of intimate discourse, and its implications. *ELT Journal, 48,* 133–141.

Cook, R. E. (1983). Why Jimmy doesn't try. *Academic Therapy, 19,*155–163.

Cooke, B. (1995). *A quality classroom: Quality teaching tools that facilitate student success.* (ERIC Document Reproduction Service No. ED383698)

Cooney, J. B., & Swanson, H. L. (1987). Memory and learning disabilities: An overview. In H. L. Swanson (Ed.), *Advances in learning and behavioral disabilities: Memory and learning disabilities* (pp. 1–40). Greenwich, CT: JAI.

Corson, D. (1983). Social dialect, the semantic barrier, and access to curricular knowledge. *Language in Society, 12*(2), 213–222.

Coull, J. T. (1998). Neural correlates of attention and arousal: Insights from elec-trophysiology, functional neuroimaging and psychopharmacology. *Progress in Neurobiology, 55,* 343–361.

Courson, R. H., & Heward, W. L. (1988). Increasing active student response through the effective use of paraprofessionals. *Pointer, 33,* 27–31.

Coyne, M. D., Kame'enui, E. J., & Simmons, D. C. (2001). Prevention and intervention in beginning reading: Two complex systems. *Learning Disabilities Research & Practice, 16*(2). Retrieved December 24, 2002, from Academic Search Premier database. (AN 34978129)

Craik, F., & Lockhart, R. (1972). Levels of processing: A framework for memory research. *Journal of Verbal Learning and Verbal Behavior, 11,* 671–684.

Crank, J. N., & Bulgren, J. A. (1993). Visual depictions as information organizers for enhancing achievement of students with learning disabilities. *Learning Disabilities Research and Practice, 8,*140–147.

Crowhurst, M. (1988). *Research review: Patterns of development in writing persuasive/argumentative discourse.* (ERIC Document Reproduction Service No. ED299596)

Cruickshank, W. M. (1977). Myths and realities in learning disabilities. *Journal of Learning Disabilities, 10,* 51–58.

Cunningham, J. W., & Moore, D. W. (1993). The contribution of understanding academic vocabulary to answering comprehension questions. *Journal of Reading Behavior, 25,* 171–180.

Curtain, H., & Haas, M. (1995). *Integrating foreign language and content instruction in grades K–8* (ERIC Digest). (ERIC Document Reproduction Service No. ED381018)

Curtis, C. Y. (2008). *Socially mediated vs. contextually driven vocabulary strategies: Which are most effective?* Unpublished doctoral dissertation, University of Oregon.

D'Amico, A., & Passolunghi, M. C. (2009). Naming speed and effortful and automatic inhibition in children with arithmetic learning disabilities. *Learning & Individual Differences, 19*(2), 170–180.

Darch, C., & Eaves, R. (1986). Visual displays to increase comprehension of high school learning disabled students. *Exceptional Children, 20,* 309–318.

David, P., & Pierson, M. M. (1998). Public affairs decision-making in the U.S. Air Force: An application of multiattribute utility theory. *Journalism & Mass Communication Quarterly, 75,* 606–627.

Davis, M. (2005). The effects of selected activities to promote generative processes during notetaking in a standard college lecture. *Dissertation Abstracts International Section A: Humanities and Social Sciences, 55*(7-A), Jan, 1840.

Denison, G. L. (1995). *Storyboarding: A brief description of the process.* Paper presented at the annual international convention of the Council for Exceptional Children, Indianapolis, IN. (ERIC Document Reproduction Service No. ED384171)

Dennis, J. W. (2007). *Middle school students' conceptions of authorship in history texts.* Unpublished doctoral dissertation, The Ohio State University. Available from http://etd.ohiolink.edu

Desberg, P., et al. (1981, September). *The effect of humor on retention of lecture material* [Abstract]. Paper presented at the annual meeting of the American Psychological Association, Montreal, Quebec, Canada. (ERIC Document Reproduction Service No. ED223118)

Dev, P. C. (1998). Intrinsic motivation and the student with learning disabilities. *Journal of Research and Development in Education, 31*(2), 98–108.

DeWispelaere, C., & Kossack, J. (1996). *Improving student higher order thinking skills through the use of graphic organizers.* Master's thesis, Saint Xavier University. (ERIC Document Reproduction Service No. ED400684)

DiCecco, V. M., & Gleason, M. M. (2002). Using graphic organizers to attain relational knowledge from expository text. *Journal of Learning Disabilities, 35*(4). Retrieved December 31, 2002, from Academic Search Premier database.

Dickson, K. L., Miller, M. D., & Devoley, M. S. (2005). The effect of textbook study guides on student performance in introductory psychology. *Teaching of Psychology, 32*(1), 34–39.

DiGennaro, M., & Picciarelli, V. (1992). Incidental science knowledge in fifth grade children. *Research in Science & Technological Education, 10*(1), 117. Retrieved January 1, 2003, from Academic Search Premier database.

DiLella, C. A. (1992, March). *Popcorn story frames.* Paper presented at the 5th Annual Midwest Regional Reading and Study Skills Conference, Kansas City, MO. (ERIC Document Reproduction Service No. ED344184)

DiVesta, F., & Gray, G. S. (1972). Listening and note taking. *Journal of Educational Psychology, 63*(1), 8–14.

DiVesta, F. J., & Smith, D. A. (1979). The pausing principle: Increasing the efficiency of memory for ongoing events. *Contemporary Educational Psychology, 4,* 288–296.

Downing, J. (1970, December). *Specific cognitive factors in the reading process.* Paper presented at the National Reading Conference, St. Petersburg, FL. (ERIC Document Reproduction Service No. ED046639)

Downing, J. A., Bakken, J. P., & Whedon, C. K. (2002). Teaching text structure to improve reading comprehension. *Intervention in School & Clinic, 37*(4). Retrieved December 16, 2002, from Academic Search Premier database.

Dreyer, L. J. (1974, November). *Yes! Individualized instruction for international students is possible in the conventional classroom—It is a formula for holding power.* Paper presented at the 64th annual meeting of the National Council of Teachers of English, New Orleans, LA. (ERIC Document Reproduction Service No. ED101369)

Duffelmeyer, F. A. (1980). The influence of experience-based vocabulary instruction on learning word meanings. *Journal of Reading, 24,* 35–40.

Duffelmeyer, F. A., Baum, D. D., & Merkley, D. J. (1987). Maximizing reader-text confrontation with an extended anticipation guide. *Journal of Reading, 31,*146–150.

Duggan, G. B., & Payne, S. J. (2001). Interleaving reading and acting while following procedural instructions. *Journal of Experimental Psychology: Applied, 7*(4), 297–307.

Duit, R. (1991). On the role of analogies and metaphors in learning science. *Science Education, 75,* 649–672.

Duke, B. L. (2004). The influence of using cognitive strategy instruction through writing rubrics on high school students' writing self-efficacy, achievement goal orientation, perceptions of classroom goal structures, self-regulation, and writing achievement. *Dissertation Abstracts International Section A: Humanities and Social Sciences, 64*(10-A).

Dunston, P. J. (1992). A critique of graphic organizer research. *Reading Research and Instruction, 31*(2), 57–65.

Dye, G. A. (2002). Graphic organizers to the rescue: Helping students link—and remember—information. In K. L. Freiberg, (Ed.), *Annual editions: Educating exceptional children. 2002/2003.* Guilford, NJ: McGraw/Hill-Dushkin.

Dyrli, O. E. (1999). Gil Dyrli's "sweet sixteen" time-tested teaching techniques. *Curriculum Administrator, Part I of II,35*(11), 60. Retrieved April 9, 2009, from Professional Development Collection database. (AN 2514821).

Dyson, B. J. (2008). Assessing small-scale interventions in large-scale teaching: A general methodology and preliminary data. *Active Learning in Higher Education, 9*(3), 265–282.

Eaton, M. D., & Hansen, C. L. (1978). Classroom organization and management. In N. G. Haring, T. C. Lovitt, M. D. Eaton, & C. L. Hansen (Eds.), *The fourth R: Research in the classroom* (pp. 191–217). Upper Saddle River, NJ: Merrill/Prentice Hall.

Ediger, M. (1998). *Grammar revisited in the English curriculum.* (ERIC Document Reproduction Service No. ED421713)

Edwards, W., & Newman, J. R. (1982). *Multiattribute evaluation.* Thousand Oaks, CA: Sage.

Egan, M. (1999). Reflections on effective use of graphic organizers. *Journal of Adolescent & Adult Literacy, 42*(8), 641–645.

Eisenman, G., & Payne, B. D. (1997). Effects of the higher order thinking skills program on at-risk young adolescents' self-concept, reading achievement, and thinking skills. *Research in Middle Level Education Quarterly, 20*(3), 1–25.

Ellis, E. S. (1992). *LINCS: A starter strategy for vocabulary learning.* Lawrence, KS: Edge Enterprises.

Ellis, E. S., & Graves, A. W. (1990). Teaching students with learning disabilities: A paraphrasing strategy to increase comprehension of main ideas. *Rural Special Education Quarterly, 10*(2), 2–10.

Englert, C. S., Mariage, T. V., & Okolo, C. M. (2009). Informational writing across the curriculum. In G. Troia (Ed.), *Writing instruction and assessment for struggling writers: From theory to evidence-based practices* (pp. 132–164). New York: Guilford Press.

Englert, C. S., & Thomas, C. C. (1987). Sensitivity to text structure in reading and writing: A comparison between learning disabled and non-learning disabled students. *Learning Disability Quarterly, 10*(2), 93–105.

Erven, J. L. (1991). *Increasing the social studies performance of middle school special education students using multisensory strategies.* Unpublished master's thesis, Nova University.

Escoe, A. S. (1981). *Schooling and scheming: From research in reading instruction toward information processing.* Paper presented at the annual meeting of the International Reading Association, New Orleans, LA. (ERIC Document Reproduction Service No. ED204735)

Espin, C. A., & Deno, S. L. (1993). Content-specific and general reading disabilities: Identification and educational relevance. *The Journal of Special Education, 27,* 321–337.

Espin, C. A., & Deno, S. L. (2000). Introduction to the special issue of *Learning Disabilities Research & Practice:* Research to practice: Views from researchers and practitioners. *Learning Disabilities Research & Practice, 15*(2), 67–69.

Espin, C. A., & Foegen, A. (1996). Validity of general outcome measures for predicting secondary students' performance on content-area tasks. *Exceptional Children, 62,* 497–514.

Evans, S. W., Pelham, W., & Grudberg, M. V. (1995). The efficacy of notetaking to improve behavior and comprehension of adolescents with attention deficit hyperactivity disorder. *Exceptionality, 5*(1), 1–17.

Faber, J. E., Morris, J. D., & Lieberman, M. G. (2000). The effects of notetaking on ninth grade students' comprehension. *Reading Psychology, 21,* 257–270.

Fahmy, J. J., & Bilton, L. (1990a). *Lecture comprehension and note-taking for L2 students.* Paper presented at the 9th World Congress of Applied Linguistics sponsored by the International Association of Applied Linguistics, Thessaloniki, Greece. (ERIC Document Reproduction Service No. ED323785)

Fahmy, J. J., & Bilton, L. (1990b). Listening and notetaking in higher education. In A. Sarinee (Ed.), *Language teaching methodology for the nineties. Anthology series 24.* (ERIC Document Reproduction Service No. ED366189)

Felton, R. H. (2001). Students with three types of severe reading disabilities: Introduction to the case studies. *Journal of Special Education, 35,*122–124.

Fisher, J. B., Schumaker, J. B., & Deshler, D. D. (1995). Searching for validated inclusive practices: A review of the literature. *Focus on Exceptional Children, 28*(4), 1–20.

Flack, J., & Sullivan, M. (1995). Science-oriented picture books for middle school students. *Teaching Pre K–8, 26*(3), 48. Retrieved July 4, 2009, from Academic Search Complete database. (AN 9510273288)

Flavell, J. H. (1971). What is memory development the development of? *Human Development, 14,* 272–278.

Flavell, J. H. (1979). Metacognitive and cognitive monitoring: A new area of cognitive-developmental inquiry. *American Psychologist, 34,* 906–911.

Flavell, J. H. (1999). Cognitive development: Children's knowledge about the mind. *Annual Review of Psychology, 50,* 21–45.

Fleckenstein, K. S. (1995). Writing and the strategic use of metaphor. *Teaching English in the Two-Year College, 22*(2), 110–115.

Flynn, L. L., Dagostino, L., & Carifio, J. (1995). Learning new concepts independently through metaphor. *Reading Improvement, 32*(4), 200–219.

Flynt, E. S. & Brozo, W. G. (2008) Developing academic language: Got words? *The Reading Teacher* 61:6, 500–502.

Foil, C. R., & Alber, S. R. (2002). Fun and effective ways to build your students' vocabulary. *Intervention in School & Clinic, 37*(3). Retrieved February 1, 2003, from Academic Search Premier database.

Fontana, J. L., Scruggs, T., & Mastropieri, M. A. (2007). Mnemonic strategy instruction in inclusive secondary social studies classes. *Remedial & Special Education, 28*(6), 345–355. Retrieved from Professional Development Collection database. (AN 27616050)

Forness, S. R., Kavale, K. A., Blum, I. A., & Lloyd, J. W. (1997). Mega-analysis of meta-analyses: What works in special education and related services. *Teaching Exceptional Children, 29*(6), 4–9.

Foss, J. M. (2001). *Nonverbal learning disability: How to recognize it and minimize its effects* (ERIC Digest E619). (ERIC Document Reproduction Service No. ED461238)

Fox, J. R., Park, B., & Lang, A. (2007). When available resources become negative resources: The effects of cognitive overload on memory sensitivity and criterion bias. *Communication Research, 34*(3), 277–296.

Frank, G. (1984). *Alleviating auditory figure-ground disability in kindergarten and first-grade children using rehabilitative and nonrehabilitative techniques.* Ed.D. Practicum Report, Nova University, Fort Lauderdale, FL. (ERIC Document Reproduction Service No. ED256096)

Frayer, D. A., Frederick, W. C., & Klausmeier, H. J. (1969). *A schema for testing the level of concept mastery* (Working Paper No. 16). Madison: University of Wisconsin, Wisconsin Research and Development Center for Cognitive Learning.

Freedman, G., & Reynolds, E. G. (1980). Enriching basal reader lessons with semantic webbing. *Reading Teacher, 33,* 677–684.

Frostig, M., & Maslow, P. (1969). Reading, developmental abilities, and the problem of the match. *Journal of Learning Disabilities, 2,* 572–574.

Fulk, B. M., Brigham, F. J., & Lohman, D. A. (1998). Motivation and self-regulation: A comparison of students with learning and behavior problems. *Remedial and Special Education, 19,* 300–309.

Fulk, B. M., & Stormont-Spurgin, M. (1995). Fourteen spelling strategies for students with learning disabilities. *Intervention in School and Clinic, 31*(1), 16–20.

Gagnepain, P., Chételat, G., Landeau, B., Dayan, J., Eustache, F., & Lebreton, K. (2008). Spoken word memory traces within the human auditory cortex revealed by repetition priming and functional Magnetic Resonance Imaging. *Journal of Neuroscience, 28*(20), 5281–5289.

Gajria, M., Jitendra, A. K., Sood, S., & Sacks, G. (2007). Improving comprehension of expository text in students with LD: A research synthesis. *Journal of Learning Disabilities, 40*(3), 210–225. (ERIC Document Reproduction Service No. EJ766677)

Gajria, M., & Salvia, J. (1992). The effects of summarization instruction on text comprehension of students with learning disabilities. *Exceptional Children, 58,* 508–516.

Gallagher, J. J., & Aschner, M. J. (1963). A preliminary report on analyses of classroom interaction. *Merrill-Palmer Quarterly, 9,*183–194.

Ganguly, I. (1995, October). *Scientific thinking is in the mind's eye. Eyes on the future: Converging images, ideas, and instruction.* Selected readings from the 27th annual conference of the International Visual Literacy Association, Chicago, IL. (ERIC Document Reproduction Service No. ED391504)

García, J.-N. & Fidalgo, R. (2008). Orchestration of writing processes and writing products: A comparison of sixth-grade students with and without learning disabilities. *Learning Disabilities—A Contemporary Journal, 6*(2), 77–98.

Garner, R., & Taylor, N. (1982). Monitoring of understanding: An investigation of attentional assistance needs at different grades and reading proficiency levels. *Reading Psychology, 3,* 1–6.

Gasser, J. (2000). Logic and metaphor. *History and Philosophy of Logic, 20,* 227–238.

Gates, R. W. (1970). *An analysis of student outcomes using audiotapes to supplement reading in the Level One Course of the Intermediate Science Curriculum Study.* Doctoral dissertation, University of Iowa. (ERIC Document Reproduction Service No. ED091149)

Gazzaniga, M. (1998). *The mind's past.* Berkeley, CA: University of California Press.

Gellevij, M., Van Der Meij, H., De Jong, T., & Pieters, J. (2002). Multimodal versus unimodal instruction in a complex learning context. *Journal of Experimental Education, 70*(3), 215–240.

Geoffrey B., & Payne, S. J. (2001). Interleaving reading and acting while following procedural instructions. *Journal of Experimental Psychology: Applied, 7*(4), 297–307.

Gersten, R., & Baker, S. (1999). *Teaching expressive writing to students with learning disabilities.* A paper presented at Two Decades of Research in Learning Disabilities: Reading Comprehension, Expressive Writing, Problem-Solving, Self-Concept. Keys to Successful Learning: A National Summit on Research in Learning Disabilities. (ERIC Document Reproduction Service No. ED430365)

Gersten, R., Baker, S., & Edwards, L. (1999). *Teaching expressive writing to students with learning disabilities* (ERIC/OSEP Digest E590). Retrieved February 1, 2003, from http://www.ldonline.org

Gersten, R., Baker, S. K., & Marks, S. U. (1998). Strategies for teaching English-language learners. In K. R. Harris, S. Graham, & D. Deshler (Eds.), *Teaching every child every day: Learning in diverse schools and classrooms* (Advances in teaching and learning series). Cambridge, MA: Brookline Books.

Gfeller, K. E. (1983). The use of melodic-rhythmic mnemonics with learning disabled and normal students as an aid to retention. *Dissertation Abstracts International, 43*(9-A).

Gfeller, K. E. (1986). Musical mnemonics for learning disabled children. *Teaching Exceptional Children, 19*(1), 28–30.

Gijlers, H., Saab, N., Van Joolingen, W. R., De Jong, T., & Van Hout-Wolters, B. H. A. M. (2009). Interaction between tool and talk: How instruction and tools support consensus building in collaborative inquiry-learning environments. *Journal of Computer Assisted Learning, 25*(3), 252–267.

Gilhool, M., Byer, J., Parmer, L., Howe, M., Dana, M., & Cliburn, A. (1996). *A qualitative study: The effect of modeling nonfiction text strategies on third and fourth grade students' nonfiction writing.* Hattiesburg: University of Southern Mississippi. (ERIC Document Reproduction Service No. ED403589)

Gilles, D. C. (1972). *An exploration of perceptual and cognitive processes involved in piano study with implications for learning disabled children.* (ERIC Document Reproduction Service No. ED119435)

Gizer, I. R., Waldman, I. D., Abramowitz, A., Barr, C. L., Yu, F., Wigg, K. G., et al. (2008). Relations between multi-informant assessments of ADHD symptoms, DAT1, and DRD4. *Journal of Abnormal Psychology, 117*(4), 869–880.

Gleason, M. M. (1988). Study skills. *Teaching Exceptional Children, 20*(3), 52–57.

Glen, M. L., & Miller, K. (1977, February). *Inservice diffusion of reading into technical areas.* Paper presented at the annual meeting of the Midwest Regional Conference on English in the Two-Year College, Dayton, OH. (ERIC Document Reproduction Service No. ED141747)

Glynn, S. M. (1996). *Effects of instruction to generate analogies on students' recall of science text. Reading Research Report No. 60.* Washington, DC: Office of Educational Research and Improvement (ED).

Goldberg, R. L., & Zern, D. S. (1982). *Learning styles, learning abilities and learning problems in college: An exploration of learning disabilities in college students. Final Report.* (ERIC Document Reproduction Service No. ED247682)

Goldenberg, E. P., & Kliman, M. (1988). *Metaphors for understanding graphs: What you see is what you see.* (ERIC Document Reproduction Service No. ED303369)

Good, T. L., & Brophy, J. E. (1984). *Looking in classrooms* (3rd ed.). New York: Harper & Row.

Gordon, M. S., Daneman, M., & Schneider, B. A. (2009). Comprehension of speeded discourse by younger and older listeners. *Experimental Aging Research, 35,* 277–296.

Gorlewski, J. (2009). Shouldn't they already know how to read? Comprehension strategies in high school English. *English Journal, 98*(4), 127–132.

Gottesman, R. L. (1994). The adult with learning disabilities: An overview. *Learning Disabilities: A Multidisciplinary Journal, 5,* 1–14.

Graham, S., MacArthur, C., Schwartz, S., & Page-Voth, V. (1992). Improving the compositions of students with learning disabilities using a strategy involving product and process goal setting. *Exceptional Children, 58,* 322–334.

Graves, A., Semmel, M., & Gerber, M. L. (1994). The effects of story prompts on the narrative production of students with and without learning disabilities. *Learning Disability Quarterly, 17,*154–164.

Graves, M. E. (1984). Selecting vocabulary to teach in the intermediate and secondary grades. In J. Flood (Ed.), *Promoting reading comprehension.* Newark, DE: International Reading Association.

Graves, M. E. (1985). *A word is a word . . . Or is it?* New York: Scholastic.

Graves, M. F., & Penn, M. C. (1986). Costs and benefits of various methods of teaching vocabulary. *Journal of Reading, 29,* 596–609.

Gray, A. R., Topping, K. J., & Carcary, W. B. (1998). Individual and group learning of the Highway Code: Comparing board game and traditional methods. *Educational Research, 40*(1), 45–54. Retrieved July 8, 2009, from Academic Search Complete database. (AN 357422)

Gray, T. (2000). *Documents related to Churchill and FDR. The Constitution community: The Great Depression and World War II (1929–1945).* Washington, DC: National Archives and Records Administration. (ERIC Document Reproduction Service No. ED463208)

Greene, G. (1992). Multiplication facts: Memorization made easy. *Intervention in School and Clinic, 27*(3), 150–154.

Greenwood, S. C. (2002). Making words matter: Vocabulary study in the content areas. *Clearing House, 75,* 258–263.

Grobecker, B. (1997). Partitioning and unitizing in children with learning differences [Abstract]. *Learning Disability Quarterly, 20,* 317–337.

Grobecker, B. (1998, April). *The evolution of proportional structures in children with and without learning differences.* Paper presented at the annual meeting of the American Educational Research Association, San Diego, CA. (ERIC Document Reproduction Service No. ED421820)

Grobecker, B. (1999). The evolution of proportional structures in children with and without learning differences [Abstract]. *Learning Disability Quarterly, 22,* 192–211.

Grobecker, B., & Lawrence, R. (2000). Associativity and understanding of the operation of addition in children with learning differences [Abstract]. *Learning Disability Quarterly, 23,* 300–313.

Groot, A. D. d. (1965). *Thought and choice in chess.* The Hague, The Netherlands: Mouton.

Grossen, B., Caros, J., Carnine, D., Davis, B., Deshler, D., Schumaker, J., et al. (2002). OSEP Research Institutes: Bridging research and practice. Big ideas (plus a little effort) produce big results. *Teaching Exceptional Children, 34*(4), 70–73.

Grossen, B. J. (2002). The BIG accommodation model: The direct instruction model for secondary schools. *Journal of Education for Students Placed at Risk, 7,* 241–264.

Guastello, E. F. (2000). Concept mapping effects on science content comprehension of low-achieving inner-city seventh graders. *Remedial & Special Education, 21*(6), 356. Retrieved January 23, 2003, from Academic Search Premier database.

Guha, S. (2000). *Temperate facts in fictitious time.* (ERIC Document Reproduction Service No. ED437290)

Gunn, B. K., & Others (1995). *Emergent literacy: Curricular and instructional implications for diverse learners. Technical Report No. 20.* (ERIC Document Reproduction Service No. ED386867)

Gurlitt, J., & Renkl, A. (2008). Are high-coherent concept maps better for prior knowledge activation? Differential effects of concept mapping tasks on high school vs. university students? *Journal of Computer Assisted Learning, 24*(5), 407–419.

Guyer, B. P., & Sabatino, D. (1989). The effectiveness of a multisensory alphabetic phonetic approach with college students who are learning disabled. *Journal of Learning Disabilities, 22*(7), 430–434.

Guyton, G. (1968, February). *Individual programming for children with learning disabilities as determined by screening, identification, and differential diagnosis.* Paper presented at the Association for Children with Learning Disabilities, Boston, MA. (ERIC Document Reproduction Service No. ED029756)

Hague, S. A. (1989). Awareness of text structure: The question of transfer from L1 to L2. *National Reading Conference Yearbook, 38,* 55–64.

Hahn, A. L., & Garner, R. (1985). Synthesis of research on students' ability to summarize text. *Educational Leadership, 42*(5), 52–55.

Hakerem, G., et al. (1993, April). *The effect of interactive, three-dimensional, high speed simulations on high school science students' conceptions of the molecular structure of water.* Paper presented at the annual meeting of the National Association for Research in Science Teaching, Atlanta, GA. (ERIC Document Reproduction Service No. ED362390)

Hämäläinen, R. P., Lindstedt, M. R. K., & Sinkko, K. (2000). Multiattribute risk analysis in nuclear emergency management. *Risk Analysis: An Official Publication of the Society for Risk Analysis, 20,* 455–469.

Hamburg, D. A., & Takanishi, R. (1989). Preparing for life: The critical transition of adolescence. *American Psychologist, 44,* 825–827.

Hannah, D. C. (2009). Attitudinal study: The interaction of students taking calculus and prerequisite courses while participating in peer tutorials. *Dissertation Abstracts International Section A: Humanities and Social Sciences, 69* (7-A), 2643.

Hardy, B. W., McIntyre, C. W., Brown, A. S., & North, A. J. (1989). Visual and auditory coding confusability in students with and without learning disabilities. *Journal of Learning Disabilities, 22,* 646–651.

Harmon, J. M., Wood, K. D., Hedrick, W. B., Vintinner, J., & Willeford, T. (2009). Interactive word walls: More than just reading the writing on the walls. *Journal of Adolescent & Adult Literacy, 52*(5), 398–408.

Harniss, M. K., Dickson, S. V., Kinder, D., & Hollenbeck, K. L. (2001). Textual problems and instructional solutions: Strategies for enhancing learning from published history textbooks. *Reading & Writing Quarterly, 17*(2), 127–150. Retrieved July 12, 2009, from Academic Search Complete database. (AN 4196998)

Harrington, S. L. (1994). An author's storyboard technique as a prewriting strategy. *Reading Teacher, 48*(3), 283. Retrieved July 9, 2009, from Academic Search Complete database. (AN 9411182305)

Harris, B., Kohlmeier, K., & Kiel, R. D. (1999). *Crime scene investigation.* Englewood, CO: Teacher Ideas Press.

Harris, C., Miller, P., & Mercer, C. D. (1995). Teaching initial multiplication skills to students with disabilities in general education classrooms. *Learning Disabilities Research and Practice, 10,*180–195.

Harris, K. R., & Graham, S. (1992). *Helping young writers master the craft strategy instruction and self-regulation in the writing process.* Cambridge, MA: Brookline Books.

Harste, J. C. (1980, October). *Semantic mapping: A text perspective.* Paper presented at the annual meeting of the Midwestern Educational Research Association, Toledo, OH. (ERIC Document Reproduction Service No. ED195959)

Hartman, K. A., & Stewart, T. C. (2001). It's a wrap: Writing, reading, and art projects for developmental college students. *Research and Teaching in Developmental Education, 18*(1), 79–83.

Hawkey, R. (1998). Have you heard the one about . . . science? *School Science Review, 80*(290), 29–36.

Hawkins, J., & Brady, M. (1994). The effects of independent and peer guided practice during instructional pauses on the academic performance of students with mild handicaps. *Education and Treatment of Children, 17,* 1–28.

Hayes, D. A. (1986, April). *Readers' use of analogic and visual aids for understanding and remembering complex prose.* Paper presented at the 67th annual meeting of the American Educational Research Association, San Francisco, CA. (ERIC Document Reproduction Service No. ED271735)

Hayes, O. C. (2009). *The use of melodic and rhythmic mnemonics to improve memory and recall in elementary students in the content areas.* (ERIC Document Reproduction Service No ED504997)

Hebb, D. (1949). *The organization of behavior.* New York: Wiley.

Heimlich, J. E., & Pittelman, S. D. (1986). *Semantic mapping: Classroom applications (Reading Aids Series, IRA Service Bulletin).* Newark, DE: International Reading Association.

Hemmerich, H., Lim, W., & Neel, A. (1994). *Prime time: Strategies for life-long learning in mathematics and science in the middle and high school grades.* Portsmouth, NH: Heinemann.

Hendricks, K. (1995). Research using higher order thinking skills to improve reading comprehension. *Middle Level Education Quarterly, 20*(3), 1–25.

Hendricks, K., Newman, L., & Stropnik, D. (1995). *Using higher order thinking skills to improve reading comprehension. Action research project.* Chicago, IL: Saint Xavier University. (ERIC Document Reproduction Service No. ED398538)

Hennings, D. G. (2000). Contextually relevant word study: Adolescent vocabulary development across the curriculum. *Journal of Adolescent & Adult Literacy, 44,* 268–279.

Herbel-Eisenmann, B. A. (2002). Using student contributions and multiple representations to develop mathematical language. *Mathematics Teaching in the Middle School, 8*(20). Retrieved May 23, 2003, from Professional Development database.

Herbel-Eisenmann, B. A. (2007). From intended curriculum to written curriculum: Examining the "voice" of a mathematics textbook. *Journal for Research in Mathematics Education, 38*(4), 344–369.

Herber, H. L. (1970). *Teaching reading in the content areas.* Englewood Cliffs, NJ: Prentice Hall.

Hew, K. (2009). Use of audio podcast in K–12 and higher education: A review of research topics and methodologies. *Full Educational Technology Research & Development, 57*(3), 333–357. Retrieved from Academic Search Complete database. (AN 39767997)

Heward, W. L., Gardner, R., III, & Barbetta, P. M. (1996). Everyone participates in this class. *Teaching Exceptional Children, 28*(2), 4.

Higgins, K., & Boone, R. (1990). Hypertext computer study guides and the social studies achievement of students with learning disabilities, remedial students, and regular education students. *Journal of Learning Disabilities, 23*(9), 529–540. Retrieved January 4, 2003, from Academic Search Premier database.

Highsmith, V. (1988). *Remediating handwriting skills for learning disabled students.* (ERIC Document Reproduction Service No. ED299783)

Hirsch, E. D., Jr. (2003). Reading comprehension requires knowledge—of words and the world. *American Educator, 27*(1), 10–13, 16–22, 28–29, 48.

Hisama, T. (1976). Achievement motivation and the locus of control of children with learning disabilities and behavior disorders. *Journal of Learning Disabilities, 9,* 387–392.

Hitchcock, C. (2001). Balanced instructional support and challenge in universally designed learning environments. *Journal of Special Education Technology, 16*(4), 23–30.

Hodges, D. L. (1982). *Findings from cognitive psychology and their applications to teaching.* (ERIC Document Reproduction Service No. ED220154)

Hoffman, J. (1992). Critical reading/thinking across the curriculum: Using I-charts to support learning. *Language Arts, 69*(2), 121–127.

Hogarth, R. M., & Karelaia, N. (2005). Simple models for multiattribute choice with many alternatives: When it does and does not pay to face trade-offs with binary attributes. *Management Science, 51*(12), 1860–1872.

Hollingsworth, M., & Woodward, J. (1993). Integrated learning: Explicit strategies and their role in problem-solving instruction for students with learning disabilities. *Exceptional Children, 59*(5), 444–456.

Holmes, C. T. & Keffer, R. L. (1995). A computerized method to teach Latin and Greek root words: Effect on verbal SAT scores. *Journal of Educational Research, 89* (1), 47–50.

Holt, G. M. (1995). *Teaching low-level adult ESL learners* (ERIC Digest). (ERIC Document Reproduction Service No. ED379965)

Honnert, A. M., & Bozan, S. E. (2005). Summary frames: Language acquisition for special education and English language learners. *Science Activities: Classroom Projects and Curriculum Ideas, 42*(2), 19.

Hood, S. (2008). Summary writing in academic contexts: Implicating meaning in processes of change. *Linguistics and Education: An International Research Journal, 19*(4), 351–365.

Hoone, C. J. (1989). Teaching timelines to fourth, fifth, and sixth graders. *Social Studies and the Young Learner, 2*(2), 13–15.

Horn, L., & Berktold, J. (1999). *Students with disabilities in postsecondary education: A profile of preparation, participation, and outcomes.* Washington DC: National Center for Education Statistics. Retrieved November 24, 2002, from http://nces.ed.gov/pubsearch/index.asp

Horton, S. V., & Lovitt, T. C. (1989). Using study guides with three classifications of secondary students. *Journal of Special Education, 22*(4), 447–462.

Horton, S. V., Lovitt, T. C., & Bergerud, D. (1990). The effectiveness of graphic organizers for three classifications of secondary students in content area classes. *Journal of Learning Disabilities, 23*(1), 12–22. Retrieved January 12, 2003, from Academic Search Premier database.

Horton, S. V., Lovitt, T. C., & Christensen, C. C. (1991). Notetaking from textbooks: Effects of a columnar format on three categories of secondary students. *Exceptionality, 2*, 19–40.

Horton, S. V., Lovitt, T. C., Givens, A., & Nelson, R. (1989). Teaching social studies to high school students with academic handicaps in a mainstreamed setting: Effects of a computerized study guide. *Journal of Learning Disabilities, 22*(10), 2–107.

Horton, S. V., Lovitt, T. C., & Slocum, T. (1988). Teaching geography to high school students with academic deficits: Effects of a computerized map tutorial. *Learning Disability Quarterly, 11*, 371–379.

Huang, J. T.-L. (2008). Critical features for teaching the five-paragraph essay to middle school Chinese speaking English learners. *Dissertation Abstracts International Section A: Humanities and Social Sciences, 68*(10-A), 4231.

Hudson, P. J., Schwartz, S., Sealander, K. A., Campbell, P., & Hensel, J. (1988). Successfully employed adults with handicaps: Characteristics and transition strategies [Abstract]. *Career Development for Exceptional Individuals, 11*, 7–14.

Hughes, C. A. (1991). Studying for and taking tests: Self-reported difficulties and strategies of university students with learning disabilities. *Learning Disabilities, 2*, 65–71.

Hughes, C. A., Hendrickson, J. M., & Hudson, P. J. (1986). The pause procedure: Improving factual recall from lectures by low and high achieving middle school students. *International Journal of Instructional Media, 13*, 217–226.

Hughes, C. A., & Smith, J. O. (1990). Cognitive and academic performance of college students with learning disabilities: A synthesis of the literature. *Learning Disability Quarterly, 13*, 66–79.

Hughes, C. A., & Suritsky, S. K. (1993). Notetaking skills and strategies for students with learning disabilities. *Preventing School Failure, 38*(1), 7–12. Retrieved February 2, 2003, from Academic Search Premier database.

Hughes, C. A., & Suritsky, S. K. (1994). Notetaking skills of university students with and without learning disabilities. *Journal of Learning Disabilities, 27*(1), 20–25. Retrieved February 2, 2003, from Academic Search Premier database.

Hulland, C., & Munby, H. (1994). Science, stories, and sense-making: A comparison of qualitative data from a wetlands unit. *Science Education, 78*, 117–136.

Hurford, D. P., & Shedelbower, A. (1993). The relationship between discrimination and memory ability in children with reading disabilities. *Contemporary Educational Psychology, 18,*101–113.

Hursh, D. E., Schumaker, J. B., Fawcett, S. B., & Sherman, J. A. (2000). A Comparison of the effects of written versus direct instructions on the application of four behavior change processes. *Education & Treatment of Children, 23*(4). Retrieved April 9, 2009, from Academic Search Complete database. (AN 4261145)

Hurst, D., & Smerdon, B. (Eds.). (2000a). Postsecondary students with disabilities: Enrollment, services, and persistence. *Education Statistics Quarterly, 2*(3), 55–58.

Hurst, D., & Smerdon, B. (2000b). *Post secondary students with disabilities: Enrollment, services, and persistence: Stats in brief.* Washington DC: National Center for Education Statistics. (ERIC Document Reproduction Service No. ED 444329)

Irvin, J. L. (1990). *Vocabulary knowledge: Guidelines for instruction.* Washington, DC: National Education Association.

Itier, R. J., & Batty, M. (2009). Neural bases of eye and gaze processing: The core of social cognition. *Neuroscience & Biobehavioral Reviews, 33*(6), 843–863.

Ivie, S. D. (1998). Ausubel's learning theory: An approach to teaching higher order thinking skills. *High School Journal, 82*(1), 35–43.

Jackson, L. (2000). *Increasing critical thinking skills to improve problem-solving ability in mathematics.* Master's action research project, Saint Xavier University and Skylight Professional Development. (ERIC Document Reproduction Service No. ED 446995)

Jacobson, A. (1987). *Essential learning skills across the curriculum.* (ERIC Document Reproduction Service No.ED295127)

Jacobson, J., Lapp, D., & Flood, J. (2007). A seven-step instructional plan for teaching English-Language Learners to comprehend and use homonyms, homophones, and homographs. *Journal of Adolescent & Adult Literacy, 51*(2), 98–111.

Jacobucci, L., Richert, J., Ronan, S., & Tanis, A. (2002). *Improving reading comprehension by predicting, monitoring, comprehension, remediation, and personal response strategies.* (ERIC Document Reproduction Service No. ED473054)

James, D. L. (2001). *Split a gut and learn: Theory and research.* (ERIC Document Reproduction Service No. ED458671)

Jitendra, A. K., Edwards, L. L., Sacks, G., & Jacobson, L. A. (2004). What research says about vocabulary instruction for students with learning disabilities. *Exceptional Children, 70*(3), 299–322.

Jitendra, A. K., Nolet, V., Xin, Y. P., Gomez, O., Renouf, K., Iskold, L., & DaCosta, J. (2001). An analysis of middle school geography textbooks: Implications for students with learning problems. *Reading and Writing Quarterly: Overcoming Learning Difficulties, 17*(2), 151–173.

Johnson, D., Cantrell, R. J., Willis, K. L., & Josel, C. A. (1997). Open to suggestion. *Journal of Adolescent & Adult Literacy, 40,* 390–395.

Johnson, D., & Myklebust, H. R. (1967). *Learning disabilities: Educational principles and practices.* New York: Grune and Stratton.

Johnson, G. (1999). Kidney role-plays. *School Science Review, 80*(292), 93–97.

Johnson, S. D., & Thomas, R. (1992). Technology education and the cognitive revolution. *Technology Teacher, 51*(4), 7–12.

Jones, E. D., & Wilson, R. (1997). Mathematics instruction for secondary students with learning disabilities. *Journal of Learning Disabilities, 30*(2), 151–164. Retrieved January 4, 2003, from Academic Search Premier database.

Jones, M. B., & Miller, C. R. (2001). Chemistry in the real world. *Journal of Chemical Education, 78*(4), 484–487.

Jones, R. W. (1975, January). *The target groups: Description of learning disabled and normal subjects participating in prototype evaluation studies.* Paper presented at the 2nd conference of the International Scientific Federation of Learning Disabilities, Brussels, Belgium. (ERIC Document Reproduction Service No. ED113859)

Jordan, D. R. (2000). *Understanding and managing learning disabilities in adults.* Professional Practices in Adult Education and Human Resource Development Series. Melbourne, FL: Krieger.

Jordan, L., Miller, M. D., & Mercer, C. D. (1999). The effects of concrete to semi-concrete to abstract instruction in the acquisition and retention of fraction concepts and skills. *Learning Disabilities: A Multidisciplinary Journal, 9*(3), 115–122.

Jordan, M. K. (1983, June). *Developing the listening speaking component in English for academic purposes.* Paper presented at the Second Language Acquisition and Second Language Teaching Conference, Tampa, FL. (ERIC Document Reproduction Service No. ED236927).

Josel, C. A. (1997). Abbreviations for notetaking. *Journal of Adolescent and Adult Literacy, 40*(5), 393–395.

Jung, E. H. (2003). The role of discourse signaling cues in second language listening comprehension. *Modern Language Journal, 87*(4), 562–577.

Kagan, S. (1992). *Cooperative learning* (7th ed.). San Juan Capistrano, CA: Resources for Teachers.

Kalispell School District 5, MT. (1987). *CRISS: Content reading in secondary schools. National Diffusion Network Programs.* (ERIC Document Reproduction Service No. ED377455)

Kamalski, J., Sanders, T., & Lentz, L. (2008). Coherence marking, prior knowledge, and comprehension of informative and persuasive texts: Sorting things out. *Discourse Processes, 45*(4–5). Special issue: Cognitive and Linguistic Factors in Interactive Knowledge Construction. pp. 323–345.

Kame'enui, E. J., & Carnine, D. W. (1998). *Effective teaching strategies that accommodate diverse learners.* Columbus, OH: Merrill, Prentice Hall.

Kame'enui, E. J., & Simmons, D. C. (1990). *Designing instructional strategies: The prevention of academic learning problems.* Columbus, OH: Merrill.

Kame'enui, E. J., & Simmons, D. C. (1999). *Toward successful inclusion of students with disabilities: The architecture of instruction. Volume 1: An overview of materials adaptations.* ERIC/OSEP Mini-Library Preview. (ERIC Document Reproduction Service No. ED429381)

Kamps, D. M., Greenwood, C., Arreaga-Mayer, C., Veerkamp, M. B., Utley, C., Tapia, Y., Bowman-Perrott, L., & Bannister, H. (2008). The efficacy of ClassWide Peer Tutoring in middle schools. *Education & Treatment of Children, 31*(2), 119–152. Retrieved July, 6, 2009, from Academic Search Complete database. (AN 31943130)

Kariuki, P. N. K., & Bush, E. D. (2008, November). *The effects of Total Physical Response by Storytelling and the traditional teaching styles of a foreign language in a selected high school.* Paper presented at the annual conference of the Mid. South Educational Research Association, Knoxville, TN. (Document Reproduction Service No. ED503364)

Karlin, R. (1964). *Teaching reading in high school.* New York: Bobbs-Merrill.

Karpicke, J.D., & Roediger, H.L. (2007). Repeated retrieval during learning is the key to long-term retention. *Journal of Memory and Language, 57,* 151-162

Katayama, A. D., & Robinson, D. H. (2000). Getting students "partially" involved in note-taking using graphic organizers. *Journal of Experimental Education, 68*(2), 119–33.

Katayama, A. D., & Crooks, S. M. (2003). Online notes: Differential effects of studying complete or graphically organized notes. *Journal of Experimental Education, 7*(4), 293–312.

Katims, D. S., & Harmon, J. M. (2000). Strategic instruction in middle school social studies: Enhancing academic and literacy outcomes for at-risk students. *Intervention in School & Clinic, 35*(5). Retrieved January 4, 2003, from Academic Search Premier database.

Kavale, K. A. (1982). Meta-analysis of the relationship between visual perceptual skills and reading achievement. *Journal of Learning Disabilities, 15*(1), 42–51.

Kavale, K. A. (1993). How many learning disabilities are there? A commentary on Stanovich's "Dysrationalia: A new specific learning disability." *Journal of Learning Disabilities, 26,* 520–523.

Kavale, K. A., & Forness, S. R. (1999). *Efficacy of special education and related services* (Monograph of the American Association on Mental Retardation). Washington, DC: American Association on Mental Retardation.

Ke, F. (2008). Computer games application within alternative classroom goal structures: Cognitive, metacognitive, and affective evaluation. *Educational Technology Research and Development, 56*(5–6), 539–556. (ERIC Document Reproduction Service No. EJ815294)

Keel, M. C., Dangel, H. L., & Owens, S. H. (1999). Selecting instructional interventions for students with mild disabilities in inclusive classrooms. *Focus on Exceptional Children, 31*(8), 1–16.

Keenan, J. M., Betjemann, R. S., Wadsworth, S. J., DeFries, J. C., & Olson, R. K. (2006). Genetic and environmental influences on reading and listening comprehension. *Journal of Research in Reading, 29*(1), 75–91. Retrieved July 10, 2009, from Academic Search Complete database. (AN 19426944)

Kelly, G. J., Chen, C., & Prothero, W. (2000). The epistemological framing of a discipline: Writing science in university oceanography. *Journal of Research in Science Teaching, 37*(7), 691–718.

Kelley, M. J., & Clausen-Grace, N. (2007). *Comprehension shouldn't be silent: From strategy instruction to student independence.* Newark, DE: International Reading Association.

Kendal, M., & Stacey, K. (2000). Acquiring the concept of derivative: Teaching and learning with multiple representations. In T. Nakahara & M. Koyama (Eds.), *Proceedings of the 24th conference of the international group for the psychology of mathematics education.* Vol. 3 (pp. 127–134). Hiroshima, Japan: Hiroshima University.

Kerber, J. E. (Ed.). (1980). Vocabulary development. *Ohio Reading Teacher, 14*(2), 1–32. (ERIC Document Reproduction Service No. ED181413)

Kerka, S. (1992). *Higher order thinking skills in vocational education.* (ERIC Digest No. 127). (ERIC Document Reproduction Service No. ED350487)

Kidd, J. W. (1970). The discriminatory repertoire—the basis of all learning. *Journal of Learning Disabilities, 3,* 530–533.

Kiewra, K. A. (1985). Learning from a lecture: An investigation of notetaking, review, and attendance at a lecture. *Human Learning, 44,* 73–77.

Kim, A., Vaughn, S., Wanzek, J., & Wei, S. (2004). Graphic organizers and their effects on the reading comprehension of students with LD. *Journal of Learning Disabilities, 37*(2), 105–118.

Kinder, D., & Bursuck, W. (1991). The search for a unified social studies curriculum: Does history really repeat itself? *Journal of Learning Disabilities, 24*(5), 270–275, 320.

King, A. (1992a). Comparison of self-questioning, summarizing, and notetaking-review as strategies for learning from lectures. *American Educational Research Journal, 29*(2), 303–323.

King, A. (1992b). Facilitating elaborative learning through guided student generated questioning. *Educational Psychologist, 27,* 111–126.

King, C. (2002). Teaching through explanatory stories: "The dynamic Earth's crust." *School Science Review, 83*(304), 63–72.

King, K. D. (2001). Conceptually-oriented mathematics teacher development: Improvisation as a metaphor. *For the Learning of Mathematics, 21*(3), 9–15.

King-Sears, M. E., Mercer, C. D., & Sindelar, P. T. (1992). Toward independence with keyword mnemonics: A strategy for science vocabulary instruction. *Remedial and Special Education, 13,* 22–33.

Kintsch, E. (1989). *Macroprocesses and microprocesses in the development of summarization skill.* (ERIC Document Reproduction Service No ED305613).

Kintsch, E. (1990). Macroprocesses and microprocesses in the development of summarization skill. *Cognition & Instruction, 7*(13), 161–195. Retrieved February 21, 2009, from Academic Search Complete database. (AN 7383307)

Kintsch, W. (2002). On the notions of theme and topic in psychological process models of text comprehension. In M. Louwerse & W. van Peer (Eds.), *Thematics* (pp. 157–170). Amsterdam: John Benjamins Publishing.

Kintsch, W., & van Dijk, T. A. (1978). *Toward a model of text comprehension and production.* Unpublished manuscript, University of Colorado, Boulder, Department of Psychology.

Kirkpatrick, L. C., & Klein, P. D. (2009). Planning textstructure as a way to improve students' writing from sources in the compare-contrast genre. *Learning & Instruction, 19*(4), 309–321. Retrieved from Academic Search Complete database. (AN 37158322)

Klein, M. L. (1988). *Teaching reading comprehension and vocabulary.* Englewood Cliffs, NJ: Prentice Hall.

Kline, C. (1986). *Effects of guided notes on academic achievement of learning disabled high school students.* Unpublished master's thesis, Ohio State University.

Klorman, R. (1991). Cognitive event-related potentials in attention deficit disorder. *Journal of Learning Disabilities, 24*(3), 130–140.

Kobayashu, K. (2006). Combined effects of note-taking/-reviewing on learning and the enhancement through interventions: A meta-analytic review. *Educational Psychology, 26* (3), 459–477.

Kops, C., & Belmont, I. (1985). Planning and organizing skills of poor school achievers. *Journal of Learning Disabilities, 18,* 8–14.

Kornblum, R. B. (1982). *A perceptuo-cognitive-motor approach to the special child.* (ERIC Document Reproduction Service No. ED223016)

Kotulak, R. (1996). *Inside the brain: Revolutionary discoveries of how the mind works.* Kansas City, KS: McMeel.

Kronick, D. (1978). An examination of psychosocial aspects of learning disabled adolescents. *Learning Disability Quarterly, 1*(4), 86–93.

Kruger, R. J., Kruger, J. J., Hugo, R., & Campbell, N. G. (2001). Relationship patterns between central auditory processing disorders and language disorders, learning disabilities, and sensory integration dysfunction. *Communication Disorders Quarterly, 22*(2), 87–98.

Kubina, R. M., Jr., & Cooper, J. O. (2000). Changing learning channels: An efficient strategy to facilitate instruction and learning. *Intervention in School and Clinic, 35*(3), 161–166.

Kumar, D., & Wilson, C. L. (1997). Computer technology, science education, and students with learning disabilities. *Journal of Science Education and Technology, 6,*155–160.

Ladas, H. (1980). Summarizing research: A case study. *Review of Educational Research, 50*(4), 597–624.

Lai, S. K., & Hopkins, L. D. (1995). Can decision makers express multiattribute preferences using AHP and MUT? An experiment. *Environment & Planning B: Planning & Design, 22*(1), 21–35.

Lancaster, S., Mellard, D., & Hoffman, L. (2001). *Experiences of students with disabilities in selected community and technical colleges. The individual accommodations model: Accommodating students with disabilities in post-secondary settings.* (ERIC Document Reproduction Service No. ED452617)

Lancioni, G. E., O'Reilly, M. F., & Oliva, D. (2001). Self-operated verbal instructions for people with intellectual and visual disabilities: Using instruction clusters after task acquisition. *International Journal of Disability, Development & Education, 48*(3), 303–312. Retrieved April 8, 2009, from Academic Search Complete database. (AN 5107721)

Langan-Fox, J., Waycott, J. L., & Albert, K. (2000). Linear and graphic advance organizers: Properties and processing. *International Journal of Cognitive Ergonomics, 4*(1), 19–35.

Lapp, D., Fisher, D., & Flood, J. (1999). Integrating the language arts and content areas: Effective research-based strategies. *California Reader, 32*(4), 35–38.

Larson, K. A., & Gerber, M. M. (1987). Effects of social metacognitive training for enhancing overt behavior in learning disabled and low achieving delinquents. *Exceptional Children, 54,* 201–211.

Lasley, T. J., Williams, S. J., & Hart, P. M. (1991). Nonexamples: Why teachers don't use them and why teacher educators should. *Mid-western Educational Researcher, 4*(3), 2–6.

Lazarus, B. D. (1988). Using guided notes to aid learning-disabled adolescents in secondary mainstream settings. *Pointer, 33*(1), 32–35.

Lazarus, B. D. (1991). Guided notes, review, and achievement of secondary students with learning disabilities in mainstream content courses. *Education and Treatment of Children, 14*(2), 112–127.

Lazarus, B. D. (1996). Guided notes: Effects with secondary and post secondary students with mild disabilities. *Education and Treatment of Children, 16*(3), 272–289. Retrieved December 17, 2002, from Professional Development Collection database.

Lebzelter, S., & Nowacek, E. J. (1999). Reading strategies for secondary students with mild disabilities. *Intervention in School & Clinic, 34*(4), 212–219.

Lee, C.-C., Bopry, J., & Hedberg, J. (2007). Methodological issues in using sequential representations in the teaching of writing. *ALT-J: Research in Learning Technology, 15*(2), 131–141. (ERIC Document Reproduction Service No. EJ815334)

Lee, G. (2003). Kamishibai: A vehicle to multiple literacies. *Voices from the Middle, 10*(3), 36–42. (ERIC Document Reproduction Service No.EJ664289)

Lenz, B. K., & Alley, G. R. (1983). *The effect of advance organizers on the learning and retention of learning disabled adolescents within the context of a cooperative planning model. Final Report.* (ERIC Document Reproduction Service No. ED257247)

Lenz, B. K., Alley, G. R., & Schumaker, J. B. (1987). Activating the inactive learner: Advance organizers in the secondary content classroom. *Learning Disability Quarterly, 10*(1), 53–67.

Lenz, B. K., Ehren, B. J., & Smiley, L. R. (1991). A goal attainment approach to improve completion of project type assignments by adolescents with learning disabilities. *Learning Disabilities Research and Practice, 6,*166–176.

Lenz, K. (1998). How SIM addresses what is unique about teaching students with LD. *Stratenotes, 6*(7), 1–8.

Levin, J. R. (1988). Elaboration-based learning strategies: Powerful theory = powerful application. *Contemporary Educational Psychology, 13,*191–205.

Levine, M. G. (1994). Effective ways to involve limited English students in the study of history. *Social Studies Review, 33*(2), 16–22.

Litt, J., Taylor, H. G., Klein, N., & Hack, M. (2005). Learning disabilities in children with very low birthweight: Prevalence, neuropsychological correlates, and educational interventions. *Journal of Learning Disabilities, 38*(2), 130–141. Retrieved July 2, 2009, from Academic Search Premier database. (AN 16266228)

Litteral, D. B. (1998). *Improving instruction, motivation, and writing skills to foster content mastery among 11th grade chemistry students.* (ERIC Document Reproduction Service No. ED436369)

Lloyd, J., Saltzman, N. J., & Kauffman, J. M. (1981). Predictable generalization in academic learning as a result of preskills and strategy training [Abstract]. *Learning Disability Quarterly, 4,* 4203–4216.

Lomika, L. L. (1998). "To gloss or not to gloss": An investigation of reading comprehension online. *Language Learning & Technology, 1*(2), 41–50.

Lorayne, H., & Lucas, J. (1974). *The memory book.* New York: Stein and Day.

Lovitt, T. C., & Horton, S. V. (1987). How to develop study guides. *Journal of Reading, Writing, and Learning Disabilities International, 3*(4). 333–343. (ERIC Document Reproduction Service No. EJ375002)

Lovitt, T. C., & Horton, S. V. (1994). Strategies for adapting science textbooks for youth with learning disabilities. *RASE: Remedial & Special Education, 15*(2).

Lovitt, T. C., Rudsit, J., Jenkins, J., Pious, C., & Benedetti, D. (1985). Two methods of adapting science materials for learning disabled and regular seventh graders. *Learning Disability Quarterly, 8,* 275–285.

Lowry, C. M. (1990). *Teaching adults with learning disabilities* (ERIC Digest No. 99). (ERIC Document Reproduction Service No. ED321156)

Määtt, S., Nurmi, J.-E., & Stattin, H. (2007). Achievement orientations, school adjustment, and well-being: A longitudinal study. *Journal of Research on Adolescence, 17*(4), 789–812.

Maccini, P., & Hughes, C. A. (2000). Effects of a problem-solving strategy on the introductory algebra performance of secondary students with learning disabilities. *Learning Disabilities Research and Practice, 15*(1), 10–21.

Maccini, P., McNaughton, D., & Ruhl, K. L. (1999). Algebra instruction for students with learning disabilities: Implications from a research review. *Learning Disability Quarterly, 22*(2), 113–126.

Maccini, P., & Ruhl, K. L. (2000). Effects of a graduated instructional sequence on the algebraic subtraction of integers by secondary students with learning disabilities. *Education & Treatment of Children, 23*(40), 465–490.

MacGregor, T. J. (2007). Try this system to keep your multiple-POV novel on track. *Writer, 120*(5), 27–29. Retrieved from Academic Search Complete database. (AN 24671527)

MacKinnon, G. R. (2006).Contentious issues in science education: Building critical thinking patterns through two-dimensional concept mapping. *Journal of Educational Multimedia and Hypermedia, 15*(4), 433–445.

Maddrell, A. M. C. (1994). A scheme for the effective use of role plays for an emancipator geography. *Geography in Higher Education, 18*(2), 155–162.

Makany, T., Kemp, J., & Dror, I. E. (2009). Optimising the use of note-taking as an external cognitive aid for increasing learning. *British Journal of Educational Technology, 40* (4), 619–635.

Malcolm, C. B., Polatajko, H. J., & Simons, J. (1990). A descriptive study of adults with suspected learning disabilities. *Journal of Learning Disabilities, 23,* 518–520.

Maley, A. (1993). Repetition revisited. *Guidelines, 15(1),* 1–11.

Malmquist, S. K. (1998). *The effects of study skills instruction on the U.S. history achievement of secondary-aged students with mild disabilities.* Unpublished doctoral thesis, University of Oregon.

Malone, L. D., & Mastropieri, M. A. (1992). Reading comprehension instruction: Summarization and self-monitoring training for students with learning disabilities. *Exceptional Children, 58,* 270–279.

Marder, C., & D'Amico, R. (1992). *How well are youth with disabilities really doing? A comparison of youth with disabilities and youth in general.* A report from the National Longitudinal Transition Study of Special Education Students. (ERIC Document Reproduction Service No. ED369233)

Marshall, K. J., Lussie, R., & Stradley, M. (1989). Social studies. In G. A. Robinson, J. R. Patton, E. A. Polloway, & L. R. Sargent (Eds.), *Best practices in mild mental disabilities* (pp. 155–178). Reston, VA: The Division on Mental Retardation of the Council for Exceptional Children.

Marshall, R. M., & Hynd, G. W. (1997). Academic achievement in ADHD subtypes. *Journal of Learning Disabilities, 30,* 635.

Martin, D. C., & Blanc, R. A. (1994). VSI: A pathway to mastery and persistence. *New Directions for Teaching and Learning, 60,* 83–91.

Massey, D. D., & Heafner, T. L. (2004). Promoting reading comprehension in social studies. *Journal of Adolescent and Adult Literacy, 48*(1), 26–40.

Mastropieri, M. A., Emerick, K., & Scruggs, T. E. (1988). Mnemonic instruction of science concepts. *Behavioral Disorders, 14,* 48–56.

Mastropieri, M. A., & Scruggs, T. E. (1989). Constructing more meaningful relations: Mnemonic instruction for special populations. *Educational Psychology Review, 1*(2), 83–111.

Mastropieri, M. A., & Scruggs, T. E. (1991). *Teaching students ways to remember: Strategies for learning mnemonically.* Cambridge, MA: Brookline Books.

Mastropieri, M. A., & Scruggs, T. E. (1994). Applications of mnemonic strategies with students with mild disabilities. *Remedial & Special Education, 15*(1). Retrieved December 29, 2002, from Academic Search Premier database.

Mastropieri, M. A., Scruggs, T. E., & Butcher, K. (1997). How effective is inquiry learning for students with mild disabilities? *Journal of Special Education, 31*(2), 199–211. Retrieved December 29, 2002, from Academic Search Premier database.

Mastropieri, M. A., Scruggs, T. E., & Mushinski, B. J. T. (1990). Teaching abstract vocabulary with the keyword method: Effects on recall and comprehension. *Journal of Learning Disabilities, 23*(2), 92–96,107.

Mateos, M., Martin, E., Villalon, R., & Luna, M. (2008). Reading and writing to learn in secondary education: Online processing activity and written products in summarizing and synthesizing tasks. *Reading and Writing: An Interdisciplinary Journal, 21*(7), 675–697. (ERIC Document Reproduction Service No. EJ808368)

Mays, F., & Imel, S. (1982). *Adult learning disabilities.* Overview (ERIC Fact Sheet No. 9). (ERIC Document Reproduction Service No. ED237797)

McCarthy, D. S. (2008). Communication in mathematics: Preparing preservice teachers to include writing in mathematics teaching and learning. *School Science & Mathematics, 108*(7), 334–340. Retrieved February 28, 2009, from Academic Search Complete database. (AN 35340525)

McCoy, J. D., & Ketterlin-Geller, L.R. (2004). Rethinking instructional delivery in a diverse age: Serving all learners with concept-based instruction. *Intervention in School and Clinic, 40*(2), 71–93.

McCrudden, M. T., Schraw, G., & Lehman, S. (2009). The use of adjunct displays to facilitate comprehension of causal relationships in expository text. *Instructional Science: An International Journal of the Learning Sciences, 37*(1), 65–86.

McDermott, P. C., & Rothenberg, J. J. (1999, April). *Teaching in high poverty, urban schools—learning from practitioners and students.* Paper presented at the annual meeting of the American Educational Research Association, Montreal, Quebec, Canada. (ERIC Document Reproduction Service No. ED431058)

McDorman, M. B. E. (1976). *The effects of directionality and complexity on learning disabled and normal subjects' learning sentence sequence, comprehending sentences and recognizing sentence relationships* [Abstract]. Doctoral dissertation, University of Georgia. (ERIC Document Reproduction Service No. ED140220)

McGinty, R. L., & Van Beynen, J. G. (1985). Activities: Deductive and analytical thinking. *Mathematics Teacher, 78*(3), 188–194.

McGlaughlin, S. M., Knoop, A. J., & Holliday, G. A. (2005). Differentiating students with mathematics difficulty in college: Mathematics disorders versus no diagnosis. *Learning Disability Quarterly, 28*(3), 223–232.

McGrady, H. J., & Olson, D. A. (1967). *Visual and auditory learning processes in normal children and children with specific learning disabilities. Final report* [Abstract]. (ERIC Document Reproduction Service No. ED025894)

McInnes, A., Bedard, A. C., Hogg-Johnson, S., & Tannock, R. (2007). Preliminary evidence of beneficial effects of Methylphenidate on listening comprehension in children with Attention-Deficit/Hyperactivity Disorder. *Journal of Child & Adolescent Psychopharmacology, 17*(1), 35–49. Retrieved from Academic Search Complete database. (AN 24321210)

McKay, E. (1999). Exploring the effect of graphical metaphors on the performance of learning computer programming concepts in adult learners: A pilot study. *Educational Psychology, 19,* 471–488.

McKeown, M. G., Beck, I. L., Omanson, R. C., & Pople, M. T. (1985). Some effects of the nature and frequency of vocabulary instruction on the knowledge and use of words. *Reading Research Quarterly, 20*(5), 522–535.

McKinney, D., Dyck, J. L., & Luber, E. S. (2009). iTunes University and the classroom: Can podcasts replace professors? *Computers & Education, 52*(3), 617–623.

McLeod, J. (1966). Psychological and psycholinguistic aspects of severe reading disability in children: Some experimental studies. Proceedings of the third annual International Conference of the ACLD, Tulsa, OK. In S. Kirk & J. M. McCarthy (Eds.), *Learning disabilities: Selected papers* (pp. 286–305). Boston: Houghton Mifflin.

McLeskey, J. (1977, December). *Learning set acquisition by reading disabled and normal children.* Paper presented at the 27th annual meeting of the National Reading Conference, New Orleans, LA. (ERIC Document Reproduction Service No. ED151754)

McMillen, M. M., Kaufman, P., & Klein, S. (1997). *Dropout rates in the United States: 1995.* Washington, DC: U.S. Government Printing Office. (ERIC Document Reproduction Service No. ED410370)

McMurray, N. E. (1974). *The effects of four instructional strategies on the learning of a geometric concept by elementary and middle school EMR students.* Doctoral dissertation, University of Wisconsin, Madison. (ERIC Document Reproduction Service No. ED110334)

McNamara, J. K. (1999). *Social information processing in students with and without learning disabilities.* (ERIC Document Reproduction Service No. ED436867)

Mellard, D. F., & Alley, G. R. (1981). *Production deficiency vs. processing dysfunction: An experimental assessment of LD adolescents.* (ERIC Document Reproduction Service No. ED217650)

Melzer, J., & Hamann, E. T. (2006). Literacy for English learners and regular students. *Education Digest: Essential Readings Condensed for Quick Review, 71*(8), 32–40.

Meyer, V., & Keefe, D. (1998). Supporting volunteer tutors: Five strategies. *Adult Basic Education, 8*(2), 59–67.

Meyrowitz, J. (1980, November). *Analyzing media: Metaphors as methodologies.* Paper presented at the New England Conference on Teaching Students to Think, Amherst, MA. (ERIC Document Reproduction Service No. ED206030)

Michalak, L. (2000). *The story of Joseph from the Koran. Lessons from ORIAS Institute on history through literature in the 6th grade/7th grade core classrooms, 1998–2000.* (ERIC Document Reproduction Service No. ED463195)

Miles, C. (1981). The 4th "R" revisited. *Journal of Developmental & Remedial Education, 5*(1), 2–4.

Miller, D. L. (1993). Making the connection with language. *Arithmetic Teacher, 40*, 311–316.

Miller, G. A. (1956). The magical number seven, plus or minus two: Some limits on our capacity for processing information. *Psychological Review, 63*, 81–97.

Miller, S. P., & Mercer, C. D. (1993). Using data to learn about concrete-semiconcrete-abstract instruction for students with math disabilities. *Learning Disabilities Research and Practice, 8*(2), 89–96.

Mislevy, R. J., Yamamoto, K., & Anacker, S. (1991). Toward a test theory for assessing student understanding. (ERIC Document Reproduction Service No. ED392817)

Mitchell, M. (Ed.). (1996). *School completion rates for children with disabilities: The role of economic and demographic factors. A Project ALIGN issue brief.* Richmond, VA: Donald Oswald, Commonwealth Institute for Child and Family Studies. (ERIC Document Reproduction Service No. ED408771)

Moffatt, C. W., et al. (1995, March). Discrimination of emotion, affective perspective-taking and empathy in individuals with mental retardation. *Education and Training in Mental Retardation and Developmental Disabilities, 30*(1), 76–85.

Molino, J. (1979). Metaphores, modeles et analogies dans les sciences (Metaphors, models, and analogies in the sciences). *Languages, 54*, 83–102.

Monroe, E. E. (1997). *Using graphic organizers to teach vocabulary: How does available research inform mathematics instruction?* (ERIC Document Reproduction Service No. ED414256)

Monroe, E. E., & Orme, M. P. (2002). Developing mathematical vocabulary. *Preventing School Failure, 46*(3), 139–142.

Monroe, E. E., & Pendergrass, M. R. (1997). *Effects of mathematical vocabulary instruction on fourth grade students.* Paper presented at the 1997 BYU Public School Partnership Symposium on Education. (ERIC Document Reproduction Service No. ED414182)

Montague, M. (1992). The effects of cognitive and metacognitive strategy instruction on the mathematical problem solving of middle school students with learning disabilities. *Journal of Learning Disabilities, 25*(4), 230–248.

Moon, K. (1992). Flowing through the American Revolution. *Social Studies Texan, 8*(1), 37.

Moore, D. W., & Readence, J. E. (1984). A quantitative and qualitative review of graphic organizer research. *Journal of Educational Research, 78*, 11–17.

Moore, D. W., Readence, J. E., & Rickelman, R. J. (1989). *Prereading activities for content area reading and learning* (2nd ed.). Newark, DE: International Reading Association.

Moran, M. (1980). *An investigation of the demands on oral language skills of learning disabled students in secondary classrooms* (Report No. 1). Lawrence, KS: University of Kansas, Institute for Research in Learning Disabilities.

Moreno, V., & DiVesta, R. J. (1994). Analogies (adages) as aids for comprehending structural relations in text. *Contemporary Educational Psychology, 19*(2), 179–198.

Morin, V. A., & Miller, S. R. (1998). Teaching multiplication to middle school students with mental retardation. *Education and Treatment of Children, 21*(1), 22–36.

Mortimore, T., & Crozier, R. W. (2006). Dyslexia and difficulties with study skills in higher education. *Studies in Higher Education, 31*(2), 235–251.

Moseley, B., & Brenner, M. E. (1997). *Using multiple representations for conceptual change in pre-algebra: A comparison of variable usage with graphic and text based problems.* (ERIC Document Reproduction Service No. ED413184)

Mosher, D. J. (1999). *Improving vocabulary knowledge and reading attitudes in 4th grade students through direct vocabulary instruction.* Master's Action Research Project, Saint Xavier University. Chicago, IL: IRI/Skylight.

Moskal, B. M. (2000). *Scoring rubrics part I: What and when* (ERIC/AE Digest). (ERIC Document Reproduction Service No. ED446110)

Most, T., & Greenbank, A. (2000). Auditory, visual, and auditory-visual perception of emotions by adolescents with and without learning disabilities and their relationship to social skills. *Learning Disabilities: Research & Practice, 15*, 171–178.

Murray, J., & Whittenberger, D. (1983). The aggressively, severely behavior disordered child. *Journal of Learning Disabilities, 16*, 76–80.

Murrihy, R. C., Byrne, M. K., & Gonsalvez, C. J. (2009). Testing an empirically derived mental health training model featuring small groups, distributed practice and patient discussion. *Medical Education, 43*(2), 140–145.

Muscari, P. G. (1988). The metaphor in science and in the science classroom. *Science Education, 72*, 423–431.

Myer, B. J., & Ganschow, L. (1988). Profiles of frustration: Second language learners with specific learning disabilities. In J. F. Lalande II (Ed.), *Shaping the future of language education: FLES, articulation, and proficiency. Report of Central States Conference on the Teaching of Foreign Language.* (ERIC Document Reproduction Service No. ED292335)

Myrah, G. E., & Erlauer, L. (1999). The benefits of brain research: One district's story. *High School Magazine, 7*(1), 34–40.

Narjaikaew, P., Emarat, N., & Cowie, B. (2009). The effect of guided note taking during lectures on Thai university students' understanding of electromagnetism. *Research in Science & Technological Education, 27*(1), 75–94.

National Center to Improve the Tools of Educators. (1998). NCITE's principles for evaluating and adapting curricula. *Teaching Exceptional Children, 31*(1), 84.

National Center to Improve the Tools of Educators, National Council of Teachers of Mathematics Standards. (1995). *Vocabulary acquisition: Curricular and instructional implications for diverse learners* (Technical Report No. 14). Retrieved November 25, 2002, from http://www.idea.uoregon.edu/~ncite/ documents/techrep /reading.html

National Information Center for Children and Youth with Disabilities. (2000). *Reading and learning disabilities. Briefing paper 17 (FS17)* (3rd ed.). Available from http://www.nichcy.org

National Institute for Literacy. (2007). *What content area teachers should know about adolescent literacy.* Washington, DC: Author. Available from http://www.nifl.gov

Nesbit, J. C., & Adesope, O. O. (2006). Learning with concept and knowledge maps: A meta-analysis. *Review of Educational Research, 76*(3), 413–448.

Neumark, V. (2001, March 23). Forging confident connections. *TES Magazine, 9.*

Nevid, J. S., & Mahon, K. (2009). Mastery quizzing as a signaling device to cue attention to lecture material. *Teaching of Psychology, 36*(1), 29–32.

Newport, R., & Howarth, S. (2009). Social gaze cueing to auditory locations. *Quarterly Journal of Experimental Psychology, 62*(4), 625–634.

No Child Left Behind Act, Pub. L. No. 107–110 (2001). Retrieved November 10, 2002, from http://www.nclb.gov

Noice, H., Noice, T., & Kennedy, C. (2000). Effects of enactment by professional actors at encoding and retrieval. *Memory, 8*(6), 353–363.

Norton, S. J., McRobbie, C. J., & Ginns, I. S. (2007). Problem solving in a middle school Robotics Design Classroom. *Research in Science Education, 37*(3), 261–277 (ERIC Document Reproduction Service No. EJ785031)

Novak, J.D. (2004). Reflections on a half-century of thinking in science education and research: Implications from a twelve-year longitudinal study of children's learning. *Canadian Journal of Science, Mathematics, & Technology Education, 4*(1), 23–41. Retrieved from Professional Development Collection database. (AN 12526486)

Novak, J. D., & Musonda, D. (1991). A twelve-year longitudinal study of science concept learning. *American Educational Research Journal, 28*(1), 117–153.

Novemsky, L., & Gautreau, R. (1997, October). Perception in the invisible world of physics. In *VisionQuest: Journeys toward visual literacy.* Selected readings from the annual conference of the International Visual Literacy Association, Cheyenne, WY. (ERIC Document Reproduction Service No. ED408978)

Nussbaum, E. M. (2008). Using argumentation vee diagrams (AVDs) for promoting argument-counterargument integration in reflective writing. *Journal of Educational Psychology, 100*(3), 549–565.

Nussbaum, E. M., & Schraw, G. (2007). Promoting argument-counterargument integration in students' writing. *Journal of Experimental Education, 76*(1), 59–92. Retrieved March 31, 2009, from Academic Search Complete database. (AN 26848916)

Oakhill, J., & Patel, S. (1991). Can imagery training help children who have comprehension problems? *Journal of Research in Reading, 14,* 106–115.

Oetting, J. B., & Rice, M. L. (1995). Quick incidental learning (QUIL) of words by school-age children with and without SLI. *Journal of Speech & Hearing Research, 38*(2), 434. Retrieved January 4, 2003, from Academic Search Premier database.

Ogle, D. M. (1986). K-W-L: A teaching model that develops active reading of expository text. *Reading Teacher, 39,* 564–570.

Oja, L. A. (1996). Using story frames to develop reading comprehension. *Journal of Adolescent & Adult Literacy, 40,* 129–130.

Okolo, C. M., & Bahr, C. M. (1995). Increasing achievement motivation of elementary school students with mild disabilities. *Intervention in School and Clinic, 30*(5), 279–286, 312. Retrieved December 21, 2002, from Professional Development Collection database.

Ollmann, H. E. (1989). Cause and effect in the real world. *Journal of Reading, 33,* 224–225.

Olson, J. K. (2008). Concept-focused teaching: Using big ideas to guide instruction in science. *Science and Children, 46*(4), 45–49.

Olson, M. W. (1980, January). *Pattern guides: An alternative for content teachers.* Paper presented at the 89th annual meeting of the Southwest Regional Conference of the International Reading Association, Albuquerque, NM. (ERIC Document Reproduction Service No. ED185580)

Orlow, M. (1974). Low tolerance for frustration: Target group for reading disabilities. *Reading Teacher, 27,* 669–674.

Paivio, A. (1990). *Mental representations: A dual coding approach.* New York: Oxford University Press.

Paivio, A., & Walsh, M. (1994). Concreteness effects on memory: When and why? *Journal of Experimental Psychology/Learning, Memory & Cognition, 20*(5), 1196–1205.

Papastergiou, M. (2009). Digital game-based learning in high school computer science education: Impact on educational effectiveness and student motivation. *Computers & Education, 52*(1), 1–12.

Pauk, W. (1978). A notetaking format: Magical but not automatic. *Reading World, 18*(1), 96–97.

Peters, C. (1974). A comparison between the Frayer model of concept attainment and the textbook approach to concept attainment. *Reading Research Quarterly, 10,* 252–254.

Peterson, S. K., Mercer, C. D., Tragash, J., & O'Shea, L. (1987). *Comparing the concrete to abstract teaching sequence to abstract instruction for initial place value skills* (Monograph #19). Gainesville, FL: University of Florida, Shands Teaching Hospital. (ERIC Document Reproduction Service No. ED301777)

Pimm, D. (1981). Metaphor and analogy in mathematics. *For the Learning of Mathematics, 1*(3), 47–50.

Pimm, D. (1988). Mathematical metaphor. *For the Learning of Mathematics, 8*(1), 30–34.

Piolat, A., Barbier, M. L., & Roussey, J. Y. (2008). Fluency and cognitive effort during first- and second-language note-taking and writing by undergraduate students. *European Psychologist, 13*(2), 114–125.

Piolat, A., Olive, T., & Kellogg R. T. (2005). Cognitive effort of notetaking. *Applied Cognitive Psychology, 19,* 291–312.

Pittelman, S. D., Heimlich, J. E., Berglund, R. L., & French, M. P. (1991). *Semantic feature analysis: Classroom applications.* Newark, DE: International Reading Association.

Plaut, S. (2006). "I just don't get it": Teachers' and students' conceptions of confusion and implications for teaching and learning in the high school English classroom. *Curriculum Inquiry, 36*(4), 391–421. Retrieved from Academic Search Premier database. (AN 23848130)

Poirier, C. R., & Feldman, R. S. (2007). Technology and teaching: Promoting active learning using individual response technology in large introductory psychology classes. *Teaching of Psychology, 34*(3), 194–196.

Pollio, H. R. (1990). *Remembrances of lectures past: Notes and note-taking in the college classroom. Teaching/Learning Issues.* Knoxville, TN: University of Tennessee, Learning Research Center. (ERIC Document Reproduction Service No. ED364179)

Polloway, E. A., Patton, J. R., Epstein, M. H., Aquah, T., Decker, T. W., & Carse, C. (1991). *Characteristics and services in learning disabilities: A report on elementary programs.* (ERIC Document Production Service No. ED342158)

Polloway, E. A., Patton, J. R., & Serna, L. (2001). *Strategies for teaching learners with special needs.* Upper Saddle River, NJ: Merrill/Prentice Hall.

Porter, A. C., & Brophy, J. (1988). Synthesis of research on good teaching: Insights from the work of the Institute for Research on Teaching. *Educational Leadership, 45*(8), 74–85.

Porter, P. (1993). Activities for social math. Pull-out feature. *Social Studies and the Young Learner, 6*(1), 1–4.

Potts, B. (1993). *Improving the quality of student notes* (ERIC/AE Digest). (ERIC Document Reproduction Service No. ED366645)

Powell, M. B., & Thomson, D. M. (1996). Children's memory of an occurrence of a repeated event: Effects of age, repetition, and retention interval across three question types. *Child Development, 67*(5), 1988–2004.

Powers, M. H. (1984). A computer assisted problem solving method for beginning chemistry students. *Journal of Computers in Mathematics and Science Teaching, 4*(1), 13–19.

Prager, I. G., Deckelbaum, G., & Cutler, B. L. (1989). Improving juror understanding for intervening causation instructions. *Forensic Reports, 2*(3), 187–193.

Prain, V., Tytler, R., & Peterson, S. (2009). Multiple representation in learning about evaporation. *International Journal of Science Education, 31*(6), 787–808.

Prawat, R. S. (1989). Promoting access to knowledge, strategy, and disposition in students: A research synthesis. *Review of Educational Research, 59*(1), 1–41.

Preddy, L. B. (2003). Student inquiry in the research process, Part 4: Inquiry Research Investigation. *School Library Media Activities Monthly, 19*(6), 26–28. (ERIC Document Reproduction Service No. EJ666574)

Pressley, M., & Harris, K. R. (1990). What we really know about strategy instruction. *Educational Leadership, 48*(1), 31–34.

Prigo, R. (2007). *Making physics fun: Concepts, classroom activities, and everyday examples, grades K–8.* Thousand Oaks, CA: Corwin Press.

Pugh, K. R., Frost, S. J., Sandak, R., Landi, N., Rueckl, J. G., Constable, R. T., et al. (2008). Effects of stimulus difficulty and repetition on printed word identification: An fMRI comparison of nonimpaired and reading-disabled adolescent cohorts. *Journal of Cognitive Neuroscience, 20*(7), 1146–1160. Retrieved April 7, 2009, from Academic Search Complete database. (AN 32897229)

Putnam, M. L. (1992a). Characteristics of questions on tests administered by mainstream secondary classroom teachers. *Learning Disabilities Research & Practice, 7,* 129–136.

Putnam, M. L. (1992b). The testing practices of mainstream secondary classroom teachers. *Remedial and Special Education, 13*(3), 11–21.

Putnam, M. L., Deshler, D. D., & Schumaker, J. B. (1993). The investigation of setting demands: A missing link in learning strategy instruction. In L. S. Meltzer (Ed.), *Strategy assessment and instruction for students with learning disabilities* (pp. 325–354). Austin, TX: PRO-ED.

Ranzijn, F. J. A. (1991). The number of video examples and the dispersion of examples as instructional design variables in teaching concepts. *The Journal of Experimental Education, 59*(4), 320–330.

Raphael, T. E., & Kirschner, B. M. (1985). *The effects of instruction in compare/ contrast text structure on sixth-grade students' reading comprehension and writing products* (Research Series No. 161). (ERIC Document Reproduction Service No. ED264537)

Rauschenbach, J. (1994). Checking for student understanding—four techniques. *Journal of Physical Education, Recreation and Dance, 64*(4), 60–63.

Reagan, R. (2008). Direct Instruction in skillful thinking in fifth-grade American History. *Social Studies, 99*(5), 217–222. (ERIC Document Reproduction Service No. EJ812506)

Reid, D. (2002). Virtual reality and the person—environment experience. *CyberPsychology & Behavior, 5,* 559–565.

Reis, S. M., Neu, T. W., & McGuire, J. M. (1995). *Talents in two places: Case studies of high ability students with learning disabilities who have achieved* (Research Monograph 95114). (ERIC Document Reproduction Service No. ED388021)

Rekrut, M. D. (1996). Effective vocabulary instruction. *High School Journal, 80*(1), 66–75.

Renick, M. J. (1985, April). *Assessing learning disabled children's motivational orientations in the classroom.* Paper presented at the biennial meeting of the Society for Research in Child Development, Toronto, Ontario, Canada. (ERIC Document Reproduction Service No. ED260568)

Resnick, L. B., & Zurawsky, E. (Eds.). (2007). Science education that makes sense. *American Educational Research Association Research Points, 5*(1). (ERIC Document Reproduction Service No. ED497647)

Resnick, M., & Wilensky, U. (1998). Diving into complexity: Developing probabilistic decentralized thinking through role-playing activities. *Journal of the Learning Sciences, 7*(2), 153–172.

Rice, M. L., & Buhr, J. A. (1992). Specific-language-impaired children's quick incidental learning of words: The effect of a pause. *Journal of Speech & Hearing Research, 35*(5), 1040. Retrieved December 18, 2002, from Academic Search Premier database.

Rice, M. L., & Oetting, J. B. (1994). Frequency of input effects on word comprehension of children with specific language impairment. *Journal of Speech & Hearing Research, 37*(1), 106–123. Retrieved December 18, 2002, from Academic Search Premier database.

Richards, G. P., Samuels, J., Ternure, J. E., & Ysseldyke, J. E. (1990). Sustained and selective attention in children with learning disabilities. *Journal of Learning Disabilities, 23,*129–136. Retrieved January 14, 2003, from Academic Search Premier database.

Ritger, S. D., & Cummins, R. H. (1991). Using student-created metaphors to comprehend geologic time. *Journal of Geological Education, 39*(1), 9–11.

Robb, L. (1999). Identify, preteach, connect. *Instructor, 108*(8), 6.

Robb, L. (2002). Tackling tough words. *Instructor, 110*(3), 35–36, 38.

Roberts, F. A. (2009). The effect of instruction in orthographic conventions and morphological features on the reading fluency and comprehension skills of high-school freshmen. *Dissertation Abstracts International Section A, 69,* Retrieved from PsycINFO database.

Robinson, D. L. H., Katayama, A. D., Beth, A., Odom, S., Ya-Ping, H., & Vanderveen, A. (2006). Increasing text comprehension and graphic note taking using a partial graphic organizer. *Journal of Educational Research, 100*(2), 103–111.

Rohrer, D., & Taylor, K. (2006). The effects of overlearning and distributed practice on the retention of mathematics knowledge. *Applied Cognitive Psychology, 20*(9), 1209–1224.

Rosell-Aguilar, F. (2007). Top of the pods—in search of a podcasting "podagogy" for language learning. *Computer Assisted Language Learning, 20*(5), 471–492. Retrieved from Academic Search Complete database. (AN 27754265)

Rosen, C. L. (1968). An investigation of perceptual training and reading achievement in first grade [Abstract]. *American Journal of Optometry, 45,* 322–332. (ERIC Document Reproduction Service No. ED025400)

Rosner, S. R. (1971). The effects of rehearsal and chunking instructions on children's multitrial free recall. *Journal of Experimental Child Psychology, 11*(1), 93–105.

Rowe, M. B. (1976). The pausing principle: Two invitations to inquiry. *Research on College Science Teaching, 5,* 258–259.

Rowe, M. B. (1980). Pausing principles and their effects on reasoning in science. *New Directions in Community College, 31,* 27–34.

Rowe, M. B. (1983). Getting chemistry off the killer course list. *Journal of Chemical Education, 60,* 954–956.

Rowell, R. M. (1975, March). *Children's concepts of natural phenomena: Use of a cognitive mapping approach to describe these concepts.* Paper presented at the 48th annual meeting of the National Association for Research in Science Teaching, Los Angeles, CA. (ERIC Document Reproduction Service No. ED106117)

Rubenstein, R. N. (2000). Word origins: Building communication connections. *Mathematics Teaching in the Middle School, 5*(8), 493. Retrieved January 1, 2003, from Academic Search Premier database.

Rubman, C. N., & Waters, H. S. (2000). A, B seeing: The role of constructive processes in children's comprehension monitoring. *Journal of Educational Psychology, 92,* 503–514.

Ruhl, K. L. (1996). Does nature of student activity during lecture pauses affect notes and immediate recall of college students with learning disabilities? *Journal of Postsecondary Education and Disability, 12*(2), 16–27.

Ruhl, K. L., Hughes, C. A., & Gajar, A. H. (1990). Efficacy of the pause procedure for enhancing learning disabled and nondisabled college students' long- and short-term recall of facts presented through lecture. *Learning Disability Quarterly, 13,* 55–64.

Ryan, M., Miller, D., & Witt, J. C. (1984). A comparison of the use of orthographic structure in word discrimination by learning disabled and normal children. *Journal of Learning Disabilities, 17,* 38–40.

Ruhl, K. L., & Suritsky, S. (1995). The pause procedure and/or an outline: Effect on immediate free recall and lecture notes taken by college students with learning disabilities. *Learning Disability Quarterly, 18*(1), 2–11.

Saddler, B., & Andrade, H. (2004). The writing rubric. *Educational Leadership, 62*(2), 48–52. Retrieved February 14, 2009, from Academic Search Complete database. (AN 14635595)

Saenz, L. M., & Fuchs, L. S. (2002). Examining the reading difficulty of secondary students with learning disabilities: Expository versus narrative text. *Remedial and Special Education, 23*(1), 31–42.

Sakurai, Y., Dohi, S., Tsuruta, S., & Knauf, R. (2009). Modeling academic education processes by dynamic storyboarding. *Journal of Educational Technology & Society, 12*(2), 307–333. Retrieved July 3, 2009, from Academic Search Complete database. (AN 38422412)

Salend, S. J., & Gajria, M. (1995). Increasing the homework completion states of students with mild disabilities. *Remedial and Special Education, 16,* 271–278. Retrieved January 4, 2003, from Academic Search Premier database.

Salinas, C., Fránquiz, M. E., & Reidel, M. (2008). Teaching world geography to late-arrival immigrant students: Highlighting practice and content. *Social Studies, 99*(2), 71–76. Retrieved from Academic Search Complete database. (AN 31891771)

Salyer, B. K., Curran, C., & Thyfault, A. (2002, March). What can I use tomorrow? Strategies for accessible math and science curriculum for diverse learners in rural schools. In *No Child Left Behind: The vital role of rural schools.* 22nd Annual National Conference Proceedings of the American Council on Rural Special Education (ACRES), Reno, NV. (ERIC Document Reproduction Service No. ED463109)

Sánchez, J. N. G., & Pérez, C. R. P. (2007). Influencia del intervalo de registro y del organizador gráfico en el proceso-producto de la escritura y en otras variables psicológicas. [Influence of the recording interval and a graphic organizer on the writing process/product and on other psychological variables]. *Psicothema, 19*(2), 198–205.

Sanders, T. J. M., & Noordman, L. G. M. (2000). The role of coherence relations and their linguistic markers in text processing. *Discourse Processes, 29*(1), 37–60. Retrieved July 11, 2009, from PsycINFO database.

Santa, C. M. (1988). *Content reading including study systems: Reading, writing and studying across the curriculum* [Abstract]. Dubuque, IA: Kendall/Hunt. (ERIC Document Reproduction Service No. ED372363)

Sanza, J. (1982). *Category priming in the lexical decision task and evidence of repetition effects.* Paper presented at the 28th annual meeting of the Southeastern Psychological Association, New Orleans, LA. (ERIC Document Reproduction Service No. ED215337)

Satcher, J. (1990). *Accommodating workers with learning disabilities.* (ERIC Document Reproduction Service No. ED320099)

Scerbo, M. W., Warm, J. S., & Dember, W. N. (1992). The role of time and cuing in a college lecture. *Contemporary Educational Psychology, 17*(4), 312–328.

Schallert, D. L., & Tierney, R. J. (1980). *Learning from expository text: The interaction of text structure with reader characteristics.* (ERIC Document Reproduction Service No. ED221833)

Scheuermann, A. M., Deshler, D. D., & Schumaker, J. B. (2009). The effects of the explicit inquiry routine on the performance of students with learning disabilities on one-variable equations. *Learning Disability Quarterly, 32*(2), 103–120.

Schiff, M. M., Kaufman, A. S., & Kaufman, N. L. (1981). Scatter analysis of WISC-R profiles for learning disabled children with superior intelligence. *Journal of Learning Disabilities, 14(7),* 400–404. Retrieved January 1, 2003, from the Professional Development Collection database.

Schiff, P. (2000). Shakespeare answering machines: A popular culture and creative dramatics exercise. *Exercise Exchange, 45*(2), 6–7.

Schiff, R., Bauminger, N., & Toledo, I. (2009). Analogical problem solving in children with verbal and nonverbal learning disabilities. *Journal of Learning Disabilities, 42* (1), 3–13.

Schirmer, B. R., & Bailey, J. (2000). Writing assessment rubric: An instructional approach with struggling writers. *Teaching Exceptional Children, 33*(1), 52–58.

Scholes, C. (1998). General science: A diagnostic teaching unit. *Intervention in School and Clinic, 34,* 107–114. Retrieved January 4, 2003, from Academic Search Premier database.

Schug, M. C., Western, R. D., & Enochs, L. G. (1997). Why do social studies teachers use textbooks: The answer may lie in economic theory. *Social Education, 6,* 97–101.

Schur, J. B. (1980). *EJ* workshop: Helping students to visualize what they read. *English Journal, 69*(2), 64–65.

Schwartz, R. M., & Raphael, T. E. (1985). Concept of definition: A key to improving students' vocabulary. *Reading Teacher, 39,*198–205.

Schwarz, R., & Burt, M. (1995). *ESL instruction for learning disabled adults* (ERIC Digest). (ERIC Document Reproduction Service No. ED379966)

Schweitzer, K., Zimmermann, P., & Koch, W. (2000). Sustained attention, intelligence, and the crucial role of perceptual processes. *Learning and Individual Differences, 12*(3), 271–287. Retrieved February 13, 2003, from the Professional Development Collection database.

Scime, M., & Norvilitis, J. M. (2006). Task performance and response to frustration in children with attention deficit hyperactivity disorder. *Psychology in the Schools, 43*(3), 377–386.

Scott, K. S. (1993). Multisensory mathematics for children with mild disabilities. *Exceptionality, 4*(2), 97–111.

Scott, T. M., & Nelson, C. M. (1998). Confusion and failure in facilitating generalized social responding in the school setting: Sometimes 2 + 2 = 5. *Behavioral Disorders, 23,* 264–275.

Scruggs, T. E., & Mastropieri, M. A. (1989). Reconstructive elaborations: A model for content area learning. *American Educational Research Journal, 26,* 311–327.

Scruggs, T. E., & Mastropieri, M. A. (1990a). The case for mnemonic instruction: From laboratory research to classroom applications. *Journal of Special Education, 24*(1), 7–33. Retrieved January 4, 2003, from Professional Development Collection database.

Scruggs, T. E., & Mastropieri, M. A. (1990b). Mnemonic instruction for students with LD: What it is and what it does. *Learning Disability Quarterly, 19,* 271–280.

Scruggs, T. E., & Mastropieri, M. A. (2007). Science learning in special education: The case for constructed versus instructed learning. *Exceptionality, 15*(2), 57–74.

Seitz, S., & Scheerer, J. (1983). *Learning feasibilities: Introduction and strategies for college teaching.* (ERIC Document Reproduction Service No. ED235864)

Seligman, M. E. P. (1975). *Helplessness: On depression, development, and death.* San Francisco: W. H. Freeman.

Semmler, C., & Brewer, N. (2002). Using a flow-chart to improve comprehension of jury instructions. *Psychiatry, Psychology and Law, 9*(2), 262–267.

Semple, J. L. (1992). *Semple math: A basic mathematics program for beginning, high-risk and/or remedial students.* Attleboro, MA: Stevenson Learning Skills.

Sencibaugh, J. M. (2007). Meta-analysis of reading comprehension interventions for students with learning disabilities: Strategies and implications. *Reading Improvement, 44*(1), 6–22.

Seung-Hoon, Y., Jun-Sang, K., & Tai-Yoo, K. (2001). Value-focused thinking about strategic management of radio spectrum for mobile communications. *Telecommunications Policy, 25*(10/11), 703–719.

Sexton, T. G., & Poling, D. R. (1973). *Can intelligence be taught?* Bloomington, IN: Phi Delta Kappa Educational Foundation.

Shambaugh, R. N. (1994). *Personalized meanings: The cognitive potentials of visual notetaking.* Paper presented at the annual Eastern Educational Research Association Conference, Sarasota, FL. (ERIC Document Reproduction Service No. ED365969)

Shields, J. M., & Heron, T. E. (1989). Teaching organizational skills to students with learning disabilities. *Teaching Exceptional Children, 21*(2), 8–13.

Siegel, D. J. (1999). *The developing mind: Toward a neurobiology of interpersonal experience.* New York: Guilford.

Siegler, R. S. (1998). *Children's thinking* (3rd ed.). Upper Saddle River, NJ: Erlbaum.

Silbert, J., Carnine, D., & Stein, M. (1990). *Direct instruction mathematics* (2nd ed.). Columbus, OH: Merrill.

Simbo, F. K. (1988). The effects of notetaking approaches on student achievement in secondary school geography. *Journal of Educational Research, 81*(6), 377–381.

Simpson, S. B. (1992). The impact of an intensive multisensory reading program on a population of learning-disabled delinquents. *Annals of Dyslexia, 42,* 54–66.

Simpson, T. J. (1997). Tri-coding of information. In *VisionQuest: Journeys toward visual literacy.* Selected readings from the 28th annual conference of the International Visual Literacy Association, Cheyenne, WY. (ERIC Document Reproduction Service No. ED408953)

Singer, H., & Donlan, D. (1980). *Reading and learning from text.* Boston, MA: Little Brown.

Sisterhen, D. H., & Gerber, P. J. (1989). Auditory, visual, and multisensory nonverbal social perception in adolescents with and without learning disabilities. *Journal of Learning Disabilities, 22,* 245–249, 257. Retrieved January 25, 2003, from Academic Search Premier database.

Skrtic, T. M. (1980). *Formal reasoning abilities for learning disabled adolescents: Implications for mathematics instruction.* (ERIC Document Reproduction Service No. ED217624)

Smagorinsky, P. (2000). *What English educators have to say to assessment specialists.* (ERIC Document Reproduction Service No. ED446050)

Smith, D. D. (1981). *Teaching the learning disabled.* Englewood Cliffs, NJ: Prentice Hall.

Smith, P. L. (1986, January). *The effects of organizational cues on learners' processing of instructional prose.* Paper presented at the annual convention of the Association for Educational Communications and Technology, Las Vegas, NV.

Smith, P. L., & Friend, M. (1986). Training learning disabled adolescents in a strategy for using text structure to aid recall of instructional prose. *Learning Disabilities Research, 2*(1), 38–44.

Smith, S. W. (1992). Effects of a metacognitive strategy on aggressive acts and anger behavior of elementary and secondary-aged students. *Florida Educational Research Council Research Bulletin, 24,* 1–2. (ERIC Document Reproduction Service No. ED355687)

Soles, D. (2001, March). *Sharing scoring guides.* Paper presented at the 52nd annual meeting of the Conference on College Composition and Communication, Denver, CO. (ERIC Document Reproduction Service No. ED450379)

Somers, C. L., Owens, D., & Piliawsky, M. (2008). Individual and social factors related to urban African American adolescents' school performance. *High School Journal, 91*(3), 1–11.

Sparks, R. L., & Ganschow, L. (1993). The effects of multisensory structured language instruction on native language and foreign language aptitude skills of at-risk high school foreign language learners: A replication and follow-up study. *Annals of Dyslexia, 43,* 94–216.

Stacey, J. (2001). The effects of combined content enhancement on the performance of students with learning disabilities. Master of Science thesis, Utah State University. (ERIC Document Reproduction Service No. ED458765.)

Stalder, D. R. (2005). Learning and motivational benefits of acronym use in Introductory Psychology. *Teaching of Psychology, 32*(4), 222–228.

Stanovich, K. E. (1986). Matthew Effects in reading: Some consequences of individual differences in the acquisition of literacy. *Reading Research Quarterly, 21*(4), 360–407.

Stanovich, K. E. (1993). Dysrationalia: A new specific learning disability. *Journal of Learning Disabilities, 26,* 501–515.

Steele, M. M. (2007). Teaching social studies to high school students with learning problems. *Social Studies, 98*(2), 59–63. Retrieved from Academic Search Complete database. (AN 25127305)

Stein, H. (1988). On that note. . . . *Science and Children, 26*(3), 16–18.

Stencel, J., & Barkoff, A. (1993). Protein synthesis: Role playing in the classroom. *American Biology Teacher, 55*(2), 102–103.

Stenhoff, D. M., & Lignugaris, B. (2007). A review of the effects of peer tutoring on students with mild disabilities in secondary settings. *Exceptional Children, 74*(1), 8–30. Retrieved July 7, 2009, from Academic Search Complete database. (AN 26361614)

Sternberg, R. J. (1993). Would you rather take orders from Kirk or Spock? The relation between rational thinking and intelligence. *Journal of Learning Disabilities, 26,* 516–519. Retrieved December 23, 2002, from Academic Search Premier database.

Sternberg, R. J. (1994). What if the construct of dysrationalia were an example of itself? *Educational Researcher, 23*(4), 22–23.

Stevenson, H. W., Hofe, B. K., & Randall, B. (1999). *Middle childhood: Education and schooling.* Unpublished manuscript, University of Michigan, Ann Arbor, Department of Psychology.

Stone, C. A., Forman, E. A., Anderson, C. J., Matthews, F., Rupert, J., & Fyfe, B. (1984). *Assessment and remediation of complex reasoning in specific subgroups of learning disabled adolescents. Final Report.* (ERIC Document Reproduction Service No. ED261505)

Stratford, B., & Metcalfe, J. A. (1982). Recognition, reproduction and recall in children with Down's syndrome. *Australia and New Zealand Journal of Developmental Disabilities, 8*(3), 125–132.

Stratford, B., & Mills, K. (1984). Colour discrimination in mentally handicapped children with particular reference to Down's syndrome. *Australia and New Zealand Journal of Developmental Disabilities, 10*(3), 151–155.

Stull, A. T., & Mayer, R. E. (2007). Learning by doing versus learning by viewing: Three experimental comparisons of learner-generated versus author-provided graphic organizers. *Journal of Educational Psychology, 99*(4), 808–820.

Sturm, W., & Zimmermann, P. (2000). Aufmerksamkeitsstorungen (Attention deficits). In W. Sturm, M. Herrmann, & C. W. Wallesch (Eds.), *Lehrbuch der klinischen Neuropsychologie* (pp. 345–365). Lisse, The Netherlands: Swets and Zeitlinger.

Suh, J. M. (2007). Tying it all together: Classroom practices that promote mathematical proficiency for all students. *Teaching Children Mathematics, 14*(3), 163–169.

Sultana, Q., & Klecker, B. M. (1999a). *Evaluation of first-year teachers' lesson objectives by Bloom's Taxonomy.* Paper presented at the annual meeting of the Mid-South Educational Research Association, Point Clear, AL. (ERIC Document Reproduction Service No. ED436524)

Sultana, Q., & Klecker, B. M. (1999b). *Two decades of research in learning disabilities: Reading comprehension, expressive writing, problem solving, self-concept.* Paper presented at Keys to Successful Learning: A National Summit on Research in Learning Disabilities, Washington, DC. (ERIC Document Reproduction Service No. ED430365). Available from National Center for Learning Disabilities Web site, http://www.ncld.org.

Sundeen, T. H. (2007). So what's the big idea? Using graphic organizers to guide writing for secondary students with learning and behavioral issues. *Beyond Behavior, 16*(3), 29–37. (ERIC Document Reproduction Service No. EJ840253)

Suritsky, S. K. (1992). Notetaking difficulties and approaches reported by university students with learning disabilities. *Journal of Postsecondary Education and Disability, 10,* 3–10.

Suritsky, S. K., & Hughes, C. A. (1991). Benefits of notetaking: Implications for secondary and post-secondary students with learning disabilities. *Learning Disability Quarterly, 14,* 7–18.

Swanson, H. L. (1994). Short-term memory and working memory: Do both contribute to our understanding of academic achievement in children and adults with learning disabilities? *Journal of Learning Disabilities, 27,* 34–50. Retrieved December 31, 2002, from Academic Search Premier database.

Swanson, H. L. (1999, May). *Intervention research for adolescents with learning disabilities: A meta-analysis of outcomes related to higher-order processing.* A paper presented at Keys to Successful Learning: A National Summit on Research in Learning Disabilities, Washington, DC. (ERIC Document Reproduction Service No. ED430365)

Swanson, H. L. (2001). Research on interventions for adolescents with learning disabilities: A meta-analysis of outcomes related to higher order processing. *Elementary School Journal, 101,* 331–349.

Swanson, H. L., & Hoskyn, M. (2001). Instructing adolescents with learning disabilities: A component and composite analysis. *Learning Disabilities Research and Practice, 16*(2), 109–120.

Swanson, H. L., Xinhua, Z., & Jerman, O. (2009).Working memory, short-term memory, and reading disabilities. *Journal of Learning Disabilities, 42*(3), 260–287.

Swanson, J. E. (1972). *The effects of number of positive and negative instances, concept definition, and emphasis of relevant attributes on the attainment of three environmental concepts by sixth-grade children: Report from the conditions of learning and instruction component of program 1* (Technical Report No. 244). (ERIC Document Reproduction Service No. ED073412)

Swartz, E. (2003). How to teach how-to writing. *Teaching Pre K–8, 34*(2), 77–78. Retrieved from Academic Search Complete database. (AN 10856877)

Swiderek, B. (1996). Metacognition. *Journal of Adolescent & Adult Literacy, 39*(5), 418–419.

Talbot, D. C. (1997). Metacognitive strategy training for reading: Developing second language learners' awareness of expository text patterns. *Dissertation Abstracts International Section A: Humanities and Social Sciences, 57*(10-A), 4310.

Tam, B. K. Y., & Scott, M. L. (1996). Three group instructional strategies for students with limited English proficiency in vocational education. *Journal for Vocational Special Needs Education, 19*(1), 31–36.

Tarquin, P., & Walker, S. (1997). *Creating success in the classroom: Visual organizers and how to use them.* Englewood, CO: Teacher Ideas Press.

Taylor, B. M., & Frye, B. J. (1992). Comprehension strategy instruction in the intermediate grades. *Reading Research and Instruction, 32*(1), 39–48. (ERIC Document Reproduction Service No. EJ454293)

Taylor, D. B., Mraz, M., Nichols, W. D., Rickelman, R. J., & Wood, K. D. (2009). Using explicit instruction to promote vocabulary learning for struggling readers. *Reading & Writing Quarterly, 25*(2–3), 205–220.

Teachers' Curriculum Institute. (1999). *History alive! Engaging all learners in the diverse classroom* (2nd ed.). Mountain View, CA: Author.

Tennyson, R. D., Merrill, M. D., & Woolley, F. R. (1971). *Exemplar and nonexemplar variables which produce correct concept classification behavior and suspected classification errors.* A paper presented at the annual meeting of the American Educational Research Association, New York, New York.

Terepocki, M., Kruk, R. S., & Willows, D. M. (2002). The incidence and nature of letter orientation errors in reading disability. *Journal of Learning Disabilities, 35,* 214–233. Retrieved December 18, 2002, from the Academic Search Premier database.

Terrill, M. C., Scruggs, T. E., Mastropieri, M. A. (2004). SAT vocabulary instruction for high school students with learning disabilities. *Intervention in School & Clinic, 39*(5), 288–294. Retrieved April 11, 2009, from Academic Search Complete database. (AN 12760412)

Thaut, M. H., Peterson, D. A., McIntosh, G. C. (2005). Temporal entrainment of cognitive functions: Musical mnemonics induce brain plasticity and oscillatory synchrony in neural networks underlying memory. In G. Avanzini, L. Lopez, S. Koelsch, & M. Manjno (Eds.), *The neurosciences and music II: From perception to performance* (pp. 243–254). New York: New York Academy of Sciences.

Thomas, R. G. (1992). *Cognitive theory-based teaching and learning in vocational education* (Information Series No. 349). (ERIC Document Reproduction Service No. ED345109)

Tileston, D. W. (2000). *10 best teaching practices: How brain research, learning styles, and standards define teaching competencies.* Thousand Oaks, CA: Corwin.

Titsworth, B. (2001). The effects of teacher immediacy, use of organizational lecture cues, and students' notetaking on cognitive learning. *Communication Education, 50,* 283–297.

Titsworth, B., & Kiewra, K. (1998, April). *By the numbers: The effect of organizational lecture cues on notetaking and achievement.* Paper presented at the American Educational Research Association Convention, San Diego, CA.

Titsworth, B. S., & Kiewra, K. A. (2004). Spoken organizational lecture cues and student notetaking as facilitators of student learning. *Contemporary Educational Psychology, 29*(4), 447–461.

Tobin, K. (1990). *Metaphors and images in teaching. What research says to the science and mathematics teacher* (No. 5). (ERIC Document Reproduction Service No. ED370786)

Todd, R. W., Chaiyasuk, I., & Tantisawetrat, N. (2008). A functional analysis of teachers' instructions. *RELC Journal: A Journal of Language Teaching and Research, 39*(1), 25–50.

Tolfa, D., Scruggs, T. E., & Mastropieri, M. A. (1985). *Extended mnemonic instruction with learning disabled students.* (ERIC Document Reproduction Service No. ED267544)

Tominey, M. R (1996). *Attributional style as a predictor of academic success for students with learning disabilities and/or Attention Deficit Disorder in postsecondary education* [Abstract]. (ERIC Document Reproduction Service No. ED407815)

Toms-Bronowski, S. (1982). *An investigation of the effectiveness of semantic mapping and semantic feature analysis with intermediate grade level children. Program Report 83-3.* (ERIC Document Reproduction Service No. ED224000)

Torgesen, J. K. (1982). The learning disabled child as an inactive learner: Educational implications. *Topics in Learning and Learning Disabilities, 2,* 45–52.

Torgesen, J. K. (1988). Studies of children with learning disabilities who perform poorly on memory span tasks. *Journal of Learning Disabilities, 21,* 605–612. Retrieved December 30, 2002, from Academic Search Premier database.

Toro, P. A., Weissberg, R. P., Guare, J., & Libenstein, N. L. (1990). A comparison of children with and without learning disabilities on social problem-solving skill, school behavior, and family background. *Journal of Learning Disabilities, 23,*115–120. Retrieved December 28, 2002, from Academic Search Premier database.

Troyer, S. J. (1994). *The effects of three instructional conditions in text structure on upper elementary students' reading comprehension and writing performance.* (ERIC Document Reproduction Service No. ED373315)

Tsal, Y., Shalev, L., & Mevorach, C. (2005). The diversity of attention deficits in ADHD: The prevalence of four cognitive factors in ADHD versus controls. *Journal of Learning Disabilities, 38*(2), 142–157. Retrieved June 29, 2009, from Academic Search Complete database. (AN 16266331)

Tsamir, P., Tirosh, D., & Levenson, E. (2008). Intuitive nonexamples: The case of triangles. *Educational Studies in Mathematics, 69*(2), 81–95.

Tuzun, H., Yilmaz-Soylu, M., Karakus, T., Inal, Y., & Kizilkaya, G. (2009). The effects of computer games on primary school students' achievement and motivation in geography learning. *Computers & Education, 52*(1), 68–77.

Tversky, A. (1969). Intransitivity of preferences. *Psychological Review, 76,* 31–48.

Tversky, A. (1972). Elimination by aspects: A theory of choice. *Psychological Review, 79,* 281–299.

Tversky, A., & Sattath, S. (1979). Preference trees. *Psychological Review, 86*(6), 542–573.

Tyas, T., & Cabot, J. (1999). A role-play to illustrate the energy changes occurring in an exothermic reaction. *School Science Review, 80*(293), 113–114.

Utzinger, J. (1982). *Logic for everyone. Alternative techniques for teaching logic to learning disabled students in the university. A part of the HELDS Project (Higher Education for Learning Disabled Students).* (ERIC Document Reproduction Service No. ED234549)

Vacca, R. T., & Vacca, A. L. (1996). *Content area reading* (5th ed.). New York: Harper Collins/College.

Valas, H. (2001). Learned helplessness and psychological adjustment II: Effects of learning disabilities and low achievement. *Scandinavian Journal of Educational Research, 45*(2), 101–114. Retrieved December 23, 2002, from Professional Development Collection database.

Van Dyke, R. (1995). Activities: A visual approach to deductive reasoning. *Mathematics Teacher, 88,* 481–486, 492–494.

van Someren, M. W., Reimann, P., Boshuizen, H. P. A., & de Jong, T. (Eds.). (1998). *Learning with multiple representations* (Advances in learning and instruction series). (ERIC Document Reproduction Service No. ED437929)

VanVoorhis, C. R. W. (2002). Stat jingles: To sing or not to sing. *Teaching of Psychology, 29*(3), 249–250.

Veerkamp, M. B., Kamps, D. M., & Cooper, L. (2007). The effects of classwide peer tutoring on the reading achievement of urban middle school students. *Education and Treatment of Children, 30*(2), 21–51. (ERIC Document Reproduction Service No. EJ778089)

Vine, F. L. (1999). *Self-esteem within children, adolescents, and adults diagnosed with attention-deficit hyperactivity disorder: A review of the literature.* Doctoral research paper, Biola University, La Mirada, CA. (ERIC Document Reproduction Service No. ED437768)

Vinther, J. (2004). Can parsers be a legitimate pedagogical tool? *Computer Assisted Language Learning, 17*(3), 267–288.

Viscovich, S. A. (2002). The effects of three organizational structures on the writing and critical thinking of fifth graders. In P. E. Linder, M. B. Sampson, J. A. R. Dugan, & B. Brancato (Eds.), *Celebrating the faces of literacy.* Readyville, TN: College Reading Association.

Vocke, K. S. (2007). *"Where do I go from here?" Meeting the unique educational needs of migrant students.* Berkley: University of California, National Writing Project. (ERIC Document Reproduction Service No. ED504749)

Vygotsky, L. S. (1962). *Thought and language* (E. Hanfmann & G. Vakar, Eds. & Trans.). Cambridge, MA: M. I. T. Press.

Waber, D. P., Weiler, M. D., Wolff, P. H., Bellinger, D., Marcus, D. J., Ariel, R., et al. (2001). Processing of rapid auditory stimuli in school-age children referred for evaluation of learning disorders. *Child Development, 72*(1), 37–49.

Wagner, E. P. (2001). A study comparing the efficacy of a mole ratio flow chart to dimensional analysis for teaching reaction stoichiometry. *School Science and Mathematics, 101*(1), 10–22.

Wagner, M., Newman, L., Cameto, R., Levine, P., & Garza, N. (2006). *An overview of findings from wave 2 of the National Longitudinal Transition Study-2 (NLTS2).* Menlo Park, CA: SRI International. Available at www.nlts2.org/reports/2006_08/nlts2_report_2006_08_complete.pdf

Walker, B., Shippen, M. E., Alberto, P., Houchins, D. E., & Cihak, D. F. (2005). Using the Expressive Writing Program to improve the writing skills of high school students with learning disabilities. *Learning Disabilities Research & Practice, 20*(3), 175–183.

Walker, J. (1989). Getting them unstuck: Some strategies for the teaching of reading in science. *School Science and Mathematics, 89* (2), 130–135.

Walton, S., & Hoblitt, R. (1989). Using story frames in content-area classes. *Social Studies, 80*(3), 103–106.

Wang, M. C. (1987). Toward achieving educational excellence for all students: Program design and instructional outcomes. *Remedial and Special Education, 8*(3), 25–34.

Wang, M. C., Haertel, G. D., & Walberg, H. J. (1993/1994). What helps students learn? *Educational Leadership, 51*(4), 74–79.

Ward-Lonergan, J. M., Liles, B. Z., & Anderson, A. M. (1998). Listening comprehension and recall abilities in adolescents with language-learning disabilities and without disabilities for social studies lectures. *Journal of Communication Disorders, 31*(1), 1–32.

Warwick, P., Stephenson, P., & Webster, J. (2003). Developing pupils' written expression of procedural understanding through the use of writing frames in science: Findings from a case study approach. *International Journal of Science Education, 25*(2), 173. Retrieved February 15, 2009, from Academic Search Complete database. (AN 9121848)

Washington, V. M. (1989). Semantic mapping: A heuristic for helping learning disabled students write reports. *Journal of Reading, Writing, and Learning Disabilities International, 4*(1), 17–25.

Watson, B. U. (1991). Some relationships between intelligence and auditory discrimination. *Journal of Speech and Hearing Research, 3,* 621–627.

Watson, R. T., Chiyasuk, I., & Tantisawetrat, N. (2008). A functional analysis of teachers' instructions. *RELC Journal: A Journal of Language Teaching and Research, 39*(1), 25–50.

Webb, N. (1995). The textbook business: Education's big dirty secret. *Harvard Education Letter, 11*(4), 1–3.

Webster, R. E., Hall, C. W., Brown, M. B., & Bolen, L. M. (1996). Memory modality differences in children with attention deficit hyperactive disorder with and without learning disabilities. *Psychology in the Schools, 33,*193–201.

Weiler, M. D., Harris, N. S., Marcus, D. J., Bellinger, D., Kosslyn, S. M., & Waber, D. P. (2000). Speed of information processing in children referred for learning problems: Performance on a visual filtering test. *Journal of Learning Disabilities, 33,* 538–550. Retrieved January 1, 2003, from Academic Search Premier database.

Weisberg, R., & Balajthy, E. (1989). *Effects of topic familiarity and training in generative learning activities on poor readers' comprehension of comparison/contrast expository text structure: Transfer to real-world materials.* Paper presented at the 34th annual meeting of the International Reading Association, New Orleans, LA. (ERIC Document Reproduction Service No. ED305618)

Welch, M. (1992). The PLEASE strategy: A metacognitive learning strategy for improving the paragraph writing of students with mild learning disabilities. *Learning Disability Quarterly, 15,*119–128.

Welch, O. M. (1984). *The role of simplicity in deaf education.* (ERIC Document Reproduction Service No. ED253012)

Werker, J. F., Bryson, S. E., & Wassonberg, K. (1985, April). *Consonant errors of severely disabled readers.* Paper presented at the meeting of the Society for Research in Child Development, Toronto, Ontario, Canada. (ERIC Document Reproduction Service No. ED259318)

Westendorf, D. K., Cape, E. L., & Skrtic, T. M. (1982). *A naturalistic study of post-secondary setting demands.* Unpublished manuscript, University of Kansas. Retrieved February 2, 2003, from Academic Search Premier database.

Whitin, P., & Whitin, D. J. (2000). *Math is language too: Talking and writing in the mathematics classroom.* Urbana, IL: National Council of Teachers of English.

Whitman, N. A. (1982). *There is no gene for good teaching: A handbook on lecturing for medical teachers.* (ERIC Document Reproduction Service No. ED233624)

Wiens, J. W. (1983). Metacognition and the adolescent passive learner. *Journal of Learning Disabilities, 16,*144–149.

Wikberg, K. (1992). *Diversifying procedural discourse.* (ERIC Document Reproduction Service No.ED359762)

Willerman, M., & Mac Harg, R. A. (1991). The concept map as an advance organizer. *Journal of Research in Science Teaching, 28*(8), 705–712.

Williams, B. (2007). *Higher order thinking skills: Challenging all students to achieve.* Thousand Oaks, CA: Corwin.

Williams, J. P., Stafford, K. B., & Lauer, K. D. (2009). Embedding reading comprehension training in content-area instruction. *Journal of Educational Psychology, 101*(1), 1–20. (ERIC Document Reproduction Service No. EJ829235)

Williams, M. L. (1995). The conundrum of Federalism: Can there be strong state governments and a strong national government? Teaching Strategy. *Update on Law-Related Education, 19*(3), 9–11.

Wilson, D. R., & David, W. J. (1994). Academic intrinsic motivation and attitudes toward school and learning of learning disabled students. *Learning Disabilities Research and Practice, 9*(3), 148–156.

Wilson, E. K. (1997). A trip to historic Philadelphia on the Web. *Social Education, 61,*170–175.

Wilterdung, J. H., & Luckie, D. B. (2002). *Journal of College Science Teaching, 31*(5). Retrieved from Academic Search Complete database. (AN 6019107)

Wing, H. (1980). Age, sex, and repetition effects with an abilities test battery. *Applied Psychological Measurement, 4*(2), 141–155.

Winograd, P. (1984). Strategic difficulties in summarizing texts. *Reading Research Quarterly 19*(4), 404–425.

Winograd, P., & Hare, V. C. (1988). Direct instruction of reading comprehension strategies: The nature of teacher explanation. In C. E. Weinstein, E. T. Goetz, & P. A. Alexander (Eds.), *Learning and study strategies: Issues in assessment, instruction, and evaluation* (pp. 121–139). San Diego, CA: Academic Press.

Witzel, B., Smith, S. W., & Brownell, M. T. (2001). How can I help students with learning disabilities in algebra? *Intervention in School and Clinic, 37*(2), 101–105.

Wixson, K. K. (1986). Vocabulary instruction and children's comprehension of basal stories. *Reading Research Quarterly, 21,* 317–329.

Wolfe, D. E., & Jones, G. (1982). Integrating total physical response strategy in a Level I Spanish class. *Foreign Language Annals, 15*(4), 273–280.

Wolfe, P. (2001). *Brain matters: Translating research into classroom practice.* Alexandria, VA: Association for Supervision and Curriculum Development.

Wolgemuth, J. R., Cobb, R. B., & Alwell, M. (2008). The effects of mnemonic interventions on academic outcomes for youth with disabilities: A systematic review. *Learning Disabilities Research & Practice. 23*(1), 1–10. Retrieved April 12, 2009, from Academic Search Complete database. (AN 30448249)

Wong, B. Y. L. (1985). Metacognition and learning disabilities. In T. J. Waller, D. Forrest-Pressley, & E. MacKinnon (Eds.), *Metacognition, cognition, and human performance* (pp. 137–180). New York: Academic Press.

Wong, B. Y. L. (1986). Metacognition and special education: A review of a view. *Journal of Special Education, 20*(1), 9–29.

Wong, B. Y. L. (2000). Writing strategies instruction for expository essays for adolescents with and without learning disabilities. *Topics in Language Disorders, 20*(4), 29–44.

Wong, B. Y. L., & Jones, W. (1982). Increasing metacomprehension in learning-disabled and normally-achieving students through self-questioning training. *Learning Disability Quarterly, 5,* 228–240.

Wood, D. D. (1988). Guiding students through informational text. *Reading Teacher, 41*(9), 912–920.

Wood, K. D. (1989, November). *The study guide: A strategy review.* Paper presented at the 33rd annual meeting of the College Reading Association, Philadelphia, PA. (ERIC Document Reproduction Service No. ED322472)

Wood, K. D. (1995). Guiding middle school students through expository text. *Reading & Writing Quarterly: Overcoming Learning Difficulties, 11*(2), 137–147.

Wood, K. D. (1989). *The study guide: A strategy review.* (ERIC Document Reproduction Service No. ED322472)

Wood, K. D., Lapp, D., & Flood, J. (1992). *Guiding readers through text: A review of study guides.* Newark, DE: International Reading Association.

Wood, S. (1995). Developing an understanding of time-sequencing issues. *Teaching History, 79,* 11–15.

Woods, J., Young, P. L., & Judd, P. A. (1985). *The expanded placement process. Work center staff training programs.* (ERIC Document Reproduction Service No. ED269949)

Woodward, A., & Elliott, D. L. (1990). Textbook use and teacher professionalism. In D. L. Elliott & A. Woodward (Eds.), *Textbooks and schooling in the U.S.* (89th Yearbook of the National Society for the Study of Education, Part 1, pp. 178–193). Chicago: National Society for the Study of Education.

Worsdell, A. S., Iwata, B. A., Dozier, C. L., Johnson, A. D., Neidert, P. L., & Thomason, J. L. (2005). Analysis of response repetition as an error-correction strategy during sight-word reading. *Journal of Applied Behavior Analysis, 38*(4), 511–527. Retrieved from Academic Search Complete database. (AN 19253631)

Worsley, D. (1988). Visualization and objective observation. *Teachers and Writers Magazine, 19*(5), 1–3.

Wray, D., & Lewis, M. (1997). *Extending literacy: Children reading and writing nonfiction.* London: Routledge.

Wright, C. M., & Conlon, E. G. (2009). Auditory and visual processing in children with dyslexia. *Developmental Neuropsychology, 34*(3), 330–335.

Wu, H.-K., Krajcik, J. S., & Soloway, E. (2001). Promoting understanding of chemical representations: Students' use of a visualization tool in the classroom. *Journal of Research in Science Teaching, 38,* 821–842.

Wyatt, M., & Hayes, D. A. (1991). *Analogies as sources of interference to learning from texts with study guides.* (ERIC Document Reproduction Service No. ED351669)

Wylie, J., & McGuinness, C. (2004). The interactive effects of prior knowledge and text structure on memory for cognitive psychology texts. *British Journal of Educational Psychology. 74*(4), 497–514. Retrieved June 30, 2009, from Academic Search Complete database. (AN 15280274)

Wyn, M. A., & Stegink, S. J. (2000). Role-playing mitosis. *American Biology Teacher, 62*(5), 378–381.

Yager, R. E., & Akcay, H. (2008). Comparison of student learning outcomes in middle school science classes with an STS approach. *RMLE Online: Research in Middle Level Education, 31*(7), 1–16. (ERIC Document Reproduction Service No. EJ801103)

Yan P. X. (2007). Word problem solving tasks in textbooks and their relation to student performance. *Journal of Educational Research,* 100(6), 347–360.

Yoho, R. R. (1985, March–April). *Effectiveness of four concept teaching strategies on social studies concept acquisition and retention.* A paper presented at the annual meeting of the American Educational Research Association, Chicago, IL. (ERIC Document Reproduction Service No. ED260993)

Yopp, H. K., & Yopp, R. H. (1996). *Literature-based reading activities* (2nd ed.). Des Moines, IA: Allyn and Bacon.

Young, B. N., Whitley, M. E., & Helton, C. (1998, November). *Students' perceptions of characteristics of effective teachers.* Paper presented at the annual meeting of the Mid-South Educational Research Association, New Orleans, LA. (ERIC Document Reproduction Service No. ED426962)

Zeaman, D., & House, B. J. (1961). *Role of attention in retardate discrimination learning. Progress Report No. 3.* (ERIC Document Reproduction Service No. ED130607)

Zera, D. A., & Lucian, D. G. (2001). Self-organization and learning disabilities: A theoretical perspective for the interpretation and understanding of dysfunction. *Learning Disability Quarterly,* 24,107–118.

Zetts, R. A., Horvat, M. A., & Langone, J. (1995). Effects of a community-based progressive resistance training program on the work productivity of adolescents with moderate to severe intellectual disabilities. *Education and Training in Mental Retardation and Developmental Disabilities, 30*(2), 166–178.

Zurcher, R. (1995). Memory and learning assessment: Missing from the learning disabilities identification process for too long. *LD Forum, 21,* 27–30.

Index

CORWIN

A SAGE Company

The Corwin logo—a raven striding across an open book—represents the union of courage and learning. Corwin is committed to improving education for all learners by publishing books and other professional development resources for those serving the field of PreK–12 education. By providing practical, hands-on materials, Corwin continues to carry out the promise of its motto: **"Helping Educators Do Their Work Better."**